CREATING HOME ECONOMICS FUTURES
THE NEXT 100 YEARS

Edited by Donna Pendergast, Sue LT McGregor and Kaija Turkki

First published in 2012
Australian Academic Press
32 Jeays Street
Bowen Hills Qld 4006
Australia
www.australianacademicpress.com.au

© 2012 Copyright for each contribution in the book rests with the identified authors.

Copying for educational purposes

The *Australian Copyright Act 1968* (Cwlth) allows a maximum of one chapter or 10% of this book, whichever is the greater, to be reproduced and/or communicated by any educational institution for its educational purposes provided that the educational institution (or the body that administers it)
has given a remuneration notice to Copyright Agency Limited (CAL) under the Act.

For details of the CAL licence for educational institutions contact:
Copyright Agency Limited, 19/157 Liverpool Street, Sydney, NSW 2000.
E-mail info@copyright.com.au

Production and communication for other purposes

Except as permitted under the Act, for example a fair dealing for the purposes of study, research, criticism or review, no part of this book may be reproduced, stored in a retrieval system, or transmitted in any form or by any means electronic, mechanical, photocopying, recording or otherwise without prior written permission of the copyright holder.

National Library of Australia Cataloguing-in-Publication entry:

Author:	Pendergast, Donna Lee.
Title:	Creating home economics futures: The next 100 years/ Donna Pendergast, Sue L. T. McGregor, Kaija Turkki.
Edition:	
ISBN:	9781921513961 (pbk.)
	9781921513978 (ebook)
Subjects:	Home economists--Forecasting.
	Home economics--Forecasting.

Other Authors/Contributors: McGregor, Sue L.T.
           Turkki, Kaija.

Dewey Number: 640

FOREWORD

In 2012 Home Economics Victoria hosted the *2012 World Congress of the International Federation for Home Economics (IFHE)* in Melbourne, Australia. It was the first congress of the next one hundred years as Home Economics as a profession celebrated the centennial of the establishment of IFHE at the World Congress in 2008. This was followed by the American Association of Family and Consumer Sciences (AAFCS) centenary in 2009.

One of the features of congress was the launch of this book entitled *Creating Home Economics futures — The Next 100 Years*, edited by Professors Donna Pendergast (Australia); Sue L. T. McGregor (Canada) and Kaija Turkki (Finland). All full registrants to the congress received a copy of the book in their conference satchels. This book offers an exciting opportunity to contribute to the thinking associated with the future of the Home Economics profession.

Home economists around the world, and those with an interest in Home Economics, were invited to contribute a chapter to the book. A stimulus chapter, by the same name as the book, was written by the editors for authors to use as a starting point from which to develop or stimulate their ideas on any aspect related to Home Economics in the next 100 years. A number of abstracts were submitted for consideration, and in this book, the final selection of chapters is presented. As editors of the book, we have been deeply impressed by the range and scope of chapters, presenting diverse and challenging ideas, and by the unexpected but welcomed synergy amongst ideas from practitioners all around the world; this synergy gives us hope for a powerful and sustainable future.

This book will make an invaluable contribution to the profession of Home Economics, and will stimulate creative, deeply intellectual and philosophical thinking about possible and preferred futures.

Editors

Professor Donna Pendergast, PhD
Professor Sue L.T. McGregor, PhD
Professor Kaija Turkki, PhD

CONTENTS

Foreword iii

Preface ix

Contributing Authors... x

Acknowledgements xvii

Dedication xviii

CHAPTER 1
    Creating Home Economics Futures: The Next 100 years....................... 1
    Donna Pendergast, Sue L. T. McGregor and Kaija Turkki

CHAPTER 2
    The Intention of Home Economics Education:.. 12
    A Powerful Enabler for Future-Proofing the Profession
    Donna Pendergast

CHAPTER 3
    Bringing a Life-Centric Perspective to Influential Megatrends.......................... 24
    Sue L. T. McGregor

CHAPTER 4
    Home Economics — A Forum for Global Learning
    and Responsible Living 38
    Kaija Turkki

CHAPTER 5
    Home Economics in Past and Present —
    Perspectives for the Future 52
    Jette Benn

CHAPTER 6
    History and Potential of Home Economics in
    the People's Republic of China 62
    Peng Chen

CHAPTER 7

Deaths, Disasters and Tasty Treats: Challenging Public
Perceptions of Home Economics 75
Jay R. Deagon

CHAPTER 8

Clothing and Crafting: A Proposal for Home Economics
Under the Perspective of Solidarity and Creative Economy 88
Rita de Cássia Pereira Farias

CHAPTER 9

Writing New Maps — Considering the Phenomenological
Attitude as a Theoretical Framework for the
Future-Orientated Field of Home Economics..101
Henna Heinilä

CHAPTER 10

Considering an Alternative Route for Home Economics
— Education for a Sustainable Future 111
Karin Hjälmeskog

CHAPTER 11

From Ice Boxes to Smart Grids: Technology in the
Homes of the Future 120
Gwendolyn Hustvedt, Christiane Pakula, Hester Steyn, Mira Ahn, and Rainer Stamminger

CHAPTER 12

Everyday Life of Families in the Global World 132
Hille Janhonen-Abruquah

CHAPTER 13

Home Economics, Mega-Crises and Continuity 143
Vuokko Jarva

CHAPTER 14

A Systems Approach to Food Future Proofs the
Home Economics Profession 157
Jane Kolodinsky

CHAPTER 15

Sustainable Consumption Through an Environmental
Lens: Challenges and Opportunities for Home Economics 170
Sylvia Lorek and Stefan Wahlen

CHAPTER 16

Anchoring Skills for Sustainable Development in
Vocational Training: Curricula for Home Economics
and Hospitality Professions 182
Nancy Mattausch, Carola Strassner and Irmhild Kettschau

CHAPTER 17

Envisioning an African-Centric Higher Education
Home Economics Curriculum for the 21st Century 195
Lois R. Mberengwa and Fungai M. Mthombeni

CHAPTER 18

Food Security, Street Food and Family Insecurity in Nigeria:
Repositioning Home Economics in the 21st Century 207
Nwakego Molokwu and Elizabeth M. Kembe

CHAPTER 19

What did we Learn from the 3-11 Disaster and How do we
Need to Reconsider a Sustainable Life? 218
Midori Otake, MichioMiyano, Kei Sasai, Kuniko Sugiyama, Yoko Ito and Noriko Arai

CHAPTER 20

Capacity-Building in the Home Economics Profession:
The Maltese Experience 228
Suzanne M. Piscopo and Karen S. Mugliett

PREFACE

This book strives to action an important statement included in the IFHE Position Statement: Home Economics for the 21st Century (IFHE, 2008, p. 2):

> The focus on the decade ahead is on future proofing, which describes the elusive process of trying to anticipate future developments, so that action can be taken to minimise possible negative consequences, and to seize opportunities. Future proofing the Home Economics profession and the Federation is a challenging task but one which is necessary to ensure a sustainable vision both for the profession, and for individual members. The International Federation of Home Economics has commenced its future-proofing strategy by focussing on questions of sustainability, advocacy and the active creation of preferred futures for Home Economics, relevant disciplinary fields, and the profession itself, while critically reflecting upon and being informed by its historical roots.

The editors, Professors Donna Pendergast (Australia), Sue L. T. McGregor (Canada) and Kaija Turkki (Finland), have worked closely with colleagues from around the globe to develop a book that takes this challenge head-on. With a stimulus chapter exploring the concept of future proofing within the context of megatrends, authors have contributed a range of creative ideas and future possibilities for the home economist, the Home Economics profession, and Home Economics professional associations in the 19 chapters that follow. They have reflected on the past and provided context-specific scenarios to illustrate how their ideas can be brought to life. The 34 authors reflect the global nature of the profession of Home Economics, with contributions from around the world.

This book, launched at the *International Federation for Home Economics World Congress in 2012*, is meant to add depth to the congress theme; Global creativity and innovation: Developing capacities for sustainable futures. The overarching focus of the congress is on global wellbeing, within a context of the transformative potential of Home Economics.

I hope you are inspired by the thinking presented in this book, a timely addition to our profession.

Professor Geraldene Hodelin, PhD
President, International Federation for Home Economics

CONTRIBUTING AUTHORS

Donna Pendergast

Professor Donna Pendergast is Dean and Head, School of Education and Professional Studies at Griffith University, Australia. She has undertaken extensive research and published widely in the field of Home Economics. Donna has actively served IFHE in roles including: Vice-President Pacific region and foundation editor of the International Journal of Home Economics. She was awarded a Fellowship of the Home Economics Institute of Australia for services to the profession including terms as President, secretary and journal editor.

Sue L.T. McGregor

Sue L. T. McGregor is a Canadian home economist (40 years) in the Faculty of Education at Mount Saint Vincent University, Canada. She has a keen interest in transdisciplinarity, integral studies, moral leadership and transformative practice as they relate to Home Economics and consumer studies. She is Docent in Home Economics at the University of Helsinki and Marjorie M. Brown Distinguished Professor.

Kaija Turkki

Kaija Turkki is a Professor in Home Economics in the Faculty of Behavioural Sciences at the University of Helsinki, Finland. She is responsible for Home Economics study programs and research from Bachelor to Doctoral levels. Kaija has devoted her teaching and research to extending our understanding of Home Economics as a multidimensional knowledge base and a forum for practice that is rooted deeply in our societies and guiding our way to the future. For the last 20 years she has shared her expertise widely at international organizations and networks.

Mira Ahn

Mira Ahn is an Assistant Professor at Texas State University-San Marcos. In addition to her background in statistics and architecture, she earned her Ph.D. from Housing at Virginia Tech. Her research focuses on home environment for the elderly. Her published research on this topic includes an examination of the role of residential technology in assisting to age in place and modification behaviour by older residents.

Noriko Arai

Noriko Arai, Ph.D., is a Professor and Vice Dean of the Faculty of Education in University of Fukui. Her major interest is to develop curriculum theory and educational strategy of Home Economics and to organize lesson study on citizenship and gender. She organized Post-2004 IFHE Congress Workshop at Kanazawa in Japan.

Jette Benn

Jette Benn is associate Professor, Ph.D. at the Institute of Education and Pedagogy, Faculty of Arts, Aarhus University, Denmark. She has undertaken research and published widely in the field of Home Economics, consumer and nutrition education. Jette has actively served IFHE in roles including: Chair of IFHE Research Committee from 2004 and as Chair of the Danish Committee. She acts as reviewer both for the IFHE journal and several others within consumer, health and nutrition areas. She has been used as reviewer of studies for the national board in Sweden and Latvia. She has been doing comprehensive studies of Home Economics within the school and through action research developed the program and developed Home Economics text books for the primary and lower secondary school.

Peng Chen

Peng Chen is Ph.D. candidate, at the International Comparative Education Research Institute, Faculty of Education, Beijing Normal University, China. She focuses on Home Economics research and will commit herself to the reestablishment of Home Economics in China.

Jay Deagon

Jay Deagon is Doctoral Candidate in the School of Education and Professional Studies, Griffith University, Brisbane, Australia. Jay is the founder of the HomeEcConnect website and researches Home Economics, spiritual health and wellbeing and Education for Sustainable Development. Jay is a 2008 and 2011 King & Amy O'Malley scholarship recipient.

Rita de Cássia Pereira Farias

Rita de Cássia Pereira Farias has an undergraduate and a masters degree in Home Economics and a doctorate degree in Social Anthropology. She teaches Clothing and Textiles in the Home Economics Course at Federal University of Viçosa Brazil. She coordinates the Graduate Program in Home Economics at that university, She researches clothing symbolism, fashion, identity, ethnicity, consumption and appearance. She wrote the book *Uniforme e Trabalho no Vale do Aço: Discursos, Práticas e Significados Simbolólicos* (Uniform and Labour in Vale do Aço: Discourses, Practices and Symbolic Meanings) published by UFV Publishers in 2012.

Henna Heinilä

Henna Heinilä, M.Sc. Home Economics teacher, 1986, Ph.D., 2007 is Principal Lecturer at HAAGA-HELIA University of Applied Sciences, School of Vocational Teacher Education, Helsinki Finland, from 2009. Her main interests are domestic skills, the rhythms of everyday life, phenomenology, inquiry-based learning and philosophical questions of Home Economics.

Karin Hjälmeskog

Karin Hjälmeskog was a teacher in Home Economics from 1978 to 1992. She completed her Doctoral degree in Education 2001 and has had assignments for the National Agency for Education, and as Political advisor at Ministry of Education. Her present position is Associate Professor and Deputy Head at the Department of Education Uppsala University. Karin was also a board member of the Swedish Committee of Home Economics and Chair of the committee 2001-2009.

Gwendolyn Hustvedt

Gwendolyn Hustvedt is an Assistant Professor in the School of Family and Consumer Sciences and Graduate Advisor for the Interdisciplinary Masters in Sustainability Studies at Texas State University-San Marcos. She earned her Ph.D. in Human Ecology from Kansas State University. Her research focuses on household sustainability with a particular emphasis on the textile supply chain and home laundering. She is actively involved in IFHE where she is a member of the Young Professional's Network and is Secretary for the Program Committee on Household Technology and Sustainability.

Yoko Ito

Yoko Ito is a Professor in the Faculty of Education at Chiba University in Japan. She received her doctorate in educational psychology from Ochanomizu University in 2003. Her current research interests are related to develop pre- parenting programs. She participates in cross-cultural studies of fathering in China, Japan, US and Sweden.

Hille Janhonen-Abruquah

Dr. Hille Janhonen-Abruquah is a Home Economics Sciences University Lecturer at the Department on Teacher Education, University of Helsinki, Finland. Currently her teaching and research interest lies on consumer education and multicultural learning. She has served IFHE as National Liaison for Finland, chaired the FIN-IFHE and an IFHE program committee.

Vuokko Jarva

Vuokko Jarva is Adjunct Professor at the University of Helsinki. Her experience includes roles as Ministry of Justice researcher in 1970s and academic researcher since early 1980s. She completed her doctorate in 1996 on consumer debt problems and was a university lecturer at the department on Home Economics and Craft Sciences between 2000 and 2009. She is specialized in futures studies and is member of the Editorial Board of Journal of Futures Studies.

Elizabeth Mngusen Kembe

Elizabeth is an Associate Professor of Home Economics, Federal University of Agriculture, Makurdi. She lectures and supervises theses and has published over 20 articles in national and international journals and 2 text books. Her current role includes Dean, College of Food Technology. Elizabeth's research interests include Family Resource Management, Home Economics Curriculum Development and Evaluation, and Women, Children in Development.

Irmhild Kettschau

Irmhild Kettschau has had a Professorship at the UASM since 1997. She is co-founder of the Institute of Teacher Training for Vocational Education at the University of Applied Sciences Münster (UASM), Germany. Since 2001 she holds the Professorship for the didactics of Home Economics and Nutrition Science and vocational pedagogy.

Jane Kolodinsky

Jane Kolodinsky, Ph.D., is Chair of the Department of Community Development and Applied Economics and Director of the Center for Rural Studies at the University of Vermont, USA. She has published 80 refereed journal articles and book chapters in the field of applied economics with a focus on the well-being of individuals and households. She has served as President of the American Council on Consumer Interests, on the editorial boards of the Journal of Consumer Affairs, International Journal of Consumer Studies and Home Economics and Journal of Family and Economic Issues.

Sylvia Lorek

Dr. Sylvia Lorek is Researcher and Policy Consultant for sustainable consumption since 1993. She has been Project Coordinator at the Wuppertal Institute for Climate, Environment and Energy. Since 2005 she is heading the Sustainable Europe Research Institute, Germany. Graduated in Home Economics as well as economics she combines the individual micro-economic and the societal macroeconomic perspective to analyse the contexts in which the scientific and societal discourses about sustainable consumption take place and to develop practical and political recommendations.

Nancy Mattausch

Nancy Mattausch, Environmental Engineer and M.Sc. graduate, is a Research Assistant at the Institute of Teacher Training for Vocational Education at the University of Applied Sciences in Muenster, Germany (UASM). She is a leading team member of the project Development of a sustainable core curriculum for professions in Home Economics and the hospitality industry.

Lois R. Mberengwa

Lois R. Mberengwa is Associate Professor in the Family and Consumer Sciences Department at the University of Botswana. She has taught at various levels of the education ladder for more than 25 years. Lois has been external examiner to several teacher-training colleges and universities in the Southern African Development Cooperation region. She has presented conference papers, written secondary school textbooks and published articles on curricular issues, family life issues including African family strengths and empowerment.

Michio Miyano

Michio Miyano is Director and Vice President of Osaka City University. He is former director of The Japan Society of Home Economics. Also, he is Vice president of Society of Social Safety Science. He has studied about safety of housing and disaster prevention on a regional scale.

Nwakego Molokwu

Nwakego Molokwu Ed.s; Ph. D Professor, Home Economics Education, Ebonyi State University Abakaliki has initiated and headed Home Economics programs. Nwakego has published over 50 journal articles, chapters in 6 books and 2 e-books. Current roles include Resource person to NUC, Universities and colleges of Education in curriculum development and evaluation. Current research interest includes Environmental Sustainability and Gender Education.

Fungai M. Mthombeni

Fungai M. Mthombeni is a Food and Nutrition Lecturer in the Department of Family and Consumer Sciences Education at University of Botswana. She taught Home Economics in Zimbabwe at high school and tertiary levels for twenty- six years before joining University of Botswana. Her research interest focuses on Family and Consumer Sciences teaching/learning environment, food product development, and maternal child dietary adequacy. Fungai is a mentor of the University Home Economics Association.

Karen Mugliett

Karen Mugliett is a Lecturer on Nutrition, Family and Consumer Studies at the University of Malta, teaching in the B.Ed, M.Ed and other courses. She sits on various international and national boards, is active in the local mass media and has authored an award-winning book on sustainable cooking.

Midori Otake

Midori Otake, Ph.D. is Vice President of Tokyo Gakugei University and Professor of the Course of Home Economics Education at Division of Integrated Education in Tokyo Gakugei University in Japan. She has served as President of the Japanese Society for Home Economists, President of Japanese Association of Home Economics Education.

Christiane Pakula

Christiane Pakula received a Diploma in Nutritional Science and Home Economics in 2008 from the University of Bonn. Since April 2008 she has been working as a Research Assistant in the Institute of Agricultural Engineering. Her work focuses on food preparation and cooking, consumer behaviour and sustainability in private households.

Suzanne Piscopo

Suzanne Piscopo, Senior Lecturer on Nutrition, Family and Consumer Studies at the University of Malta, teaches in the B.Ed, M.Ed and other courses. Author of health-related children's storybooks, Suzanne is active in the local mass media, sits on various international and national boards, and chairs 'Home Economists in Action'.

Kei Sasai

Kei Sasai is a Professor of Faculty of Human Sciences and Design at Japan Women's University. She recently works for empowering women in developing countries through clothing education. She serves as Vice President of the Japanese Society for Home Economics and Vice President of Asian Regional Association of Home Economics.

Rainer Stamminger

Professor Rainer Stamminger is Dean of the Institute of Agricultural Engineering and holds the Chair for Appliance Technology and Process Engineering at the University of Bonn. Rainer has worked in the past many years for appliance industry and is now researching extensively on the way appliances are used and how this usage can be optimized. He chairs the Program Committee on Household Technology and Sustainability within IFHE.

Hester Steyn

Professor Hester Steyn completed her Ph.D. degree at the University of the Free State in South Africa in 1995. She is currently chairperson of the department of Consumer Science at the University of the Free State. She specializes in Textile Science with focus on laundry practices and natural fibres.

Carola Strassner

Carola Strassner holds the endowed Chair of Sustainable Food Systems and Nutrition Ecology in the Faculty of Home Economics and Nutrition Science at the University of Applied Sciences, Münster (UASM) Germany. Her current research foci include the organic food system and sustainable foodservice. She pursues her business interests with her company a'verdis, sustainable foodservice solutions.

Kuniko Sugiyama

Kuniko Sugiyama is a Professor of Faculty of Education and Human Sciences at Yokohama National University in Japan. She received her doctorate in agriculture from the University of Tokyo in 1991. She serves as representative of the Association for Home Economics Education of Yokohama National University.

Stefan Wahlen

Stefan Wahlen is Lecturer in Sociology of Consumers and Households at the Wageningen University and Research Centre, the Netherlands. Results of his research are published in the *Journal of Home Economics,* the *Journal of Consumer Policy* and the *International Journal of Consumer Studies.* Stefan has served as chair of the IFHE young professionals network (YPN) including a co-opted membership to the federation's executive committee. Moreover, he has taken over responsibilities in the program committee on consumer issues and sustainability.

ACKNOWLEDGEMENTS

The editors wish to thank Joy Reynolds for her administrative contribution to this book. We also acknowledge the enthusiastic response of our colleagues who replied to the Call for Chapter Abstracts, many of whom we reluctantly were unable to include given the overwhelming response. We thank the reviewers for their insightful comments and the publishers for their confidence in this project.

We are grateful to all of the home economists who have, over the years, eagerly taken on the task of organizing the IFHE congresses. We dedicate this book to them and to our founders from over 100 years ago, to our current, vigilant practitioners and to our future practitioners, all of whom hold the profession in their capable hands as they strive for practice that will sustain and future-proof the profession

Donna Pendergast

Sue L.T. McGregor

Kaija Turkki

CHAPTER

1

Creating Home Economics Futures: The Next 100 Years

Donna Pendergast, Sue L. T. McGregor and Kaija Turkki

In 2012, the World Congress of the International Federation for Home Economics (IFHE) was hosted by Home Economics Victoria in Melbourne, Australia. It was the first congress of the *next one hundred years*. Home Economics as a profession celebrated the centennial of the establishment of IFHE at the World Congress in 2008. This was followed up by the American Association of Family and Consumer Sciences (AAFCS) centenary in 2009. As the profession commences its second century of influence, the opportunity to provide a future orientation has never been more important. This chapter provides the platform for outlining the futures orientation underlying the chapters of this book.

Home Economics in contemporary times

Contemporary Home Economics has been described by Pendergast as being at a 'convergent moment' (2006, 2009), a time of opportunity where several key societal factors are occurring simultaneously. Pendergast argues that these factors serve to provide a moment of alignment of potentially facilitating factors that, when taken together, provide an unprecedented opportunity to re-vision the Home Economics profession. These convergent factors can be seen as a catalyst for major reform, and include: (a) the past century of invention, development and changes in roles for men and women; (b) consumption and globalization patterns; (c) generational characteristics and the emergence of the digital native as the Y generation; (d) features of 'New Times' and the need to be 'expert novices' (good at learning new things); and, (e) significant changes in individual and family structures impacting globally on demographic patterns and on the family's ability to fulfil its main functions as a fundamental social institution.

1

The Home Economics profession has entered its 6th generation. It is characterized by a multigenerational cohort of professionals with the greatest number of members and the most leadership roles held by Baby Boomers; that is, people born between 1943 and 1960 (Howe & Strauss, 2000). Each generation brings to the field predictable traits, values and beliefs, along with skills, attributes, capacities and preferred modus operandi directly reflecting their generational location (see McGregor & Toronyi, 2009 and Pendergast, 2007, 2009).

At a global level, there has been important progress in the conceptual development of the profession, leading to the development of the *IFHE Position Statement — Home Economics in the 21st Century (IFHE, 2008, www.ifhe.org)*.

The position statement is a two-page document produced through a global, collaborative process with members of IFHE and more widely of the Home Economics profession (see Pendergast, 2008). It is an attempt to locate the profession in the contemporary context by serving as a platform, looking ahead to viable and progressive visions of Home Economics for the twenty-first century and beyond. It is expected to be used to provide defensible arguments for individuals and professional groups requiring such support, as they strive to validate and legitimize the role of Home Economics in solving the problems facing humanity.

Creating futures — the place of megatrends

Futurists make predications and speculate about the future. They base their future predictions on a compilation of informing factors such as: patterns of human behaviour, politics and religious beliefs, environmental trends and changes, economic context and access to resources. In fact, there is a whole field of study that thrives on predicting future trends and advising organisations, professions, businesses, countries, individuals — almost everyone and anyone, how they might survive and thrive in the context offered by alternative futures. Futures researchers always work with three types of futures: the predictable, the possible, and the preferred. *Probable futures* are likely to happen if present trends (and the interplay among them) continue. *Possible futures* might conceivably come about if nurtured. They are not bound by current, seemingly inexorable, trends or paradigms. Finally, *preferred futures* are futures we would like to come about, given our values and our priorities. Aiming to achieve preferred futures often involves challenging current worldviews and paradigms (Selby, 1999) and there is often some intentional approach to managing the likely or probable future in ways that lead to the desired outcomes.

One futurist group is the *Copenhagen Institute for Futures Study* (see http://www.cifs.dk/scripts/artikel.asp?id=1469). This group uses the idea of megatrends to consider the future. The idea of mega (great) trends (move in a direction) is in fact a megatrend in itself; that is, the idea of having great moves in a direction is a trend we are likely to see more of in the future. Theorists generally define megatrends as the great forces in societal development that will very likely affect the future in all areas over the next 10–20 years. According to Hajkowicz and Moody, a megatrend is a "... collection of trends, patterns of economic, social or environmental activity that will change the way people live and the science and technology products they demand" (2010, p. 2).

Megatrends are the identification of *probable futures*. Many companies and organizations use megatrends in their strategic work as a base for identifying probable futures and reshaping these to possible and preferred futures. The following megatrends are drawn from the future predictions made by this Institute and formed the basis for the authors of this book to develop their chapters.

Megatrends are our current knowledge about the probable future; hence, they are regarded as being predictable. Megatrends are the forces that define our present and future worlds, and the interaction between them is as important as each individual megatrend. That is why futures researchers, companies and others use megatrends when they develop and work with scenarios. Scenario is Latin *scena* (scene), an imagined situation or sequence of events, a possible course of action.

Even though megatrends say something about what we know of the future, it is not certain how society, professions or any of us will react to or shape these forces.

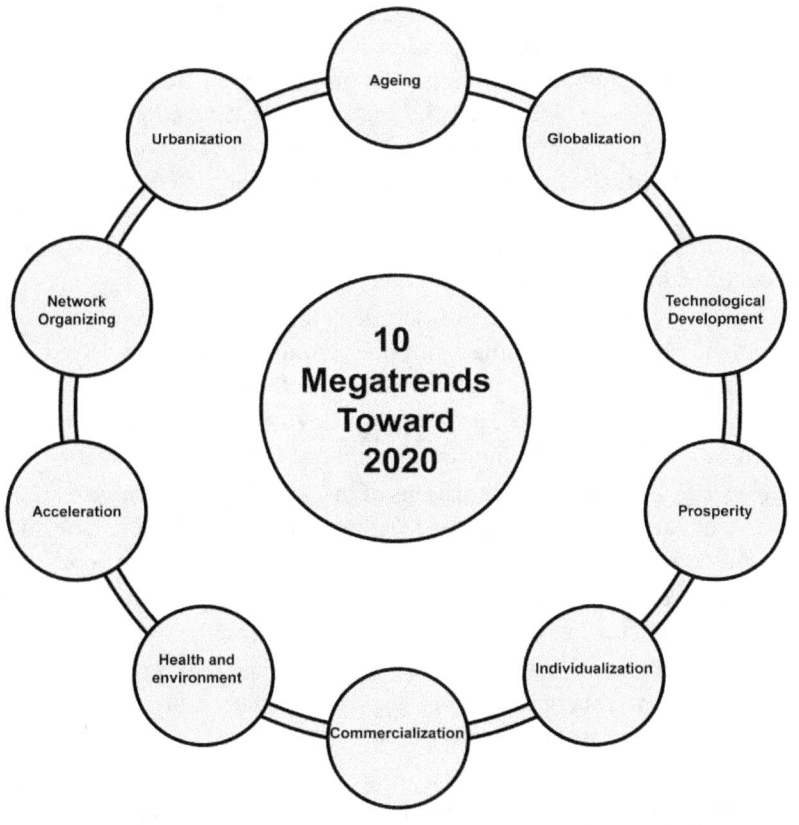

Figure 1.1

The 10 megatrends

The future is never a given, and any one of us can affect or create the future. Megatrends provide the likely predictable future, but there are other possible, alternative futures. Every megatrend can be set aside or can suddenly and fundamentally change direction. Wildcards — events that are unlikely, but that would have enormous consequences — can slow or augment a megatrend's development or create counter-forces. An excellent example of an unpredictable event is the terrorist attacks of September 11, 2001, which are recognised globally, and which temporarily stopped corporate growth and slowed some aspects of corporate-led, economic globalization.

Megatrends can be used as a method to strategically look to the future. This approach moves into the applied sphere of futures work known as future-proofing, one of the key strategies for the future highlighted in the *IFHE Home Economics Position Statement*. McGregor (2011) explains that if a profession is future-proofed, it is protected; guaranteed not to be superceded by unanticipated future developments. A future-proofed profession takes steps *now* in order to avoid having to make radical changes to practice in order to remain viable in the future. A future-proofed profession is strategically planned so it can remain effective even, especially, when things change. Figure 1.1 provides a visualisation of the 10 megatrends towards 2020, and Table 1.1 provides further detailed explanation, as formulated by the Copenhagen Institute for Futures Study. *Copenhagen Institute for Futures Study.*

The Australian Commonwealth Scientific and Industrial Research Organisation (CSIRO) recently released the report, *Our Future World: An analysis of global trends, shocks and scenarios* (Hajkowicz & Moody, 2010). This report also utilised the idea of megatrends to capture the future trends likely to shape the next decade. The authors filtered their list to five megatrends, which unsurprisingly are very similar to those developed by the *Copenhagen Institute for Futures Study*. The five interrelated megatrends identified in the Australian report are:

- *More from less.* This relates to the world's depleting natural resources and increasing demand for those resources through economic and population growth. Coming decades will see a focus on resource use efficiency.
- *A personal touch.* Growth of the services sector of western economies is being followed by a second wave of innovation aimed at tailoring and targeting services.
- *Divergent demographics.* The populations of the 32 OECD countries are ageing and experiencing lifestyle and diet related health problems. At the same time, there are high fertility rates and problems of not enough food for millions in poor countries.
- *On the move.* People are changing jobs and careers more often, moving house more often, commuting further to work and travelling around the world more often.
- *iWorld.* Everything in the natural world will have a digital counterpart. Computing power and memory storage are improving rapidly. Many more devices are getting connected to the internet (Hajkowicz & Moody, 2010, p. 3).

The CSIRO report also introduces the idea of megashocks, which are defined as "potential risks facing the global community which may be expressed via sudden, and

Table 1.1
Megatrends — Towards 2020

Megatrend	Explanation
Aging	The world population is 7 billion.
	On a global frame, the population of the world is ageing as a result of two factors: longer life expectancy and a decline in birth rates, largely through efficient birth control.
	There will be relatively more elderly than youths in the next decades.
	The aging megatrend applies particularly to developed regions of the world, and has great significance for society, the economy, business, education and individuals.
	Japan and Italy have been identified as two of the oldest populations in the world, so will lead the aging megatrend.
	A federal government report released in Australia points to some of the implications of this megatrend as follows:
	> Over the next 40 years, a number of developed countries are expected to experience long-run population decline associated with low fertility levels. Europe's total population is projected to fall by over 40 million by 2050, driven by substantial falls in the populations of Russia and Germany. Higher spending on public health care, pensions and other social services caused by population ageing is resulting in rising fiscal pressures for governments across the OECD (Australian Government, 2010, n.p.).
	Most OECD countries have the issue of an aging population at the top of their political agendas, and health care, pension systems and care for the elderly have been prioritized in many countries in recent years.
Globalization	Globalization is any range of processes, innovations and changes that increase the interconnectedness of the world.
	Globalization of the economy is bound to the expansion of new communications technologies such as the Internet, creating a global village where the traditional boundaries of time and geographic space have been negated.
	Globalization makes us more alike across the world, but it also makes us more aware of local differences.
	The global development leads to increased liberalization and expanded trade in most countries and regions.
	However, it does not seem likely that the world will be dominated by common political and ethical values in the near future.
	A probable future can therefore be a world made up of regions and nations, with global free trade but with deeper integration only at regional levels.
Technological development	Humans are the only creatures who construct and develop tools that make life more pleasant. Since the start of the industrial age, technological development has accelerated, so changes come faster and in more areas.
	The most important technological development areas in the next decades are: information technology, biotechnology, nanotechnology and energy.
	Information technology has created enormous changes in recent decades: personal computers, the Internet, mobile telephones, industrial robots, iPods, and much more. In 2020, computers will be about 200 times faster than today's computers, and will have memories 1000 times as large. Computers and robots will take on increasingly complex assignments, and the Internet will be the site for completely new, virtual industries.
	Research in biotechnology opens the door to new, future treatments in the form of gene therapy and transplantation of cloned organs. Genetically modified plants and animals (GMO) may potentially relieve world hunger. However, biotechnology raises ethical questions: Is it acceptable to manipulate life? Will biotechnology prompt unforeseen biological catastrophes?

CONTINUE NEXT PAGE

Table 1.1 (CONT)
Megatrends — Towards 2020

Megatrend	Explanation
Technological development	Nanotechnology is a general term for technology with structures on a nanometer scale (one billionth of a meter). Researchers develop nanomaterials with many fantastic characteristics such as extreme strength, special electric properties and extremely low friction. Nanoelectronics may, in a few years, replace microelectronics. A littlefurther into the future are nanomachines: microscopic robots that, for example, swim around in our veins removing cancer and plaque.
Prosperity	The majority of the population of OECD countries and large groups in formerly developing countries are growing more prosperous. Between 2% and 4% growth is assumed in the western world in coming years, and in some regions — especially North America, Latin America, and Asia — the growth rate will likely reach 10–15%. It is doubtful that Africa and the Middle East will enjoy such growth and increase in prosperity because fertility rates are expected to remain high in these regions, among other factors. The Russian middle class will grow from 50% to 85% in the next 10 years, the Chinese from 5% to 40% and the Brazilian from 25% to 50%.
	Gross National Product (GNP) is traditionally used to measure and compare the wealth of nations. The US and EU are, measured by GNP, far richer than other parts of the world, but that can change in step with the high economic growth rates and increasing employment in many developing countries.
	The economic growth will cause a change in the demand for new types of products, with a new business structure as a result. In short, most countries are going through a structural social and economic change in the transition from agricultural and/or industrial society to a knowledge society.
	As countries become more prosperous, new needs arise and consumption increases in the form of intangible products such as entertainment, experiences, services, savings and investment. More prosperity changes our consumption of traditional tangible products such as food, because affluent consumers focus on health, quality, trust, origin, animal welfare, etc.
Individualization	Individualization is the shift from more collectivist societal norms to the person.
	Individualisation of life paths refers to the never-before experienced lack of clear guidelines about future roles, the difficulties associated with long-term decision making where careers and jobs have not yet been created.
	The individualistic approach has made branding one of the key figures in modern sales and marketing.
Commercialization	Commercialization is the meeting of increasingly more human needs by the private market through trade that can be both supply and demand driven.
	Prosperity and individualization accelerate commercialization because consumers have more money and at the same time demand individually tailored products and services.
	Commercialization will probably increase in the future, and the consequences will range from even more prosperity to specialization in business and the labor market. Specialization means that companies deliver more differentiated products and services while employees work more with product development, innovation, marketing and sales. This will in turn speed up the transition to the creative knowledge economy.
	Commercialization gives the individual more choices, increases competitive pressure on many companies and organizations, and thereby creates a growing market for new products.

CONTINUE NEXT PAGE

Table 1.1 (CONT)
Megatrends — Towards 2020

Megatrend	Explanation
Health and environment	Fitness has become wellness, and so has gained a more spiritual and personality-optimizing character. New spa baths, treatment resorts and other offerings ar constantly appearing on the market.
	The health and environment megatrend will have even greater significance in the coming years. There will be more age-related illnesses, more lifestyle illnesses such as obesity and stress, and more mental illness. Men's sperm quality has fallen greatly over the last 10 years, more children suffer from allergy, and smoking is banned in more and more places. There will be focus on clean drinking water, even in the countries that until now have not had problems drinking water from the tap.
	The individual household uses more and more money on environment and health.
Acceleration	The industrial revolution was the starting signal for increased acceleration, which has continued to grow since then.
	Today there is more knowledge for the individual to consider, more to produce and consume, more to throw out, more to communicate, more to transport and many more people to interact with.
	The pace of change is the number of changes in society per unit of time, and there are no absolute numbers for it.
	Changes touch us on many levels, and we change jobs, partners, friends, interests, homes, knowledge, news and ideas faster than before. Information is not just more accessible today — the entry of new products on the market goes faster and faster.
	Modern people must make far more daily choices than ever before, and our curiosity and our aspirations for development, new knowledge and improvements will be forces that will increase the pace of change in the future.
Network organizing	Network organizing is a megatrend because network has become a central term that permeates our way of thinking.
	A network's value increases exponentially with the number of members who are in it. Changes in a network society do not happen linearly as they do in an industrial society. That means that many changes that took decades in the past now happen significantly faster.
	Network organizing greatly affects technological, societal and economic development, and this will increase.
	In 2009 Facebook announced that 250 million people used the social networking tool. In 2011 there were reportedly 800 million active users worldwide. This is an amazing statistic given that it was only created in 2004!
	Networks drive out hierarchies and create many new open and decentralized social structures. This applies to private life, especially for the younger generation, to the labor market, and business life.
	Network organizing challenges our entire way of thinking and traditional institutions such as the nation-state, the church, culture and language because people enter other and new networks more than ever before.
Urbanization	Just over 48% of the world's 7 billion people live in urban areas. The United Nations predicts that this will rise to over 53% by 2030. While the average annual rate of change in urbanization towards 2030 is predicted to be only 0.5% in more developed regions, it is predicted to be 2.3% in less developed regions, primarily in Asia and Africa.
	Rapid urbanization poses a fundamental challenge to the development of adequate infrastructure and liveable housing, and the maintenance of healthy environments. Other than that, it also put stress on traditional ways of living, family structure and cultural values — creating a growing potential for social and political unrest.

dramatic, events" (Hajkowicz & Moody, 2010, p. 15). These megashocks are categorized as: economic, geopolitical, environmental, societal and technological.

The next 100 years?

So, what might our world look like in the coming decades, in the next one hundred years, given these megatrends and megashocks? In his book, *The Next 100 Years, A forecast for the 21st Century*, George Friedman (2009) reflects on historical and geopolitical patterns dating back hundreds of years to predict what the next 100 years holds for the United States, as it interacts with the rest of the world. Among his predictions are the following:

- The US-Jihadist war will conclude, replaced with a second full-blown cold war with Russia;
- China will undergo a major extended internal crisis, and Mexico will emerge as an important world power;
- A new global war will unfold toward the middle of the century between the United States and an unexpected coalition from Eastern Europe, Eurasia and the Far East;
- Technology will focus on space, both for major military uses and for a dramatic new energy source that will have radical environmental implications; and,
- The United States will experience a Golden Age in the second half of the century (Friedman, 2009).

These rather more bold predictions about the future of the United States are also probable futures for us. So where in this story of the future does Home Economics as a profession sit? What is the role of Home Economics in these probable futures? Better yet, what future does Home Economics *prefer* given its values and priorities? *Preferred futures* are what we would *like* to see come about. Ensuring these futures means we have to be prepared to challenge current worldviews and paradigms, even to challenge the identity of the 10 megatrends described in this chapter.

Future-Proofing the Profession

The final section of the *IFHE Position Statement — Home Economics in the 21st Century* (IFHE, 2008) states the following objectives for the next decade:

> The focus on the decade ahead is on future-proofing, which describes the elusive process of trying to anticipate future developments, so that action can be taken to minimise possible negative consequences, and to seize opportunities. Future-proofing the Home Economics profession and the Federation is a challenging task but one which is necessary to ensure a sustainable vision both for the profession, and for individual members. The International Federation of Home Economics has commenced its future-proofing strategy by focussing on questions of sustainability, advocacy and the active creation of preferred futures for Home Economics, relevant disciplinary fields, and the profession itself, while critically reflecting upon and being informed by its historical roots. (IFHE, 2008, p. 2)

Those who developed the IFHE statement felt that this is the platform upon which our future should be built. By way of commencing this work, the IFHE Think Tank committee is responsible for leading the processes involved in a rebranding exercise, involving the reflection and forward visioning of Home Economics as a recognisable 'brand' into the future. A brand serves several key functions. To be more visible and accessible, we have to be able to define and articulate distinctive characteristics by which people come to know us. A brand has to empower those using it to demonstrate their identity with the profession. It should be based on a vision, a mission and ends valued by everyone who will be using the identity (brand). Promoting the brand with consistent visuals and messaging ensures that people know they are dealing with a stable and secure entity — the Home Economics profession (McGregor, 2007). Connecting with the 10 core megatrends is a proactive way to create a preferred future for the profession, by branding it as involved with megatrends.

In addition to branding the profession, McGregor (2007) proposed we consider creating Home Economics ambassadors. Ambassador stems from the Medieval Latin word *ambactia*, mission. Ambassadors are spokespersons authorized to represent the profession, and *carry its message*. They would represent the profession in areas outside the field of practice, bringing its mission, unique approaches to practice and valued ends to others' attention. Their main function would be to advance the interests of the profession. This work would occur quietly behind the scenes or in the public eye. They would be well versed in an agreed- to value statement of the profession (one example being the 2008 IFHE position statement). They would spread the word about the profession's work, our value and the contributions of the profession to the good of humanity. This idea has potential. Ambassadors of the profession can position it firmly in the centre of the complex 21st century.

Within this mission of branding the profession, and becoming ambassadors of the profession, it is important to consider *what* Home Economics might be and *how* we ensure that the profession is a part of the future of humankind. Clarity about "what is Home Economics?" has been a challenge to the profession for one hundred years. IFHE has proposed a unified position from which to engage in Home Economics work around the globe: "Home Economics is a field of study and a profession, situated in the human sciences that draws from a range of disciplines to achieve optimal and sustainable living for individuals, families and communities" (IFHE, 2008, p. 1).

Furthermore, the IFHE 2008 position statement proposed that Home Economics can be clarified by four dimensions or areas of practice (see Figure 1.2):

- as an *academic discipline* to educate new scholars, to conduct research and to create new knowledge and ways of thinking for professionals and for society;
- as an arena for *everyday living* in households, families and communities for developing human growth potential and human necessities or basic needs to be met;
- as a *curriculum area* that facilitates students to discover and further develop their own resources and capabilities to be used in their personal life, by directing their professional decisions and actions or preparing them for life; and,

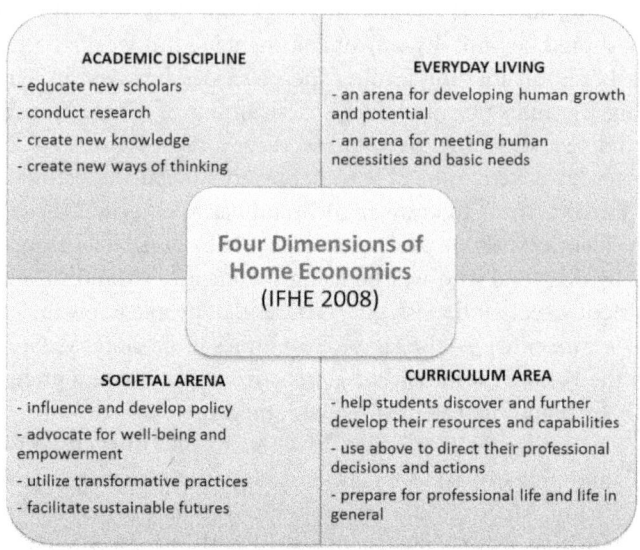

Figure 1.2

Four Dimensions of Home Economics practice

- as a *societal arena to influence and develop policy* to advocate for individuals, families and communities to achieve empowerment and wellbeing, to utilize transformative practices and to facilitate sustainable futures.

The IFHE has offered the profession a position about the four dimensions of Home Economics practice. In summary, the intent is to augment and advance the profession's knowledge base; facilitate everyday living of the family as a social institution; prepare any Home Economics student (primary, secondary and tertiary) to engage with life; and, influence policy for the improvement of family life and, by association, humanity. We now need to capture the 21st century thinking that enables us to enact this vision for the profession. If the profession of Home Economics is to survive and thrive, there must be a committed effort to adapt the incentives, the motivators, the leadership models and the overall culture of the profession to strategically target a preferred future.

The profession is responsible for making its own future and must engage with the megatrends of society as a way forward. Home Economics can be a dynamic tool to create a sustainable future. But, to do that we have to discover future making tools and renew our communication with others and with each other. Everyone in the profession has to continually learn new things and deeply trust in our commitments to families and to humanity (Turkki, 2008). The promise of Home Economics is there for the future, if we work for it.

Discussion Prompts

- How might you engage with the idea of megatrends and future proofing in the roles you play?
- What is your preferred future for Home Economics?
- What action can you take, within your sphere of influence, to shape a preferred future for Home Economics?

References

Australian Government (2010). *The 2010 Intergenerational Report.* http://www.treasury.gov.au/igr/igr2010/report/html/03_Chapter_2_Growing_the_economy.asp Retrieved 17 March, 2010.

Copenhagen Institute for Futures Study (2006) *Why megatrends matter.*http://www.cifs.dk/scripts/artikel.asp?id=1469). Retrieved 14 January, 2012.

Friedman, G. (2009). *The Next 100 Years, A forecast for the 21st Century.*

Hajkowicz, S & Moody, J (2010). *Our future world. An analysis of global trends, shocks and scenarios,* CSIRO, Canberra.

Howe, N. & Strauss, W. (2000). *Millennial's rising: The next great generation.* New York: Vintage Books.

International Federation for Home Economics (2008). *IFHE Position Statement – Home Economics in the 21st Century.* Bonn: IFHE.

McGregor, S. L. T. (2007). Practising on purpose: Becoming professional ambassadors. Workshop for the Alberta Human Ecology Association Conference/AGM. Red Deer, Alberta. Retrieved from http://www.consultmcgregor.com/documents/keynotes/Alberta_2007_Practice_on_Purpose_PD_Overheads.pdf

McGregor, S. L. T. (2011). Home Economics in higher education: Pre professional socialization. *International Journal of Consumer Studies, 35*(5), 560–568.

McGregor, S. L. T., & Toronyi, K. T. (2009). A millennial recruitment and retention blueprint for home economics professional associations. International Journal of Home Economics, *2*(2), 18–35.

Pendergast, D. (2000). The Future of Home Economics, *ECHO, 39*(2), 2–9.

Pendergast, D. (2006). Sustaining the home economics profession in new times — A convergent moment. In Rauma, A., Pollanen, S. & Seitamaa-Hakkarainen, P. (Eds), *Human Perspectives on Sustainable Future.* Joensuu: University of Joensuu.

Pendergast, D. (2007). Teaching Y generation. *Journal of the Home Economics Institute of Australia, 14*(3), 15–21.

Pendergast, D. (2008). Introducing the IFHE Position Statement, *International Journal of Home Economics, 1*(1), 3–7.

Pendergast, D. (2009). Generational theory and home economics: Future proofing the profession. *Family and Consumer Sciences Research Journal. 37*(4), 504–522.

Selby, D. (1999). Global education: Towards a quantum model of environmental education. *Canadian Journal of Environmental Education, 4,* 125–141.

Turkki, K. (2008). Home Economics — A Dynamic Tool for Creating a Sustainable Future. *International Journal of Home Economics, 1*(1), 32–42.

CHAPTER

2

The Intention of Home Economics Education: A Powerful Enabler for Future-Proofing the Profession

Donna Pendergast

This chapter highlights the contribution of Home Economics education to develop lifelong learning capabilities and to contribute to optimising individual and family well-being. The intention of Home Economics education is explored and connections to generational theory and other 'convergent factors' are heralded as key factors impacting on the future Home Economics education agenda. In order to achieve this, a review and re-presentation of some of the thinking by the author over the last decade will be featured in this chapter as the foundation to the renewed call for a focus on the capacity to develop lifelong learners, who are expert novices in and of their profession. Connections to the five interrelated megatrends presented in the stimulus chapter highlight the ways in which a proactive position can be taken to ameliorate the trends in ways that set the path for professionals and the profession on a preferred futures trajectory, leaning heavily on the argument that Home Economics education is a powerful enabler of such an achievement and can be used as a means to empower individuals to be effective agents in the techniques of future-proofing.

The intention of Home Economics education

Home Economics curriculum differs around the world, whether in a school, university or other educational location. Students undertake context- specific content in a range of domains, yet there is a shared theoretical and philosophical base and set of core practices that bind Home Economics curriculum globally. Recently, the *IFHE Position Statement — Home Economics in the 21st Century* (IFHE, 2008, p. 1) captured this shared meaning by formulating the statement that as a curriculum area, Home Economics...

> ... facilitates students to discover and further develop their own resources and capabilities to be used in their personal life, by directing their professional decisions and actions or preparing them for life.

Hence, through the engagement in Home Economics curriculum, the individual is provided the learning opportunity to develop capabilities to enhance personal empowerment to act in daily contexts. Contexts may include, but are not limited to: food; nutrition and health; textiles and clothing; shelter and housing; consumerism and consumer science; household management; design and technology; food science and hospitality; human development and family studies; and, education and community services. In the Position Statement, it is argued that the capacity to draw from such disciplinary diversity is "a strength of the profession, allowing for the development of specific interpretations of the field, as relevant to the context" (IFHE, 2008, p. 1).

Further, the *Position Statement* explains that Home Economics is:

> ... concerned with the empowerment and well-being of individuals, families and communities, and of facilitating the development of attributes for lifelong learning for paid, unpaid and voluntary work and living situations (2008, p. 1).

The key concepts of 'well-being' and 'lifelong learning' are strikingly evident as intended outcomes of Home Economics education. It is to these concepts, in the context of Home Economics education that the chapter now turns.

Well-being

The concept of well-being has been explored in the literature for decades, including in the Home Economics literature (see for example Henry, 1995; McGregor & Goldsmith, 1998; Deagon & Pendergast, 2012), which is unsurprising given that Home Economics is explicitly concerned with optimizing well-being. It is used widely in health promotion fields, yet a single definition remains elusive (McGregor, 2010). The idea of self-definition, as for family, remains the most useful as it enables a context-specific focus. As argued by Twigg and Pendergast (2012, n.p.) the "most accessible of all definitions is the simplest: well-being is good or satisfactory condition of existence, as defined by the individual or family".

In Australia and globally, considerable research has sought to identify how to optimize well-being, including in educational contexts. Two categories of factors have been identified that impact on well-being; risk factors and protective factors. Risk factors are those that are likely to negatively affect the achievement of a state of well-being; while protective factors are those that are likely to contribute positively to the enhancement of well-being. These latter factors can be grouped into five domains: personal, family, formal learning context, life events, and community and cultural domains (Mission Australia, 2005). With respect to Home Economics education, there is a particular opportunity to focus on reducing risk and enhancing protective factors through the curriculum, especially in the domains of the personal and the formal learning contexts. By way of example, with respect to the personal domain, developing problem solving skills, social competence and optimism are all powerful ways of enhancing protective factors to achieve well-being, and these are fundamental to Home Economics curriculum. With respect to the formal learning domain, developing pro-social behaviour, providing opportunities for hands-on activities and success and a sense of belonging are also protective factors that are fundamentally incorporated in Home Economics curriculum.

In Australia, for example, the new nationally developed curriculum informed by the *Melbourne Declaration on Educational Goals for Young Australians* (MCEETYA, 2008) notes the 'vital role' schools play in "promoting the intellectual, physical, social, emotional, moral, spiritual and aesthetic development and well-being of young Australians, and in ensuring the nation's ongoing economic prosperity and social cohesion" (MCEETA, 2008, p. 4). As an intended outcome of Home Economics education, individual and family well-being is a powerful aspiration. Combined with the achievement of well-being, the development of the attributes of lifelong learning is also explicitly stated to be the intention of Home Economics education.

Lifelong learning

Education systems around the world have embraced the ideals of lifelong learning since the 1980's. The aspiration of the development of attributes of lifelong learners is commonly embedded as a key component of government reports and policy documents. It is rapidly becoming a generic educational target connected with and assumed to encapsulate the desirable characteristics of members of society, both during and after their formal years of education. The focus on lifelong learning has been prompted by the emergence of knowledge economies and information societies, the key features of which are well known and documented, including: globalization and increasing trade liberalism; changing nature of work and employment opportunities; increased mobility; increasing impact of new and future ICTs; and a shift away from manufacturing towards knowledge and service economies (Bahr & Pendergast, 2007). The five interrelated megatrends outlined in Chapter 1 of this book indicate that the past trends leading to the need for the development of lifelong learning attributes continue into the predicted future, reinforcing the continued need for this aspirational outcome of education.

Lifelong learning focuses attention on the need for continual learning and on the sets of generic skills and capacities that will equip individuals and societies to embrace the expanded notion of learning and the challenges of living and working in knowledge economies and the new work order. As the Ministerial Council on Education, Employment, Training and Youth Affairs (MCEETYA 2005:5) notes in its position paper *Contemporary learning: Learning in an online world*, "continuous learning with clear purpose and connection to the real world is critical to developing the capabilities, dispositions and literacy's required to participate in society and to deal with the complexity of issues and change." From the point of view of educators, this approach means focussing on the development in students of traits associated with being 'expert novices' (Gee, Hull & Lankshear, 1996); that is, someone who is an expert at continually learning anew and in-depth.

Just what is lifelong learning? In their report prepared for the Organization for Economic Cooperation and Development (OECD), Selby Smith and Ferrier (2002) identify four key elements for education to lead to lifelong learning outcomes for contemporary societies, these being:

- Systemic view of learning — that learning, formal and informal, is linked to the full life cycle rather than 'front-loaded' into the compulsory years of schooling;
- Centrality of the learner — recognition of diversity of learners and a shift in priority towards an increased client focus;
- Motivation to learn — attention to self-directed and individualized learning; and,
- Multiple objectives of educational policies — economic, social, personal.

Perhaps the best known and most useful of the lifelong learning conceptual frameworks is offered by UNESCO's International Commission on Education for the Twenty-First Century, under the leadership of Jacques Delors. The report, *Learning: The treasure within* (Delors, 1996), outlines four characteristics of lifelong learners that are needed to set the parameters of a lifelong learning society:

- learning *to do* (acquiring and applying skills, including life skills);
- learning *to be* (promoting creativity and personal fulfilment);
- learning *to know* (an approach to learning that is flexible, critical and capable); and,
- learning *to live together* (exercising tolerance, understanding and mutual respect).

A curriculum review auditing the opportunities of *learning to do, to be, to know and to live together* offers the potential to understand the contribution disciplines make to achieving lifelong learning capabilities. Unsurprisingly, latterly, the measurement of lifelong learning attributes has become an important priority to achieve an evidence base to demonstrate the effectiveness of curriculum, pedagogy and assessment practices. For example, the *Composite Learning Index* (Canadian Council of Learning, 2010) has been designed to measure the progress of lifelong learning, using the Delors conceptual framework of *learning to do, to be, to know and to live together*. It is made up of 17 indicators and 26 specific measures.

Currently, there is limited research that has explored the effectiveness of Home Economics education to contribute to the development of lifelong learning attributes, a need for which there is a priority to build a justification for the future of the curriculum area. Although the profession has staked a claim to contribute to lifelong learning, there is little evidence to support this claim. One piece of research that does provide evidence of Home Economics as a vital subject that develops valuable lifelong learning attributes was undertaken in the Hong Kong Home Economics tertiary education context (Ma & Pendergast, 2010).

In Hong Kong, the Curriculum Development Council (CDC) set as a policy priority that the school curriculum provides learning experiences with an emphasis on the development of generic elements for lifelong learning throughout all stages of schooling and across the key learning areas (CDC, 2000). The consequential effect was the need to prepare pre-service student teachers who have the capacities to impart learning to enhance lifelong learning attributes, and to serve as lifelong learning role models. The comprehensive study of Home Economics teacher education students, specifically in the context of textiles study, revealed that students were engaged in 'RICCCH' learning activities, where the acronym represents: R — Research abilities; I — Information technology; C — Critical reflection; C — Collaboration; C — Creativity; and, H — Higher order thinking. These six attributes, typically equated with lifelong learning attributes, were evident in the experiences of the participants of these studies; the students demonstrated the ability to impart this learning to their own students, hence providing experiences that lead to the development of lifelong learning attributes.

Connecting Home Economics education and the future of the Home Economics profession

Like most overarching outcomes of education, the development of lifelong learning attributes cannot be "transplanted" (Bryce, Frigo, McKenzie & Withers, 2000, p. 30), but must be developed over time and sustained by shared commitment. So too, the achievement of well-being is a long term aspiration and intention of education. If we accept that Home Economics education contributes to the achievement of well-being and of the development of lifelong learning attributes because it intentionally sets out to do so, then there is a need for a commitment, at a policy level, to the delivery of Home Economics education over time, in the core curriculum. Yet, the current trend is away from Home Economics as a preferred area of study, especially in school settings. This trend is not necessarily a response to the subject area, but to the more pressing demands of literacy, numeracy and other high-stakes areas that are used as comparative measures for educational achievement by local, national and international stakeholders. What Home Economics has failed to achieve is recognition for the role it plays intentionally to address the optimization of well-being and the development of lifelong learning attributes as core to the discipline. It is this failure, largely due to the lack of an evidence base that may cost the profession its future.

Ironically, perhaps the best lesson that the Home Economics profession can learn about having its curriculum legitimated is one provided from outside of the field. Public discussion about the role of schools and formal curriculum to prepare young people to be food literate has received scant attention until recently, when medical experts dealing with the consequences of the obesity epidemic made the following plea: "providing a mandatory food preparation curriculum to students throughout the country may be among the best investments society could make—bring Home Economics back" (Lichtenstein & Ludwig, 2010, p. 1858). In their article related to the obesity epidemic in affluent countries, especially the United States of America, they suggest that "…girls and boys should be taught the basic principles they will need to feed themselves and their families within the current food environment: a version of hunting and gathering for the 21st century" (p. 1857). They argue that to date, most programs meant to address obesity have had limited success because they fail to connect knowledge, skills and critical decision-making, and that any solution must address the poor food quality of the average diet and how to prepare food and plan meals. They argue the need for Home Economics education for all students:

> ... Home Economics curriculum could equip young adults with the skills essential to lead long healthy lives and reverse the trends of obesity and diet-related diseases. This instruction will also help youth re-establish a healthy relationship with food, protecting them from the constant onslaught of weight-loss diets and body-building fads. (Lichtenstein & Ludwig, 2010, p. 1858).

In the United Kingdom, the school curriculum has been identified as one area to focus reform in attempts to rein in the devastating effects of poor nutrition and its contribution to child and adult obesity and related chronic health diseases. The development of the Food Competency Framework (Food Standards Agency, 2007) mandates the teaching of food skills and knowledge for children and young people for the ages of 7–16. Incorporating functional, interactive and critical food literacy, this framework includes knowing what foods to eat and why, how to read food labeling information and what it means, and how and why we need to prepare and cook food safely. This framework is being delivered in all schools in the United Kingdom by Home Economics teachers.

As a confirmatory note, Pendergast, Garvis and Kanasa (2011) recently analyzed the commentary of members of the public regarding the role of Home Economics to deliver food literacy. Respondents revealed ...

> ... the power of Home Economics to change their food literacy habits. In particular a number of males wrote of the importance of learning Home Economics at school ... Many of the males made references to using recipes they had learnt during Home Economics at school. This snapshot provides evidence of the importance of teaching Home Economics in schools for the future. Many of the male participants also wrote of building on previous skills and knowledge learned in Home Economics, demonstrating evidence of lifelong learning with food literacy (pp. 428-429).

What all of this points to is timing. It is apparent that food literacy education may provide one avenue to highlight the potential contribution of the discipline. The profession of Home Economics is closely linked to its viability as a curriculum area in schools and in universities and other places of learning. Home Economics education remains the dominant area of work for professionals in the field. Hence, the issues that impact on the profession synergistically relate to the viability of the field as a discipline of study. Being opportunistic is important for shaping the future of the profession, and timing is vital in this regard.

In 2006, Pendergast coined the concept of 'convergent moment' to capture the idea that a number of important societal and historical factors are currently aligning, providing a never before experienced opportunity to re-vision the Home Economics profession. When taken together, these factors can be seen as catalysts for major reform — making this a defining moment for the profession. The current focus on food literacy is evidence of this impetus. The six convergent factors, along with a brief explanation, are presented in Table 2.1.

It can be strongly argued that these convergent factors each have a role in the curriculum of Home Economics, as well as in shaping the future of the profession. This

Table 2.1
Convergent Factors in the Home Economics profession

Convergent Factor	Explanation
100 year history of the profession	The past century since the inception of Home Economics has been one of invention, development and changes in roles for men and women generally in society. This current decade signifies a major shift in society, with the effects of globalization and Information and Communications Technologies making this decade unlike any previously experienced. It represents a societal paradigm shift.
Consumption and globalization	The global pattern of a divide between the developed and developing countries where around 20% of the worlds' population consumes 80% of the products and services, and the remaining 80% consumes the remaining 20%, has created problems for both groups, with the effects of abundance sometimes being described as 'affluenza,' while the effects of under-provision leads to poverty, under-nutrition, lack of educational opportunity and more. There is a lack of parity between the globalizers and the globalized.
Generational theory	The socio-cultural construction of society based on generations provides a valuable insight into the current issues confronting the Home Economics profession. The future of the profession lies in the hands of the Y and Z generations, the characteristics of which must be contended with and embraced by the profession if it is to pave its preferred future
Societal context of the 'New Times'	The idea of societal paradigm shift from modernity to post modernity is played out in workplaces, schooling, new literacy's, new families and communities. Given that Home Economics engages and operates among these contexts, it must embrace and lead the fundamental dimensions of 'new times.' The Age of Terrorism and the Information Age are facets of the new times.
Family changes	Major changes occurring in individual and family characteristics around the globe. The United Nations identifies four trends that impact families around the globe: changes in family structures, demographic ageing, the rise of migration, and the HIV/AIDS pandemic.
The United Nations Decade of Education for Sustainable Development (2005-2014)	In a recently released document titled "Guidelines and recommendations for reorienting teacher education to address sustainability", the importance of the world's 59 000 000 teachers to educate for developing understandings about sustainable development is articulated and strategies for action outlined. It is argued that "the core themes of education for sustainability include lifelong learning, interdisciplinary education, partnerships, multicultural education and empowerment" (UNESCO 2005, p. 15). The approach urges a multidisciplinary approach, noting that "no one discipline can or should claim ownership of Education for Sustainable Development" (p. 27

Adapted from Pendergast (2006, 2008).

is the opportunity to reconfigure the profession as a cultural practice. However, there are a number of negative forces that need to be addressed to enable this process to flow. In Pendergast's (2001) theoretical work around Home Economics and the compliance of the profession to empower members as a reconfigured cultural practice, several consistent themes that characterise this mindset were noted, including:

- the splintering-off of specializations and of knowledge in the profession;
- research in the field typically conducted as a small and piecemeal body of work, lacking impact and cohesive potentialities;
- the loss of common professional purpose;

- anti-intellectualism;
- a reluctance on the part of many professionals to be self-reflective about their own beliefs;
- a lack of respect for the academic world;
- continuous struggles to gain legitimacy within patriarchal parameters;
- the apolitical orientation of many members of the profession;
- the dominance of transient social agendas driving Home Economics; and,
- the difficult relationship between feminism and Home Economics.

Any one of these 'problems' would be cause for a profession to (re)consider its position. Taken together, these themes tell the story of a profession and its members that appear to be constantly struggling with, and grieving for, the repeated failure of attempts to establish a legitimate identity (Pendergast & McGregor, 2007). It could be argued that Home Economics is in fact a failed institution. The profession has clearly failed to position itself as a leader, and to be progressive in its approach to defining its niche in the valued education curriculum. This predicament is astounding given the intention of the profession to enhance well-being and to optimize the development of lifelong learning attributes, both of which are key goals of education in the 21st century.

The way ahead is to make links with the opportunities. One way forward is to work closely with the megatrends predicted for the future, and to position the work of the profession, especially in the curriculum work, around these trends. Food literacy is, in fact, a good example of such as strategy, as it links strongly to megatrend 3, divergent demographics. Table 2.2 provides some examples of Home Economics curriculum relevant to the megatrends.

Home Economics as a sustainable profession

In order for home economists to be influential leaders in creating preferred, sustainable futures, there is a need to focus on the sustainability of the profession itself. This chapter has sought to consider these two significant issues in tandem, highlighting the coincidences and convergences of events that serve as catalysts to taking such action at this time. There is no doubt the profession is positioned to play a pivotal role in shaping preferred futures, which are crafted in response to the megatrends — but it must attend to its own internal questions of sustainability first. The following is a composite of key messages for shifting to a positive capital position; hence, sustaining the profession:

The name must be better rebranded. Home Economics is a great name, but it needs rebranding. Rebranding is about placing in people's minds the associations with a term, product or idea. Home Economics has not, in its 100 years history, had a clear brand that positions it to reflect its intended contribution to achieving well-being and developing lifelong learning attributes. This is an institutional capital issue for the profession and the IFHE has now committed to a rebranding strategy.

Fragmentation of the field must stop. Another inevitably failing strategy is the fragmentation of the umbrella profession into various micro-fields that lack a central

Table 2.2
Interrelated megatrends and examples of related Home Economics curriculum

Interrelated megatrends	Explanation	Examples of related Home Economics curriculum
More from less	This relates to the world's depleting natural resources and increasing demand for those resources through economic and population growth. Coming decades will see a focus on resource- use efficiency.	• Home management • Food selection, preparation and storage • Financial management • Energy efficiency • Textiles selection and care
A personal touch	Growth of the services sector of Western economies is being followed by a second wave of innovation aimed at tailoring and targeting services.	• Creativity and design to meet individual needs • Problem solving and decision making strategies
Divergent demographics	The populations of the 34 OECD countries are ageing and experiencing lifestyle and diet- related health problems. At the same time, there are high fertility rates and problems of not enough food for millions in poor countries.	• Food and nutrition literacy • Human development and relationships • Equity and resource management
On the move	People are changing jobs and careers more often, moving house more often, commuting further to work and travelling around the world more often.	• Housing • Time management
iWorld	Everything in the natural world will have a digital counterpart. Computing power and memory storage are improving rapidly. Many more devices are getting connected to the internet.	• Interpersonal relationships • Design and creativity for problem solving in a range of contexts

(Columns 1 and 2 from Hajkowicz & Moody, 2010, p. 3).

understanding and a connection with the intent of the profession, leading to the integrity of the profession being diffused. Many examples of this fragmentation exist in almost every education system around the world, not just in Home Economics.

Curriculum content at all levels should always be contested. Much has changed in the last century, and the rate of change is only increasing. Students need lifelong learning attributes, for paid, unpaid and voluntary life roles. Students must be expert novices. Students need transportable essential learning's focusing on lifelong learning capabilities. Optimizing their well-being is paramount to achieving this. While the profession makes claims about its intent, it is up to individual practitioners to ensure this intent is achieved.

Home Economics requires academic evolution, both in the classroom and in the academy. The profession must have an internationally united philosophy that shifts it to an agenda-setting position and that clearly articulates the uniqueness of the discipline (adapted from Pendergast, 2006).

Research to measure the efficacy of intentions is required. Claims made in the IFHE (2008) *Position Statement* must be validated through extensive research, and this process and attendant results must be validated through peer review.

Summary

Home Economics education is an important enabler for achieving preferred futures. With the benefit of predicted megatrends, there is an opportunity to shape the future of the profession to connect explicitly with the strategies and capabilities that are required for setting the compass towards a sustainable future for the profession. Following are the key points developed in this chapter:

- The intention of Home Economics education is to empower individuals and families to optimize their well-being and to develop lifelong learning attributes.
- These intents connect strongly with worldwide agendas about the importance and value of education.
- Little explicit evidence exists to validate the claims made by the Home Economics profession of its intended learning outcomes.
- Opportunities to validate the profession must be a priority for the profession, offering the means to undertake research that investigates the degree to which Home Economics education achieves its stated intents associated with well-being and lifelong learning.
- Recognition by those external to the profession of the valued contribution, for example the food literacy expose, are important for gaining validation.
- Rebranding the name 'Home Economics' is an important strategy for setting a future path for the profession.

Discussion Prompts

- Explore the ways in which lifelong learning can be quantified and qualified and map out a research design to undertake this research work.
- Identify a key facet of Home Economics curriculum that links to one or more of the megatrends. Conduct an audit of the lifelong learning elements *learning to do, learning to be, learning to know and learning to live together*, evident in the Home Economics curriculum for your local region.
- Design a new look for the Home Economics profession. What would be the logo; what colours, slogans and images would you associate with the profession?

References

Bahr, N., & Pendergast, D. (2007) *The millennial adolescent.* Canberra: Australian Council for Educational Research.

Bryce, J., Frigo, T., McKenzie, P., & Withers, G. (2000). *The era of lifelong learning: Implications for secondary schools*. Camberwell, Victoria: ACER.

Canadian Council of Learning. (2010). *Composite learning index*. Ottawa, ON: Author. Retrieved from http://ni.unideb.hu/learn/doc/Canadian_Learning_Index.pdf

Curriculum Development Council. (2000). *Learning to learn—The way forward in curriculum development* [Consultation Document]. Hong Kong: Government Printer.

Deagon, J., & Pendergast, D. (2012). A framework for investigating spiritual health and well-being in Home Economics. *International Journal of Home Economics, 5*(1), pages forthcoming.

Delors, J. (1996). *Learning: The treasure within*. Paris: UNESCO.

Food Standards Agency. (2007). *Food competency framework*. London: Author. Retrieved from http://www.food.gov.uk/multimedia/pdfs/competenciesconsensus.pdf

Gee, J., Hull, G., & Lankshear, C. (1996). *The new work order: Behind the language of the new capitalism*. Sydney: Allen & Unwin.

Hajkowicz, S & Moody, J (2010), *Our future world. An analysis of global trends, shocks and scenarios*, CSIRO, Canberra.

Henry, M. (1995). *Well-being, the focus of home economics: An Australian perspective*. (Unpublished doctoral dissertation). University of New England, Biddeford, Maine.

International Federation for Home Economics. (2008). *IFHE Position Statement — Home Economics in the 21st Century*. Bonn, Germany: Author.

Lichtenstein, A., & Ludwig, D. (2010). Bring back home economics education. *Journal of the American Medical Association, 303*(18), 1857–1858.

Ma, A., & Pendergast, D. (2010). Innovative pedagogies for family and consumer science/home economics education: Utilising computer based collaborative learning to foster lifelong learning attributes. *Family and Consumer Sciences Research Journal, 38*(2), 201–216.

McGregor, S. L.T. (2010). *Locating the human condition concept within home economics*. McGregor Monograph Series No. 201002. Seabright, NS: McGregor Consulting Group. Retrieved from http://www.consultmcgregor.com/documents/publications/human-condition-monograph-2010.pdf

McGregor, S.L.T., & Goldsmith, E. (1998). Extending our understanding of quality of living, standard of living and well-being. *Journal of Family and Consumer Sciences, 90*(2), 2–6, 22.

Ministerial Council on Education, Employment, Training and Youth Affairs. (2005). *Contemporary learning: Learning in an online world*. Melbourne: Curriculum Corporation.

Ministerial Council on Education, Employment, Training and Youth Affairs. (2008). *Melbourne Declaration on Educational Goals for Young Australians*. Melbourne: Curriculum Corporation.

Mission Australia. (2005). *Developing resilience at every stage of a young person's life*. Melbourne: Author.

Pendergast, D. (2001). *Virginal mothers, groovy chicks and blokey blokes: Re-thinking home economics (and) teaching bodies*. Brisbane: Australian Academic Press.

Pendergast, D. (2006). Sustaining the home economics profession in new times — A convergent moment. In A. Rauma, A. Pollanen and P. Seitamaa-Hakkarainen (Eds.), *Human perspectives on sustainable future* (pp. 3–32). Joensuu, Finland: University of Joensuu.

Pendergast, D. (2008). Generational dynamics — Y it matters 2 u & me. In D. Pendergast (Ed.), *Home economics: Reflecting the past; Creating the future* (pp. 99–114). Bonn, Germany: International Federation of Home Economics.

Pendergast, D., Flanagan, R., Land, R., Bahr, M., Mitchell, J., Weir, K., Smith, J. (2005). *Developing lifelong learners in the middle years of schooling*. Brisbane: The University of Queensland.

Pendergast, D., Garvis, S., & Kanasa, H. (2011). Public responses to the inclusion of food preparation skills in the Queensland curriculum: The role of formal and informal learning about food literacy. *Family and Consumer Sciences Research Journal, 39*(4), 415–430.

Pendergast, D. & McGregor, S. (2007). *Positioning the Profession Beyond Patriarchy*. Michigan: Kappa Omicron Nu.

Schon, D. (1983). *The reflective practitioner: How professionals think in action*. New York: Basic Books.

Selby Smith, C., & Ferrier, F. (2002). Lifelong learning and the world of work: CEET's survey for the OECD. *Paper presented at the 6th National Conference of the Monash University — ACER, Centre for the Economics of Education and Training. Victoria, Australia*. Retrieved from http://edu.monash.edu/centres/ceet/docs/conferencepapers/2002confpaperselbysmith.pdf

Twigg, D., & Pendergast, D. (2012). Social and emotional well-being of early years learners. In D. Pendergast and S. Garvis (Eds.), *Teaching early years: Rethinking curriculum, pedagogy and assessment* (pages forthcoming). Sydney: Allen & Unwin Crows Nest.

Watson, L. (2003). *Lifelong learning in Australia.* Canberra: Commonwealth of Australia, Department of Education, Science and Training

CHAPTER

3

Bringing a Life-Centric Perspective to Influential Megatrends

Sue L. T. McGregor

How the profession chooses to interpret megatrends will affect Home Economics practice into the next millennium. Indeed, megatrends have different meanings for different people, companies, organizations and professions (Larsen, 2006). This chapter shares a critique of the 10 megatrends identified in the Stimulus chapter (Anderson et al., 2006), and identifies 10 alternative megatrends discussed through a life-centric perspective. Suggestions are offered for how Home Economics practice has to change to deal with the full range of megatrends shaping family life in the future.

For clarification, a trend is a general tendency or direction for conditions or events, often pertaining to instances when something veers off in a different direction or experiences a change in momentum. Mega is Greek *megas*, great or large. *Megatrends* are large movements that become great forces in societal development; they define the present world and have the potential to shape the future. Well known examples of megatrends include globalization, aging and climate change (Anderson et al., 2006; Roland Berger Strategy Consultants, 2011; Singh, 2010).

Several features of Anderson et al.'s (2006) profile of 10 megatrends prompted the ideas shared in this chapter. First, they only focused on what the megatrends mean for businesses, consumer product innovation, marketing, and employers. Second, most of their predictions only pertained to the 34 member countries of the Organization for Economic Cooperation and Development (OECD), not the other 223 countries, most of them Majority World countries (developing or underdeveloped economies).

Third, and most compelling, Anderson et al.'s (2006) predictions were narrowly based on conventional, economic, neo-liberal, corporate-led, top-down globalization. This analytical approach hints at what Korten (2000) called the machine/clock metaphor of the universe. This metaphor assumes the universe is winding down and dying; things are scarce, thereby requiring competition for limited and finite resources, leading to win/lose scenarios. A life-centered perspective, on the other hand, assumes the universe is a living, evolving, dynamic system, replete with abundance, chaos (order emerging), creativity and potential. To offset their machine-metaphor approach (whether intended or not), this chapter brings a life-centric perspective to the 10 megatrends, balancing Anderson et al.'s predictions with other global trends not identified in their analyses.

Larsen (2006) recognized four additional points that informed the development of this chapter. First, the interaction among several megatrends is as significant as each individual megatrend. Second, when events develop that create counter forces or confounding forces, any megatrend can be set aside, change trajectory or shift momentum. Third, although megatrends are viewed as certainties, they also contain elements of uncertainty. Fourth, megatrend projections can also privilege particular ideological perspectives (noted above). Respecting the realities of confounding influences, trajectory shifts, uncertainties and dominant ideologies, 10 life-centered countertrends are now presented as possible counter forces to Anderson et al.'s (2006) 10 megatrends (see Table 3.1).

Countertrend 1— No Chance to Age

The population of the world *is* aging. By 2030, one in every eight persons in the world will be over 65 (Li, Iadarola & Maisano, 2007). Their numbers will increase by 125% by 2020. This increase represents 15% of the world's population, compared to 8% in 2010 (Singh, 2010). In 2007, 60% of those 65 and older lived in the developing world, with an expected jump to 80% by 2050 (Weinberger, 2007).

Despite this reality, Anderson et al. (2006) focused their discussion on the 34 affluent OECD countries, whose primary concerns are health care, income security and pensions and enabling environments (shelter and elder care). In addition to governments, they also addressed how this trend will affect businesses (different products

Table 3.1
Trends that counter Anderson et al.'s (2006) 10 megatrends for 2020

10 Megatrends Toward 2020 (Anderson et al., 2006)	10 Countertrends Toward 2020
Aging	No chance to age
Globalization (top down)	Localization and globalization (bottom up)
Technological development	Focal versus techno
Prosperity (GNP)	Redefining prosperity (GPI)
Individualization	The commons
Commercialization (scarcity mentality)	Abundance mentality
Health and environment connection	Human needs
Acceleration	Deceleration
Network Organizing	Kinship networks
Urbanization	Counterurbanization and ruralization

and services) and the labor market (fewer people at working age will require new forms of employment). There was no mention of families, communities or society.

When most people address the aging megatrend, they note that people are living longer, are more affluent than past generations and are healthier (due to improved health care, pharmaceuticals and technologies) (e.g., Li et al., 2007). But, as Larsen (2006) suggested, events or conditions can develop that counter the trajectory or momentum of a megatrend. Such is the case with aging, which must be juxtaposed against the megatrend of the HIV/AIDS epidemic. This epidemic has taken entire generations in some countries — children, youth, adults, seniors. People are not getting a chance to get old because they are terminally ill and dying. And, they are not affluent nor do they have access to medicines, health care or to enabling environments.

As a powerful example, in the 41 Sub-Saharan African countries, an estimated 22.5 million people were living with HIV in 2009. This number equates to 68% of all global citizens with HIV. Incidents of HIV infection in OECD countries account for only 7% of the global epidemic. As of 2009, 1.3M people in Sub-Saharan Africa had died from AIDS, amounting to 72% of all people in the world who have succumbed to this disease. This figure compares to just 2% of OECD citizens. Finally, almost 90% of the world's children orphaned by AIDS live in Sub-Saharan Africa (UNAIDS, 2010).

The incidence of HIV has fallen by 25% in the last decade. Although encouraging, people are still contracting HIV and the number of those dying of AIDS remains the same (UNAIDS, 2010). Many African nations now face a cadre of women, orphans, grandmothers and people living with AIDS (as well as others facing the reality of contracting HIV). Higher mortality rates, shorter life expectancies, compromised quality of life due to illness and a youth population of orphans are trends that buck the global megatrend of aging. Households affected by AIDS generally have less income, reduced food security and increased vulnerability. Kinship networks are disappearing (see section on kinship networks). Death and the splitting-up of families has led to weakened family ties and declining networks of support. The resultant lack of social relations in the family group has led to a lack of cooperation and trust among community members (Nombo, 2007).

Home economists need to resist uncritically extrapolating Western trends to everyone in the world. Context matters. Dying from old age or complications of aging is not the same thing as dying long before one reaches old age. The HIV/AIDS megatrend may temper expectations for continued increases in longevity (Li et al., 2007), especially in developing countries, where the most rapid pace of aging is forecasted (Weinberger, 2007).

Countertrend 2 — Localization and Globalization from the Bottom-up

One of the most compelling megatrends is globalization. Anderson et al. (2006) defined it as the "fast growing global interconnectedness reflected in the expanded flows of people, capital, goods, services, information, technologies and culture" (p. 3). They then predicated their entire framing of this megatrend on economic, corporate-led, top-down globalization. This model of globalization leads to "insecurity, instability, injustice and inequality" (Lucas, 2003, p. 263). Home economists need to be aware of two other global countertrends, localization and globalization from the bottom-up, both of which strive to address the downside of corporate-led globalization.

First, localization refers to an alternate approach to the *global* economy, one that focuses on the *local*. Hines (2000) explained that globalization favors transnational corporations (TNCs) at the expense of state autonomy and sovereignty, and the voice and agency of civil society. Localization, on the other hand, favors nation states or regional groupings of states, their citizens and the environment. Policies to bring about localization would increase control of the economy by the communities and nation states. This local control would result in an increase in social cohesion, more sustainable communities, and a reduction in poverty and inequality. Local control ensures improvement in livelihoods, social infrastructures, environmental protection, and benign technological developments (Lucas, 2003).

Second, proponents of the localization countertrend are often involved in the globalization from the bottom-up movement. Membership in this movement includes civil society members representing some combination of gender, faith, human rights, indigenous peoples, the environment, consumers, peace and justice, labor, and the humane (animal) movement. Civil society is recognized as a major, global, countervailing force in the world, pushing back against the encroaching power of the market and complicit nation states (Perlas, 2000). The dramatic proliferation in the number of civil society organizations (also referred to as non-governmental organizations, NGOs), the growth in their funding and the dramatic increase in membership bases have enabled this sector to become a powerful force in world politics (McGann & Johnstone, 2006). The number of NGOs increased 333% during the 1990s alone. However, "the real story is ... how these organizations have effectively networked and mobilized their members to reshape world politics" (McGann & Johnstone, p. 67).

Members of civil society seek the elimination of extreme poverty, injustices and inequalities. They desire sustainable development and environmental protection as well as the humane treatment of other species. They call for the reform of international financial institutions, and debt forgiveness of Majority World countries. They want enhanced worker and human rights and ecological standards in the workplace. They demand that TNCs be held accountable, better ensured if civil society members have a place and a voice at the global table. Also, they strive for localization and mindful markets in conjunction with responsible consumer behavior, and for global citizenship (McGregor, 2006). With knowledge of these two powerful counter forces to globalization from the top-down, home economists are better equipped to help families cope with, and challenge, hegemonic, capitalistic globalization.

Countertrend 3 — Focal versus Techno

Anderson et al. (2006) identified technological development as a key megatrend (see also Roland Berger Strategy Consultants, 2011). Anderson et al. acknowledged the pros and cons of this megatrend, commenting on its acceleration with the advent of the industrial age (late 1800s). They framed humans as the only creatures who use technology to make life more pleasant. Borgmann (2000) took issue with this idea when he discussed the lingering impact of technology. Before the industrial revolution, people were burdened with hard labor as they fared for themselves and their families. They were self-sufficient and community-bound for survival. He called this *focal things and practice* (focused on home, family and community).

Perceiving this *focus on focal practice* as a burden, preventing people from progressing, industrialists designed new technologies to replace the discomfort and burden of this labor. The intent was to liberate people so they could experience safety, ease, space and time (via factory-made products, home storage innovations (e.g., the fridge) and communication technologies (e.g., radio, telephone, and computers)). Borgmann (2000) described this process as the rise of the 'technological' device paradigm wherein, over time, technology led to people becoming distanced from the origins of what they were consuming, and distanced from each other. Home life was changed forever, leading to a profound loss of *focal practice*.

To counter this megatrend, Borgmann (2000) called for a *life of engagement*, ensured through: the culture of the table (home); the culture of the world; and, the culture of the arts, athletics (exercise) and philosophy. Said another way, people must become re-engaged with *focal things and practice* because such practice allows them to know the world around them and understand our time, place, heritage and hopes. Focal practice *centers people's lives*. Short of embracing the Luddite movement, home economists need to counter the juggernaut of technological advancements with a concern for the vitality and viability of the family as a social institution.

Countertrend 4 — Redefining Progress and Prosperity

As would be expected from anyone living at the cusp of the 21st century, Anderson et al. (2006) recognized prosperity as a megatrend. Unfortunately, they narrowly equated prosperity with economic growth, as measured by the Gross National Product (GNP); economic growth equals human prosperity. They also linked prosperity with consumption and the growth of the middle class, as if these are positive correlations. Furthermore, their discussion of the "enjoyment of prosperity" mainly focused on the 34 OECD countries, suggesting that the entire continent of Africa (54 countries) will not be *prosperous* because it will not be economically viable. Their discussion of prosperity completely ignored the powerful countertrend that focuses on *redefining progress* as genuine, societal and human-focused rather than as economic prosperity.

Growth does not equal progress or prosperity. The costs of economic activity are far-reaching and potentially harmful to people, communities and society: family breakdown, suicide and mortality, abuse, crime, environmental degradation and resource depletion, pollution, loss of leisure time, un/under employment, poverty, less time to volunteer and loss of civility in communities (Lawn, 2000). The redefining progress (or genuine progress) countertrend movement seeks to shift the prevailing definition of progress from one focused on a growing economy to one that resonates with people's sense of the quality of their lives. Social health cannot be measured using economic indicators. Alternative measures, especially the Genuine Progress Indicator (GPI, developed in 1995), assign value to the life-sustaining functions of households, communities and the natural environment (Cobb, Goodman & Wackernagel, 1999). Home economists have a powerful ally in the redefining progress movement.

Countertrend 5 — The Commons

Individualization was the fifth megatrend identified by Anderson et al. (2006), defined as a shift from more collective societal norms to the individual person. In conjunction with this shift is a lack of clear guidelines and predictable social scripts that used to guide people through their life transitions (from youth to teen, to adult, to elder). Although this lack of predictability is very true, Anderson et al. restricted their discussion of the import of this trend to product development, marketing ploys and labor markets. Home economists need to augment Anderson et al.'s discussion of the significance of life transition ambiguities with a family and community perspective. To do this, they can use insights gained from the global movement toward *the commons*.

The individualization of society means that rules commonly followed to enable transition from one stage of life to another, or for how to behave in different situations, are diluted or lost. People are increasingly required to construct their own lives. This process of *growing up alone* leads to less connection with and concern for the commons, defined as elements of the environment, culture and public goods that ideally are shared and enjoyed by everyone. Cultural commons include literature, music, art and heritage sites. Public commons include parks, schools, health care and infrastructures (e.g., roads and public transportation). Hybrid commons include those elements that have been partially privatized (e.g., the Internet) (Barnes, 2006).

The elements of the common are said to be *held in common*, and are viewed as gifts to the community to be shared and protected for future generations. The commons cannot be commodified or they cease to be commons. They are meant to be inclusive, not exclusive, and are meant to be preserved regardless of their monetary value (Barnes, 2006). The commons serve as an anchor for members of society. They are spaces where people encounter a community, and where *actions* can be witnessed, assigned meaning and be remembered. It is a web of relationships sustained through human interactions and stewardship (Arendt, 1958).

Nurturing the collective commons is a powerful strategy for countering the alienating impact of individualization. The familiar *tragedy of the commons* pertains to the depletion of common resources as a result of human greed. In these cases, the benefits of exploitation of the commons are enjoyed by a single group or person while the consequences are felt by the collective, for generations (Hardin, 1968). The *tragedy of the individual* occurs when people become separated from the collective; they live with fear, anger, angst and hopelessness. Such are the characteristics of today's consumer society, predicated on individualism (McGregor, 2010a). Home economists can counter the negative impact of individualization by drawing energy from the commons movement (which includes both the movements for a culture of peace and for sustainability).

Countertrend 6 — Abundance Mentality

Anderson et al. (2006) defined commercialization as meeting human needs through trade in private markets. They equated this megatrend with more individual, consumer choice, with competition and with marketing strategies necessary to reach more diverse markets. They remarked on the links between commercialization and corporate-led, economic globalization and economic prosperity. Taken together, their conceptualization of commercialization reflected the economic concept of scarcity and the attendant *scarcity mentality* of the global marketplace.

Their framing of this megatrend reflects the machine/clock metaphor mentioned earlier (Korten, 2000). The scarcity mentality feeds upon the "I am separate" mindset, and on self-interest and interpersonal competitiveness (Bagshaw & Bagshaw, 1999). Wealth is created by cut-throat competition within a win-lose mentality, characterized by a lack of trust, accountability and human immaturity (Blackstone, Gardiner & Gardiner, 1997). Winning is viewed as a compromise wherein one has to give up something (lose) in order to gain; therefore, one has to play hard and smart so one gives up as little as possible (Starck, Mackey & Adams, 1995). Predicated on classical economic theory, supply is always strictly limited, resources are always lacking, and there is never enough to go around. People assume they cannot achieve their goals if others manage to achieve theirs — so there is always competition.

Home economists can learn much from the countertrend of an *abundance mentality*. Touted by Covey (1989), it presumes there is plenty for everyone if people allow themselves to see the possibilities and opportunities inherent in every situation. People strive constantly to generate new ideas, make a commitment continually to grow and to help others grow. They remain willing to invest time, resources and self in the problem-posing and solving process, to use the synergy of the group, and to hope for long-term gains that are mutually beneficial. The intent is win-win (Vuotto, 2004). This mindset does not assume that if one person gets something, there is less for others; instead, it assumes that the more successful people are, the more likely others are affected in a positive way (Starck et al., 1995).

Within an abundance mentality, human interactions are predicated on trust, integrity and maturity, and flow from a deep sense of self-worth and security (Covey, 1989). Decisions are made within a climate of high trust, deep respect and reciprocity (Bagshaw & Bagshaw, 1999). Because people focus on what is there rather than on what is missing, this process opens possibilities, options, alternatives and creativity. They learn to appreciate their lives for the potential and the opportunities. From this stance, commercialization can be debunked and reframed (see section on redefining progress and prosperity). With an abundance mentality, people are happy when others prosper.

Countertrend 7 — Human Needs

Health and environment is another megatrend noted by Anderson et al. (2006) and by others (Roland Berger Strategy Consultants, 2011; Singh, 2010). People are presumed to be more *aware* of the connection between their health and their immediate environments. Anderson et al. referenced the new spiritual and personality-optimizing focus of fitness and wellness, age and lifestyle-related illnesses, and the portent of health pandemics. However, they again limited their discussion of increased consumer spending on health problems (exacerbated by environmental conditions) to its impact on corporations, ignoring any reference to families meeting their basic needs.

Home economists can use Anderson et al.'s (2006) insights about the link between environments and health to appreciate that the ability of near and far environments to impact personal health, well-being and wellness is mediated by people's ability to meet basic human *needs*. A need is something that is necessary for an organism to live a healthy life. Needs can be objective (e.g., food, water, shelter) or subjective (psychological, e.g., the need to belong). Needs can also refer to the *costs of being human* within society. People who do not have their needs fulfilled will function poorly in society. Indeed, not meeting a need can led to death or dysfunction (Doyal & Gough, 1991) because while wants are life-enhancing, needs are life-sustaining.

If environmental conditions prevent people from meeting their basic human needs, their ability to make responsible health-related choices is compromised; hence, the processes involved in creating wellness, and the current state of being well, may be compromised. To augment the health-environment connection (the megatrend), Home economists can extend their focus on well-being and wellness to include basic human needs (e.g., subsistence, protection, affection, understanding, participation, idleness, creation, identity and freedom) (Max-Neef, 1991; McGregor, 2010b).

Countertrend 8 — Deceleration

Referring to the megatrend of acceleration, Anderson et al. (2006) argued that change is happening faster since the advent of the industrial revolution. They defined the *pace of change* as the number of changes a society faces in a unit of time. Rightly so, they referenced the need to be change-oriented to offset the inclination to passively adjust to changes in the world. But, they narrowly focused their comments to how companies can protect their competitive power in a rapidly changing marketplace, which is supercharged with relentless innovations and excessive information.

Home economists have two options relative to this megatrend. They can accept acceleration as a trend and help families learn to be change-oriented. And/or, they can draw strength from the deceleration movement — the slow [down] movement. Regarding the first, Home economists can teach people about what it means to be change-oriented. Orientation is one's place and direction relative to one's surroundings. Change is the process of making something different (exchanging or substituting something). One's change orientation is, thus, one's predisposition to the process of making things different from what they are now. Becoming change-oriented means one accepts the process of moving from one state of being to another as a universal, inevitable part of life (Kniep, 1989).

Dealing with the pace of that change is another issue. The Slow movement advocates a cultural shift that slows down the pace of life and of change. The World Institute of Slowness (http://www.theworldinstituteofslowness.com/) strives to teach the world the way of Slow, the Slow philosophy. The main premise of the Slow movement is that, regardless of the pace of change, people's basic human needs do not change: they need to be appreciated, to belong, to be near and connected, to be cared for and to give care and to be loved. To ensure these basic needs are met, people have to strive for slowness in human relations (Guttorm Fløistad as cited in dos Reis and Wolf, 2010).

In order to deal with acceleration, people have to rediscover slowness, reflection and togetherness, where they will find renewal rather than relentless newness (Guttorm Fløistad as cited in dos Reis and Wolf, 2010). The Slow philosophy favors a state of mind that values localism, regionalism, mindfulness, sustainability, ethics and morality. Home economists can augment their practice by teaching families to be change-oriented while concurrently teaching the Slow philosophy.

Countertrend 9 — Kinship Networks

Anderson et al. (2006) identified *network organizing*, explaining that it refers to people organizing into, and connecting through, technology-mediated networks (e.g., the Internet, e-mail, chat rooms, Facebook, Twitter, YouTube). van Dijk (1991) defined *the network society* as a form of society that increasingly organizes its relationships in media networks using social networking technologies, which are gradually replacing the long-standing social networks of face-to-face communication. Anderson et al. characterized it as a new phenomenon gaining incredible momentum due to communication and media technology. They then related their entire analysis to the impact of *network organizing* on corporations. Like others, home economists know that the alienation associated with 21st century versions of social networking may have lasting and profoundly negative (at least controversial) impacts on *personal* and *familial* relationships.

But, there is also another powerful countertrend associated with networking, that being the loss of, or threat to, family and extended kinship networks. While technology-based relationships have been expanding (Anderson et al., 2006); family-based relationships mediated through kinship networks are witnessing a different trend. By way of definition, a *family* kinship network comprises relationships between people that stem from parentage or marriage (parent-children, couples, siblings and extended family members) (Scott & Carrington, 2011). *Extended* kinship networks can also include community members and friends and neighbors (Sarker, Keya & Punday, 2006).

Each individual goes through his or her life in a kinship network. The global megatrend of changing family demographics has created situations where there are fewer children, siblings, cousins, aunts and uncles and grandparents. There are more single parents, more divorced families and more blended families. These changes in family structures will affect family dynamics, changes that cannot help but cause breaks (or strains) in the threads that bind kinship networks together (Sarker et al., 2006).

The decline of family and extended kinship networks is a concern for home economists. Kinship networks connect family members, physically and emotionally. The resultant kinship cohesion or stress shapes the nature of socio-economic and psychological resources that provide emotional, informational and material support for individuals. Interpersonal interactions within a kin network directly affect the health and well-being of individuals by (a) satisfying (or not) the needs for affiliation, affection and security; and, by (b) increasing (or not) feelings of self-esteem and self-efficacy (Sarker et al., 2006).

Also, while Home Economics has always viewed the family as the cornerstone of society, those engaged with the megatrend of *network organizing* view technology as the cornerstone of society — actually saying "technology is society" (Castells, 2006). home economists must balance their approach to practice by focusing on both (a) the impact of globalization, media and *network organizing* on kinship networks; and (b) the ongoing changes in family dynamics due to the shifting profile of family kinship networks (ironically now enriched somewhat by social networking technologies). Nonetheless, home economists should not privilege technology over families, nor favor network organizing over kinship networks.

Countertrend 10 — Ruralization/Counter urbanization

Anderson et al. (2006) identified urbanization as a final megatrend. Urban refers to a city or a densely populated area, relative to rural, which is characterized by an agrarian lifestyle outside of a city. Urbanization (urban drift) is defined as the physical growth of urban areas as a result of global change. Close to 180,000 people move into cities on a daily basis. Some people are moving from the suburbs to the city and some are moving from rural areas to the city. And, yes, it is true that the urban populations of Asia, Africa and Latin America and the Caribbean will increase by an average of 94%, 152% and 52% respectively, in the next 20 years. There is no question that urbanization is a megatrend, with the projection that nearly 60% of the world's population will live in urban areas by 2030 (United Nations HABITAT, 2008).

But, this fact means that, for many years to come, the other 40% will *not* live in urbanity. This number equates to almost half of the world's population. The urban drift, the transition to urban life, occurs at different times, with diverse patterns (see Figure 3.1). In 2010, 50% of the world's population was rural. This percentage is projected to decline to 14% over the next 40 years (by the year 2050) (United Nations HABITAT, 2011); but, there is a countertrend in play.

Rosenberg (2008) questioned whether the urbanization megatrend would continue at its current pace in light of the concurrent countertrend of ruralization in Majority World (developing) countries; that is, the movement of people back to their villages. This countertrend has also been labeled *counter urbanization*, referring to when cities lose populations to rural areas (Berry, 1980; Griffiths, Christiansen &

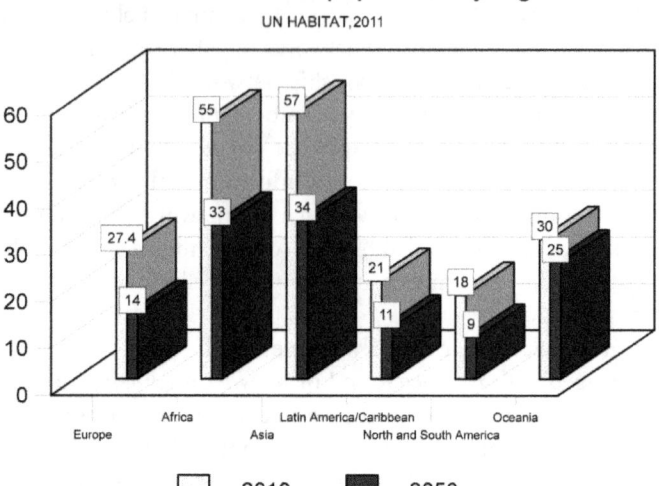

FIGURE 3.1

Predicted percentage of rural population by region

Chapman, 2010). This demographic trend was not reported in the 2011 UN HABITAT predictions nor by Anderson et al. (2006). Although 95% of future urban growth *will* occur in developing nations (United Nations, 2007; United Nations HABITAT, 2008) (see Figure 3.1), rural areas currently accommodate most of the population of developing countries, a trend that began to lessen in 2005, the tipping point (United Nations HABITAT, 2002). Home economists need to balance their focus on both aspects of dwelling realities — urban and non-urban. The complexities of rural life for individuals and families mirror that of urban living. The issues are the same, just manifested in different ways: poverty, access to goods and services, equity and opportunity, gender gaps, aging, health care, technology and so on.

Summary

The analysis shared in this chapter clearly illustrated the ambiguity of some of the megatrends. Their future is not yet determined and/or they are not always interpreted from a family-oriented perspective. The integrity of the family as a social institution behoves home economists to future-proof themselves by continuing to critique the dying-universe interpretations of global megatrends from a life-centric perspective.

This chapter identified 10 countertrends that home economists can embrace as they future-proof the profession (see Table 3.1): HIV/AIDS (not aging), localization and globalization from the bottom-up, focal practices, redefining progress, the commons, an abundance mentality, focus on human needs, deceleration and the Slow movement, declining kinship networks and counter urbanization.

Home Economics needs to extrapolate family-inspired interpretations of 21st century megatrends, rather than uncritically accepting others' interpretations. And, we need to identify countertrends and offer alternative paths for families to ponder, perhaps choose to follow.

If we want to create viable and sustainable Home Economics futures during the next 100 years, we must bring our *own perspective* to bear on global megatrends impacting home and family, for the good of humanity.

Discussion Prompts

- How readily did you accept the Copenhagen Institute for Future Studies identification and interpretation of megatrends for the next 10 years? How receptive were you to my suggestions for alternatives?
- What other megatrends can you identify, from a life-centered perspective, which families face and how do you think home economists should deal with these megachanges?
- How do you think higher education programs should change (innovate) so they can socialize new generations of home economists to be critical of non-Home Economics approaches to changes to our common future?
- What do you think is unique in our approach to helping families deal with these megachanges?
- What role do you see for IFHE given the profound changes families are facing and given the need for Home Economics to future-proof itself so it remains viable and visible in the future?

Acknowledgement

Thanks to Annette Tweedie for reading an earlier version of this chapter.

References

Anderson, K., Kruse, M., Persson, H., Mogensen, K., & Eriksen, T. (2006). *10 megatrends toward 2020*. Copenhagen, Denmark: Copenhagen Institute of Future Studies. Retrieved from http://www.cifs.dk/scripts/artikel.asp?id=1469

Arendt, H. (1958). *The human condition*. Chicago, IL: University of Chicago Press.

Bagshaw, M., & Bagshaw, C. (1999). Leadership in the twenty-first century. *Industrial and Commercial Training, 31*(6), 236–239.

Barnes, P. (2006). *Capitalism 3.0: A guide to reclaiming the commons*. San Francisco, CA: Berrett-Koehler.

Berry, B. (1980). Urbanization and counter urbanization in the United States. *The ANNALS of the American Academy of Political and Social Science, 451*(1), 1–30.

Blackstone, J., Gardiner, L., & Gardiner, S. (1997). A framework for the systemic control of organizations. *International Journal of Production Resources, 35*(3), 597–609.

Borgmann, A. (2000). The moral complexion of consumption. *Journal of Consumer Research, 26*(4), 418–422.

Castells. M. (2006). *The theory of the network society*. Cornwall, England: MPG Books.

Cobb, C., Goodman, G., & Wackernagel, M. (1999). *Why bigger isn't better: The Genuine Progress Indicator-1999 update*. San Francisco, CA: Redefining Progress. Retrieved from http://www.nber.org/~rosenbla/econ302/lecture/GPI-GDP/gpi1999.pdf

Covey, S. (1989). *The seven habits of highly effective people*. NY: Simon and Schuster.

dos Reis, M. P., & Wolf, B. (2010). Slow shopping. *Proceedings of the LeNS Conference Sustainability in Design: NOW* (pp. 1259 — 1267). Sheffield, England: Greenleaf Publishing. Retrieved from http://www.mariapaulasaba.com.br/pdf/research/paper_slowshopping_LeNS.pdf

Doyal, L., & Gough, I. (1991). *A theory of human need*. NY: Guilford Press.

Griffiths, M. B., Christiansen, F., & Chapman, M. (2010). Chinese consumers: The romantic reappraisal. *Ethnography,11*, 331–357.

Hardin, G. (1968). The tragedy of the commons. *Science, 162*(3859), 1243–1248.

Hines, C. (2000). *Localization: A global manifesto*. London: Earthscan.

Kniep, W. M. (1989). Social studies within a global education. *Social Education, 53*(6), 385, 399–403.

Korten, D. (2000). *The post-corporate world*. San Francisco, CA: Berrett-Koehler.

Larsen, G. (2003). Is your company oriented toward change? *Future Orientation, 1*. Retrieved from http://www.cifs.dk/scripts/artikel.asp?id=819&lng=2

Larsen, G. (2006). Why megatrends matter. *Future Orientation, 5*. Retrieved from http://www.cifs.dk/scripts/artikel.asp?id=1469

Lawn, P. (2000). *Toward sustainable development — An ecological economics approach*. Boca Raton, FL: CRC Press.

Li, R., Iadarola, A., & Maisano, C. (Eds.) (2007). *Why population aging matters: A global perspective*. Bethesda, MD: National Institute on Aging, National Institutes of Health. Retrieved from http://www.nia.nih.gov/NR/rdonlyres/9E91407E-CFE8-4903-9875-D5AA75BD1D50/0/WPAM.pdf

Lucas, C. (2003). Localization — An alternative to corporate-led globalization. *International Journal of Consumer Studies, 27*(4), 261–265.

Max-Neef, M. A. (1991). *Human scale development*. NY: The Apex Press. Retrieved from http://www.dhf.uu.se/pdffiler/89_1.pdf

McGann, J., & Johnstone, M. (2006). The power shift and the NGO credibility crisis. *International Journal of Not-for-Profit Law, 8*(2), 65–77.

McGregor, S. L. T. (2006). *Transformative practice*. East Lansing, MI: Kappa Omicron Nu.

McGregor, S. L. T. (2010a). *Consumer moral leadership*. Rotterdam, the Netherlands: Sense Publishers.

McGregor, S. L. T. (2010b). *Well-being, wellness and basic human needs in home economics [McGregor Monograph Series No. 201003]*. Seabright NS: McGregor Consulting Group. Retrieved from http://www.consultmcgregor.com/documents/publications/well-being_wellness_and_basic_human_needs_in_home_economics.pdf

Nombo, C. I. (2007). *When AIDS meets poverty*. (Doctoral dissertation, Wageningen University). Retrieved from http://edepot.wur.nl/2501

Padoch, C., Brondizo, E., Costa, S., Pinedo-Vasquez, M., Sears, R., & Siqueria, A. (2008). Urban forest and rural cities. *Ecology and Society, 13*(2). Retrieved from http://www.ecologyandsociety.org/vol13/iss2/art2/

Perlas, N. (2000). Civil society: The third global power. *INFO 3: Anthroposophy in Dialogue*. Retrieved from http://southerncrossreview.org/4/wto.html

Roland Berger Strategy Consultants. (2011). *Trend compendium 2030*. München, Germany: Author. Retrieved from http://www.rolandberger.com/gallery/trend-compendium/tc2030/content/assets/trendcompendium2030.pdf

Rosenberg, M. (2009, February 28). *Ruralization* [Web log post]. Retrieved from http://geography.about.com/b/2009/02/28/increased-ruralization.htm

Sarker, P., Keya, M., & Panday, P. (2006). Perceived stress in kinship network system among the people of Bangladesh. *Journal of Societal and Social Policy, 5*(2), 1–11.

Scott, J., & Carrington, P. (2011). *Handbook of social network analysis*. Thousand Oakes, CA: Sage.

Singh, S. (2010). *Top 20 global mega trends and their impact on business, cultures and society*. Toronto, ON: Frost and Sullivan. Retrieved from http://www.frost.com/prod/servlet/cpo/213016007

Starck, P., Mackey, T., & Adams, J. (1995). Nurse managed clinics. *Journal of Professional Nursing, 11*(2), 71–77.

UNAIDS. (2010). *Global report: UNAIDS report on the global AIDS epidemic.* Geneva, Switzerland: Author. Retrieved from http://www.unaids.org/globalreport/documents/20101123_GlobalReport_full_en.pdf

United Nations. (2007). *UN state of the world population: Unleashing the potential of urban growth.* Paris, France: Author. Retrieved from http://web.unfpa.org/swp/2007/english/introduction.html

United Nations HABITAT. (2002). *The rural dimension of sustainable urban development* [HS/GC/19/6]. Nairobi, Kenya: Author.

United Nations HABITAT. (2008). *State of the world's cities 2008/2009: Harmonious cities.* London: Earthscan. Retrieved from http://www.unhabitat.org/pmss/listItemDetails.aspx?publicationID=2562

United Nations HABITAT. (2011). *State of the world cities 2010/2011: Bridging the urban divide.* London: Earthscan. Retrieved from http://www.unhabitat.org/pmss/listItemDetails.aspx?publicationID=2917

van Dijk, J. (1991). *The network society.* Thousand Oaks, CA: Sage.

Vuotto, F. (2004). Information competence as a value-added product. *Reference Services Review, 32*(3), 234–248.

Weinberger, M. (2007). *Major developments and trends in global aging.* Washington, DC: AARP International. Retrieved from http://www.aarpinternational.org/usr_doc/unbsproceedings.pdf http://en.wikipedia.org/wiki/Urbanization.

CHAPTER 4

Home Economics — A Forum for Global Learning and Responsible Living

Kaija Turkki

The purpose of this chapter is to provide some tools that help us to better understand the dynamics of our daily life in a global world, but also to direct our professional expertise to meet the challenges of the present and the future. To focus on responsible living and to create Home Economics futures, let us consider a *change to be our challenge* and adopt *interrelatedness and diversity* as inspirational common arenas. We have good reasons to stand behind the basic goals and focus that our professional founders selected over a century ago, but we must also recognize the necessity to develop a new 'language' to communicate and to reposition us in relation to others, other professional communities, and the world. Home Economics has many special qualities that enable it to move in diverse directions and to cross disciplinary boundaries. Our original knowledge-creation processes are unique and fundamental to exerting an influence on personal, societal and global levels. But, we still have things to learn.

This chapter presents an approach to practicing Home Economics that views it as a forum for global learning and responsible living. The seeds for this chapter lie in my 40-year academic career, which has had a strong emphasis on restructuring university studies, working for national curricula in Home Economics, conducting research for and about Home Economics, and serving in international forums. Drawing on my research and work with our students, I have prepared many conceptual frameworks and tools to demonstrate our presence in a global context. I will present several of them in this chapter, which is highly committed to the ideas and trends introduced by the stimulus chapter of this book. I begin with a tree metaphor, followed with four ideas raised to further discussions about discovering our challenges without neglecting the richness of Home Economics history.

Tree Metaphor

Nature is a powerful teacher. It has guided me in expressing the vitality of Home Economics as that of *an old, vital tree*. I shall use this metaphor to guide us through the following four sections of this chapter. It is possible for a tree to sustain the next 100 years or even longer, if it succeeds in maintaining a balance in its living conditions and in renewing its basic structures. Furthermore, the sustainability and strength of a tree is highly dependent upon the actors around it. Finally, inevitably, trees are damaged or cut down. This has happened in Home Economics. Fortunately, stalwart Home Economics professionals have managed to plant some seeds to raise new life again (like a tree). Applying this metaphor, I will introduce some key ideas around reconsidering how to create a sustainable basis for Home Economics, and how to demonstrate our knowledge base in an innovative manner. The latter better ensures our thinking is stimulated, leading to the renewal of our educational structures and research strategies — future-proofing the profession.

Learning new language and designing new landscapes for communication

The glue of this chapter is the realization that, in most cases, very simple facts and necessities of life lay the foundation for our profession, and these same facts cause turbulence at the global level. It is a question of food, people, education, environment, energy, economics, technology and cultures. Now it is time to revisit the processes and structures of our profession and to establish knowledge forums, special bodies and/or new specialized areas that are committed to sustainability, and can acknowledge these simple everyday issues as being the most *fundamental* structures of the present and future world.

Through our daily actions, Home Economics is closely connected to most global systems. It thereby has the ability to exert a major impact on these systems (see Figure 4.1). Sustainability has always been one of the key elements in Home Economics, grounded in the human ecological heritage from our early history. However, we have been slow to utilize its plurality and to establish communication with others about this aspect of our practice. Now it is time to renew our language to better communicate with specialists from other fields and with power forums. To do this, we need to design new landscapes that demonstrate more dynamic processes and comprehensive holistic frames. Home Economics is a life-supporting arena or discipline originating in human evolution and civilization, and it follows that we can have a global message. These premises challenge us to adopt a role as central contributors in promoting global well-being — the overall theme of our IFHE 2012 World Congress. By uniting the discourses of well-being and sustainability, we can serve as key players in various forums. Another fundamental fact is that we cannot adopt this role on our own; rather, we need others, others in a broad sense. We must, therefore, develop our knowledge base as integrators, networkers and as creators of the future, and communicate it to others in such a way that they can understand it and accept it.

It is relevant and hopefully fruitful to embark on this new journey by referring to the name of our discipline and profession, because it is an important tool for identity

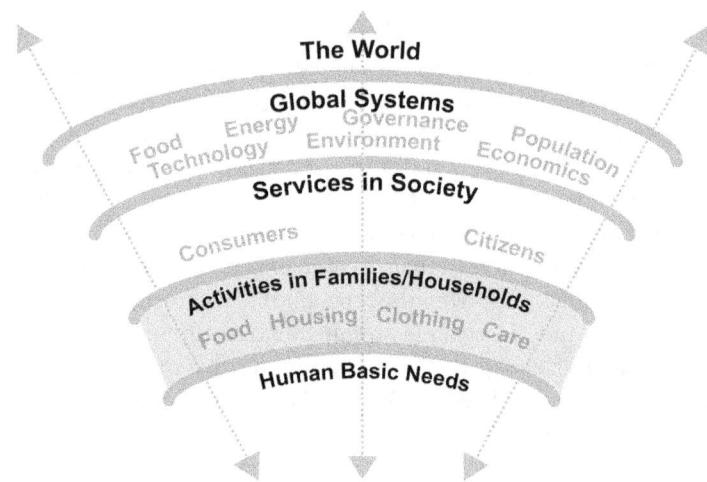

Figure 4.1

Home Economics in the World.

and for communication (McGregor 2010). The name *Home Economics* is a critical element in our history. IFHE's (2008) recent choice to use *Home Economics* as an international name for the profession is an excellent choice for our future. The connotation of those two very powerful words, home and economics, opens many doors for us. This name is an excellent example of how to move from individual to global levels, and how to cross private and public spaces. In addition, both words have a very rich etymology and touch many social and cultural phenomena and value chains. *Economics* is an important language to know, and a *home* is something to which most people attach meaning(s).

Internationally, we also have a history of another name, *Human Ecology*, which I also favor. By combining Human Ecology with Home Economics, we can extend our image of ourselves and bring this image to our interactions with power structures (see Figure 4.2). Each of the major concepts in the figure is now discussed. First, sustainability earns its place at the crossing- point in Figure 4.2 because it represents the increasing interdependence of humans and ecological systems. Our expertise and knowledge base regarding sustainability is at the very core of our profession, extending from an individual level to a global level. Second, home economists have always been strongly committed to value creation, which plays a key role in shaping the new global world.

Third, we have our own language for understanding *economics*, indicating resources to cover a wide spectrum of elements, embracing deeply embedded values to guide our daily actions. Home economists have been pioneers in establishing an approach to the economic discipline that encompasses a wide range of human and material resources, which can be included in decision-making and management

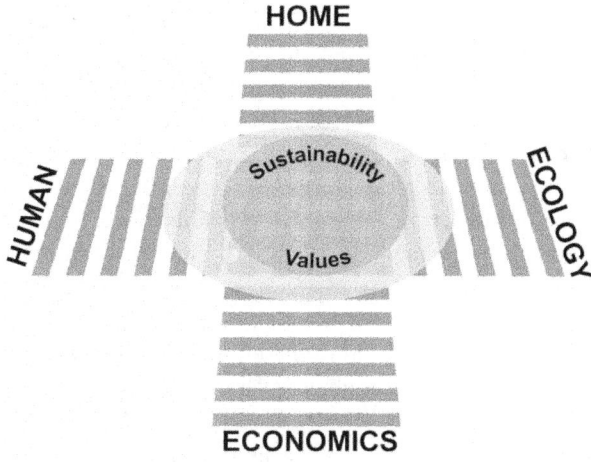

Figure 4.2

Playing with names — enriching the message.

processes. As well, our notion of economics can be related to basic human needs and the well-being of humans, at the individual and community levels. Also, economics is much more than a financial issue; other resources, such as time, knowledge, skills, utilities and networks, also play a central role in people completing their daily necessities, in both private and public arenas.

Finally, human ecology involves a comprehensive view of human institutions, culture and ideas, and their presence in human daily actions in relation to the environment. The matrix, and the space around horizontal and vertical influences, forms a complex web of mutually conditioning structures and processes that we encounter in our daily actions. Both directional dimensions and each of the four surrounding elements need to be revisited and reflected upon to extend our communication, to inform our competencies, and to raise potential for the future.

Providing solid grounds and constructing new positions in relation to others

This chapter is deeply rooted in the discussions and results of the IFHE 2008 Lucerne conference and linked to my research and teaching in Finland. The guiding principles informing this chapter include the necessity of designing concepts (a) to capture the whole and (b) to strive for holistic and integrated frameworks. These principles can be applied to any of the four dimensions or fields of practice that were set out in the *IFHE Position Statement* (IFHE, 2008): societal arena, curriculum, academic discipline and everyday living. In my opinion, these four dimensions complement each other, create a solid basis for our research and teaching and, to a large extent, place our profession within a diverse societal context, both locally and globally.

My basic tool for communicating my thoughts about the many dimensions of Home Economics is the formulation of conceptual frameworks and models, a process informed by the aforementioned principles of holism and integration. Their creation is informed by my experiences in various university assessments within Home Economics and related fields, my reviews of research applications, journal articles, professional applications, et cetera. Moreover, active participation in international networks and some future forums have left important marks on my thinking. All of these venues contribute to the ongoing renewal of these frameworks. I use these conceptual frameworks to encourage discussion by teaching, researching and communicating with others.

In previous work, I conceived Home Economics as a human science including arts, as a human ecology, as a philosophy of everyday life, as a holistic and integrative knowledge base, and as a discipline for the future (Turkki, 2004). These five approaches support each other and serve as a guide for this chapter as well. If I were to include the subject matters in the definition, we can add a sixth approach, that being the definition of Home Economics as human action in everyday life in relation to food, housing, clothing and care. My focus is on *human action* and its relation to natural, social and cultural or human-made environments. From the holistic and human points of view, Home Economics can be defined as a combination of human development, social responsibility, a healthy life-style, the sustainable use of resources and cultural diversity. All these definitions manifest in our private lives and in our services and professional arenas. Together, they influence our well-being and our society at large, at a global level.

When reflecting on these many definitions of Home Economics, it is most important to consider the questions, "What are the key grounds for our profession and our personal expertise? How do we to structure them and communicate these with others?" It is also essential to formulate our message in a way that others can relate to and touch. This is the area in which we may not have been most successful in our past. These walls must be brought down so others can hear and consider our professional messages.

My research program, entitled *Home Economics as a science and discipline,* consists of three interrelated elements that, together, have proven to be intellectually fruitful. Most of my research unites three kinds of analysis or focus: (a) to capture the phenomena and to pay attention to both (b) the processes and (c) the structures. This approach enables me to locate our knowledge base in relation to others, but it also facilitates the practice of our profession in innovative ways. In addition, it provides confidence and persistence to stand by our basic missions that will last forever. Our key competencies include the flexibility of Home Economics, our capability to transform our actions according to the current situation, and our quality or competence to serve as integrators or facilitators in uniting diverse capacities and actions towards common goals.

My central message is that we cannot escape complexity or avoid change because these form the core of our profession, and of everyday life. We can learn to approach them by selecting new focuses and/or building partnerships for moving in new direc-

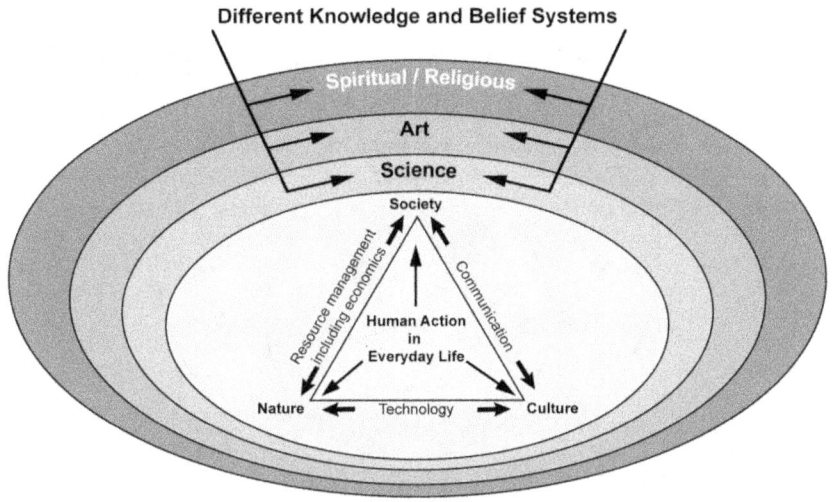

Figure 4.3

Home Economics: Our Relation to the World.

tions. To do this, we have to clarify our message and recognize the core elements of our work. I have selected several examples of my conceptual frameworks to show my approach to communicating our core elements. Figure 4.3 demonstrates our human ecological basis that reflects the key processes to shape our future. Figure 4.4 illustrates our fundamental unity and capabilities. Figure 4.5 focuses on human qualities and the essence of integrated thinking. Each is now briefly discussed.

Figures 4.3 and 4.4 were part of a plenary presentation I made with Professor Virgina Vincenti at the IFHE 2008 congress. They highlight our professional knowledge base and achievements of the past (Turkki & Vincenti, 2008). The concepts contained in the conceptual frameworks will certainly serve as a basis for our profession and will lead us in the future. Starting with Figure 4.3, when we focus on our professional practices or on human action in everyday life, we find ourselves in the middle of interactions and relations with the world, relations that direct our behavior and activities, and vice versa. We also begin to consider the nature of the entities we are dealing with, and how far we should extend our thinking and responsibility. In this context, it matters how we understand knowledge, and how we relate ourselves and our daily life to society, nature and culture. Economics, technology and communication are processes that most highly transform our environments. They provide us with prosperity, functionality and meaningfulness in life (or not). Our role as Home economists is to highlight the human side of this entity and to raise our expertise to highest possible level.

We will examine Figure 4.4 next. Turning our interest to the professional achievements that have occurred during the past century, we certainly can identify a variety of outcomes in forms of education and research, and new products and services or

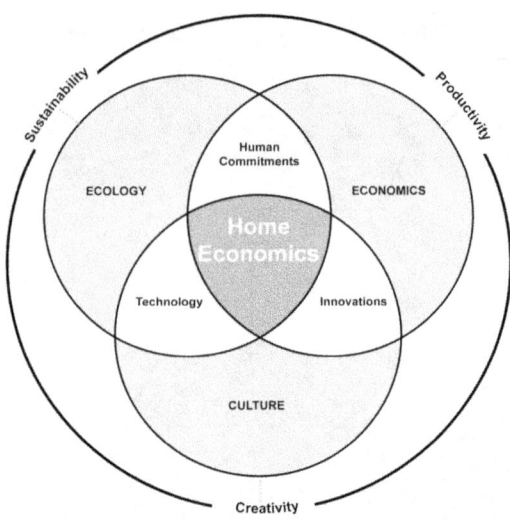

Figure 4.4

Home Economics — On our Way to Good Life.

institutional structures, which are reflected in society. By analyzing the documents and discoveries of earlier years, we can argue that Home Economics professionals have succeeded in crossing over the disciplines of economics, ecology and culture. We did so by providing new innovations, by using and developing further new tools based on available technologies, and by being committed to several human and social responsibilities in the work for the betterment of people and communities. The procedures and our ways of practice are reflected in the integration of productivity, sustainability and creativity. Figure 4.4 conceptualizes our knowledge base and ways of knowing, and represents how we have practiced following our understanding of *a good life* for individuals, families and communities, and it represents the necessity of stimulating interdependent and multidimensional relations to society, nature and culture.

Figure 4.5 expresses the same message, but indicates, in detail, some elements of the integrated thinking most of our practice includes, which, in combination, makes sustainability happen. Integrated thinking includes several value-related components that guide human actions. Our profession works to improve economic well-being by stressing the need to improve social conditions. Our focus is on *both* economics *and* the social aspects. Sustainability can happen only when these are closely connected (see Jackson, 2009). The similar connection is evident between technology and culture. We want to contribute to the use of technology, but, likewise, we want to recognize and unite technology as providing new content and quality for our culture and daily lives. It is through the human dimension and integrated thinking that this is achieved. After all, humans can create changes in a highly conscious manner because they have the ability to imagine, and this generates innovations. In earlier paragraphs, I emphasized the importance of human qualities and indicated that Home Economics

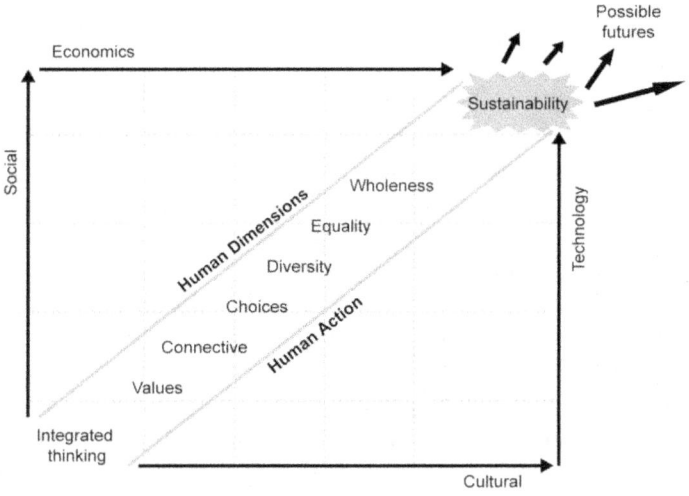

Figure 4.5

Diversity of Commitments to reach the Future.

is a human profession, and I mean *human* in its deepest sense. This is absolutely one of the key areas in which we can and should strengthen our expertise. From an historical point of view, I dare to claim this lack of integrated thinking and lack of a deep meaning of human as one of our blind spots.

Home Economics has always valued recognizing the future and its role in daily life. The importance of this is reflected in the Figure 4. 5. It is there to remind us of our visions, but also to remind us of its other contents and qualities. Based on our professional history, but also by analyzing our current practices, we certainly can convince ourselves of, and accept our role as, actors or professionals *for the future* (Lampinen & Melen-Paaso, 2009). Indeed, the future is an integral part of everyday life. Our educational programs should allocate sufficient attention to this area of knowledge because the future and innovations go hand-in-hand. Incorporating the future — in an intentional manner — as an essential part of our knowledge base, opens roads in many directions (Turkki, 2009). For this reason, I urge members of the Home Economics profession to avail themselves of the many conceptual and methodological tools created by future society organizations. The latter can be made to see that our knowledge base and approaches are central and current, and have been shown to be essential due to their strong commitment to human qualities and daily practices and services within sustainable frames.

Global learning — our promise for sustainable futures

This section discusses the concept of *global learning*. The aim of global learning is to enrich our life, our experiences, but also to increase our responsibility. In order for people to attain the goal of sustainability, it is necessary that they are connected and feel involved. Figure 4.6 demonstrates the importance of understanding the position of learning and of knowledge systems vis-a-vis global learning, given the megatrend of globalization. Learning and knowledge systems are, at same time, both stabilizing factors *and* sources for innovations and development. Our expertise in all of the areas contained within the oval circles enables us to adopt new challenges and to process daily life (lowest box) and to relate our knowledge base and visions to attaining a global mindset.

Figure 4.6 also indicates the presence of the same key processes that enact the most change and turbulence, both in one's daily life and in global contexts. However, the logistics are quite different in either of these realms and some logistics sustain processes that do not necessarily support positive development and progress. Furthermore, we still need to overcome many obstacles and barriers to attain the basic goals and visions for a sustainable future. The most important message here for our professionals is to recognize how privileged we actually are as we approach both future and global awareness. We have long been involved in serving as experts related to future knowledge and that of global education. Perhaps, the following discussion of global learning competencies will serve to convince Home economists of our uniqueness in this particular knowledge area, so key to sustainable futures.

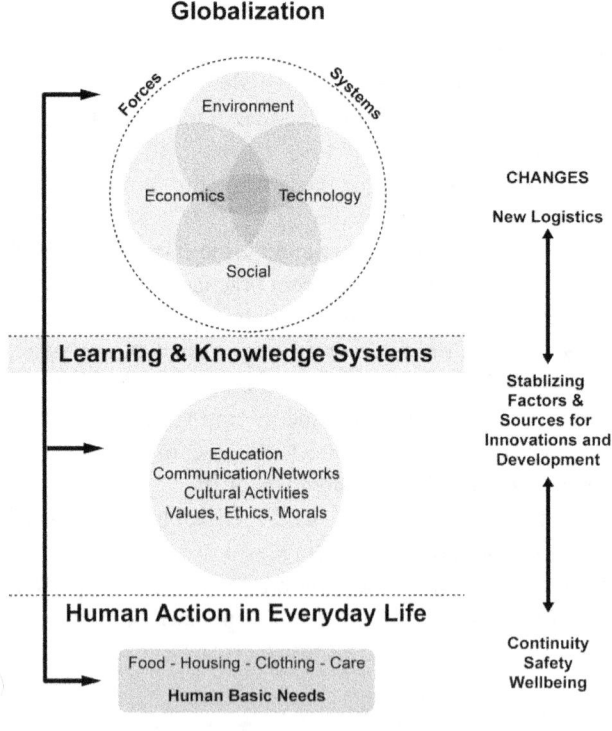

Figure 4.6

Home Economics frame for global learning.

Arguing for, and defining, *global learning*, Hartmayer (2008) emphasizes the importance of including all levels, from personal to global (akin to Home Economics integral, holistic, human ecosystem approach). His approach is strongly practice-oriented, thus serving our profession well. Hartmayer points out six important competencies that need to be covered. *Seeing global interdependence* involves the competency to see complex, global interdependencies, to understand them and to reflect on them critically. *Seeing one's own globality* means one has the ability to gain insight into one's own relations to globality in everyday life. *Assessing values* is the competency to assess values and attitudes. *Developing perspectives and visions* is the ability to develop future-oriented approach and visions. *Thinking for action in a global context* is the competency to reflect, and to develop opinions for action in a global context as well. *Readiness for communication and participation* is defined as the ability to participate in an independent and integrated way, in communication and in decision-making processes.

Additional valuable insights into what is involved in global learning can be garnered from Sahlberg's (2011) new book titled *Finnish Lessons*. He compares the Finnish educational system to key global educational reforms and identifies five characteristics or key elements, as manifested in what he called, 'The Finnish Way' of teaching. These include: customizing teaching and learning, focusing on creative learning, encouraging risk-taking, learning from the past and owing innovations and sharing responsibility and trust (Sahlberg, p. 103). His approach serves as a frame for our field because it focuses broadly on educational structures and policies, including economics in global scale. The Finnish education reform demonstrates that welfare, equality and competiveness can be united to support high- level learning results. If we extend the above analysis to Home Economics, and include our four dimensions of practice (IFHE, 2008), we can take even stronger steps in the future (Nickols et al., 2010).

Five steps for the future

The question of envisioning the future is a challenge that is as old as humankind (Malaska & Virtanen, 2009). I thought I would share with you Ståhle's (2007) approaches to seeking future success, and interpret them for the Home Economics profession. She believed future success could be achieved by: inspiring a national vision, making the Finnish success story known internationally, focusing on sources of innovation, enhancing social skills in the global arena and becoming a future pioneer in ecology. After reading the five bullets below, which interpret these five steps through a Home Economics lens, I also invite you to embark on your own journey into the profession in your country or region. The points below serve as a departure point, anticipating they might serve as an action plan for you, your national professional association and your students. By profiling five steps for the Home Economics future, you can unite the knowledge of your history, the policies of your country and the future of your choice.

Visualize a Big Dream — the need for a common vision
- We need emotional drive and engagement
- We are much more than a family and a consumer profession

Tell the Story of Home Economics in your country
- Clarify self-image and identity based on values — not only on competencies and products we produce
- Demonstrate our resource base and the entrepreneurial spirit

Consolidate the Roots of Innovations
- Focus needs to be on history, culture, education, social structures and practices
- HE/FCS could be a centre for social and cultural innovations
- Culture and values will serve as key drivers for change

Build Societal Intelligence at a Global level
- Local cases with global influences and dynamics
- HE/FCS is about communication and rich in relational capital created by connection, networks, sharing and new leadership
- Create new power structures — 'soft power' partnerships

Become a Forerunner for Human ecological principles
- Unite individual and collective sustainability and include giving and caring with new governance
- Maintain the idea of home and family and everyday life as being central and connected to health and well-being
- Unite Humans (people), Economics and Environment in terms of professional visions

A comment on theories and conceptual frameworks in Home Economics

Throughout this chapter, I have used conceptual frameworks to illustrate my ideas. Home Economics research is not very strong in terms of constructing theories. I invite you to review an overall draft framework (see Figure 4. 7) as an integrating framework which is highly connected to the research discussed in this chapter. This synthesis is designed to cover the idea of integrated theories based on a systemic thinking that encompasses the basic elements, processes and structures that are essential to knowledge in Home Economics.

In more detail, three concentric circles illustrate the necessity to cross and unite the individual, communal and societal levels, and to embrace the changing situations widely at hand. Each circle consists of *the human* element, demonstrating human processes, qualities and values. This conceptualization calls for dynamics and complexity along many dimensions to determine all qualities of *human action*. *Human commitments* refer to the values and the courage to complete one's visionary goals.

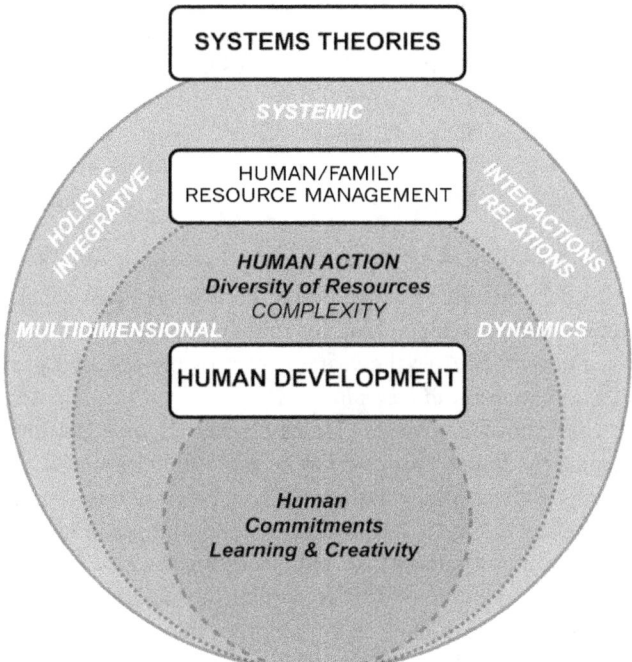

Figure 4.7

A preliminary systemic model to focus on Dynamics of Everyday Life.

People's commitments affect their *human development*. To aspire to the practice intimated in this diagram, we need to focus more on *new forms of learning* as parts of various processes — both visible and invisible — to surround and transform our daily activities. Furthermore, all the megatrends manifest in some shape or form at the parameters of each level of each circle.

This conceptualization of the profession is one response in an effort to assure that our professionals have all the capacity they need to respond to my invitation (see introduction) to regard *change as our challenge* and to make *interrelatedness and diversity* our inspirational common arenas to focus on responsible living and to create Home Economics futures.

Also, this conceptual model is in line with our human ecological heritage, the maintenance of which will be our greatest challenge during the next decades. Even though we have been forerunners in human ecological thinking (e.g., sustainable and responsible living), we have not necessarily consciously completed it through our professional activities. Each home economist has to decide how to address this major challenge. For example, you can practice Home Economics at home, in a local community, or by working as a professional and expert while being open to international and global issues. Each level (see Figure 4. 1) can nourish the others.

To recall the metaphor of *an old, vital tree*, I am sure that in the next 100 years, there will be a vital global Home Economics community which looks back to these years with varying degrees of emotions. It depends highly on us how they assess our achievements of today. Indeed, we must assume responsibility for our next generations (the seeds), if we are ever to future-proof our profession.

Summary

As we face the challenge of future-proofing the profession, the validity of Home Economics can be demonstrated by the body of knowledge upon which the discipline is based. Cushioned in the tree metaphor, this chapter profiled seven conceptual frameworks that I have developed over the years as part of my research program entitled *Home Economics as a Science and Discipline.*

Competences and knowledge bases in Home Economics serve as a powerful arena for learning and shaping the future. Our path has been life-long learning. One fundamental area for actions and services locally and globally will continue to be human action in everyday life. This relates to food and eating, housing, clothing, communication and care services. The future and innovations have always belonged to our daily lives, and value creating is one of the many human qualities to guide our practices.

I also that advocated that the profession embrace the concept of *global learning* so that we all can envision ourselves as global citizens and be able to adopt the metaphor by Ellie Vaines of the 'World is our Home' (Vaines, 2004). I embraced this *learning story* and extended it to larger environments to discover and to enrich our global challenges for sustainable futures. Home economists have to learn in relation to moving in time, in space and in values to be able to create meaningful futures. We have extensive evidence to confirm the importance of Home Economics as a future profession, but also reminders of the vulnerability it holds owing to the complexity and difficulty of formulating our message in a manner that is understood easily by outsiders. There are still many misunderstandings within the profession and outside based on narrow and false interpretations.

Global learning is now a real aspect of Home Economics. By travelling far, virtually, geographically and in our minds and thoughts, we can build a more intensive and flourishing environment around us. In other words, Home Economics is a rich learning environment for all. For me, personally, my journey has been both as a human thinker and as a traveler to the most remote corners of the globe and the universe around it. And, this journey is becoming more colorful and enjoyable day after day due to the challenge of learning new skills and of feeling like I am a partner in our common global community.

Home Economics as a profession is in unique position because of the way we *are* in the world, and the way our body of knowledge (whether or not we recognize it or are aware of it) serves as a fundamental tool for global wealth and prosperity. To safeguard this position, we need to continue to establish and sustain the educational landscape required to have well-grounded and sustainable platforms to foster the next generation of innovative Home Economics professionals, teachers and researchers.

Discussion Prompts

- What does it mean, if we designate global learning as our basic human quality, and what kind of implications could it hold concerning the four dimensions of practice in Home Economics? How do you see your role and position in this context, and which professionals would you invite to be your partners to efficiently promote global learning?
- Home Economics is about communication and networking, and it provides us a unique position for our personal and professional lives. What is the quality of the communication in your present coalitions and how could it be improved to reach higher levels of learning and creativity? How do you envision your opportunities to process the global megatrends and to extend the discussion to target the dialogue for universal values 2030.
- Higher education: Educating new professionals and conducting research play critical roles for future development. Which improvements need to happen in your country to establish a firm basis for the best possible knowledge-creation environments? How could our global communities — as the IFHE — be partners and/or facilitators in renewing the circumstances in your country and in providing forums for creativity and innovation?

References

Hartmeyer, H. (2008). *Experiencing the world*. Munster: Waxmann.

IFHE. (2008). Position statement "HE21C". *International Journal of Home Economics, 1*(1),6–7.

Jackson, T. (2009). *Prosperity without growth: Economics for a finite planet*. London: Earthscan.

Lampinen, T., & Melen-Paaso, M. (2009). *Tulevaisuus meissä — Kasvaminen globaaliin vastuuseen*. [Trans: The future in us. Education for global responsibility]. Ministry of Education Publications 2009:40. Helsinki: University Press.

Malaska, P., & Holstius, K. (2009). Modern futurist approach. Finnish Society for Futures Studies. *FUTURA, 28*(1), 85–96.

McGregor, S. (2010). Name changes and future-proofing the profession: Human sciences as a name? *International Journal of Home Economics 3*(1), 20–37.

Nickols, S.Y., Turkki, K., Pichler, G., Kirjavainen, L., Atiles, J.H. & Firebaugh, F.M. (2010). A Global Perspective for FCS. Sustaining Families, Communities, and Natural Environment by Building Social Capital. *Journal of Family and Consumer Sciences, 102*(4), 10–16.

Sahlberg, P. (2011). *Finnish Lessons. What can the world learn from educational change in Finland*. New York: Teachers College Press.

Ståhle, P. (Ed.) (2007). *Five steps for Finland's future*. Helsinki: TEKES

Turkki, K. (2004). The influence of Eleanore Vaines on home economics in Finland. In G. Smith, L. Peterat and M. deZwart (Eds.), *Home economics now: Transformative practice, ecology, and everyday life* (pp. 53–66). Vancouver, BC: Pacific Educational Press.

Turkki, K., & Vincenti. V. (2008). Celebrating the past: A critical reflection on the history of IFHE and home economics profession. *International Journal of Home Economics, 1*(2), 75–97.

Turkki, K. (2009). Koti ja kotitalous — Home and Home Economics — learning for life and responsibility. In J. Lampinen and M. Melen-Paaso (Eds.), *Tulevaisuus meissä — Kasvaminen globaaliin vastuuseen*. (pp. 100–106). [Trans: The future in us — Education for global responsibility]. Ministry of Education Publications 2009:40. Helsinki: University Press.

Vaines, E. (2004). Wholeness, transformative practices, and everyday life. In G. Smith, L. Peterat and M. deZwart (Eds.), *Home economics now:Transformative practice, ecology, and everyday life* (pp. 133–165). Vancouver, BC: Pacific Educational Press.

CHAPTER
5

Home Economics in Past and Present — Perspectives for the Future

Jette Benn

Home Economics has been a subject in school and education for more than 100 years in the Western world. Home economists have from the beginning been inspiring each other by visiting colleagues around the world, and very early the International Federation of Home Economics was established in order to broaden and deepen the knowledge of Home Economics through collaboration and exploration, and this is still the vision for IFHE, of which this book can be an example.

As part of the school curriculum and a foundation to general education, Home Economics has needed to define and be able to position the subject. Through the 100 years period the roles and valuations of the teachers have changed. Why and how the subject has changed is essential to analyze in order to understand the present situation and to give proposals for the future. Teachers within Home Economics have been and are still mainly female. This can be related to the subject itself, the home, which is a female domain. This domestic domain or sphere with its values, language and work, naturally has an impact on the school subject, the understanding, practising and education within the field.

In this chapter I will go through history to provide an understanding of the basic, essential and important aspects of Home Economics, take these aspects up to present time and make perspectives for the future.

As a start I will state some postulates to show some of the dilemmas and dialectics, which are on the agenda.

- Home Economics is a subject in a conflict between science (theory) and everyday life experiences (practice)
- Home Economics is gendered

- Home Economics is culturally dependant, society determined, individually featured
- Home Economics holds potentials, possibilities, and difficulties

These postulates are essential to bring to an open discussion for developing Home Economics in the long run. In short, the conflict of Home Economics and within the subject itself as an applied science, this has a problem of defining what Home Economics is and can be.

The gender part is based on the context home, kitchen and household, and furthermore context is culturally bound. Finally, Home Economics holds potentials both taken from history and the present. I will explore these issues through a historical critical approach, which has been part of my research for the last thirty years.

Home Economics in the past
1880s—1910

One of the Danish pioneers, Magdalene Lauridsen, expressed the mission for Home Economics as follows: *"to household (or good housekeeping) means to use what you have, in order to get what you want."* By that she meant that the aim of Home Economics was that both coming teachers and students should learn to use and handle the resources of the home and household in the most prudent way. This was both a question of cooking and cleaning following the advices, which could be extracted from the new sciences of nutrition and microbiology. The visions were *"furthermore to raise the view of the housework, improve women's education, apply scientific results, solve social problems, and understand the nature and demands of the child".* The last issue, the nature of the child, was a new understanding of the bodily needs, as the school was sitting down listening, reading, and writing and that school could profit by including practical work in the school day. This can also be related to a pedagogical movement from Germany called the working school (Der Arbeitsschule). This movement represented by Kerschensteiner, a German headmaster working with craft, saw the practical work as part of literacy or Bildung (Kerschensteiner in Husen, 1980).

The subject was seen as an applied science in Denmark, but as expressed by another Nordic pioneers Helga Helgesen: "As both natural science and mathematics are seen as part of the general education (Bildung) in the school, they cannot lose their educational ability when the pupils learn to apply the sciences in a prudent way" (Helgesen, 1900).

The introduction was influenced by different angles and visions. Pedagogical theorists such as Kerchensteiner and Dewey were among the influential. Kerchensteiner was a German headmaster concerned with how a practical subject as craft could have an educational meaning or rather a meaning for 'Bildung' on boys. Dewey was concerned with the meaning of experiences within education, or learning by doing, which has become a motto for his research (see Husen, 1978, Dewey, 1998/1938).

Spokeswomen for Home Economics education were found among conservative and liberal circles. The first mentioned group aimed at heightening the view of household work and values within the home, and they viewed the home and house-

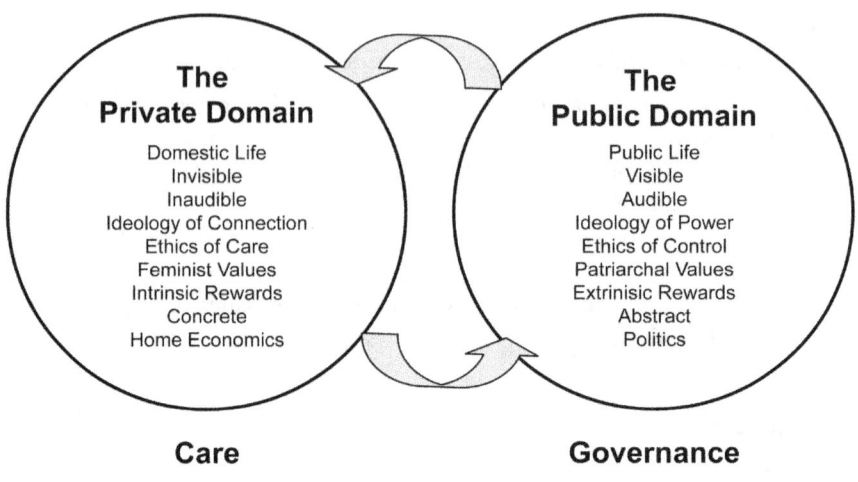

Figure 5.1

Two Systems of Human Action (Thompson, 1992 p. 31

hold as isolated from the society. This separation can be compared to the Greek society in ancient history, where oikos (the Greek word for household) was isolated from polis (the society). The values in the two domains were totally distinctive as shown by Patricia Thomson (Thompson, 1992, 1993). Patricia Thompson uses the old Greek terms oikos for household and polis for society and points out the heritage from the Greek society with the different values within the two spheres. Oikos is dominated by the practical, female housework and private world whereas polis is/was the public place for free men to discuss and work with more theoretical and artistic issues. Thompson illustrates this in her model for 2 systems of action, Figure 5.1. The model is useful in showing this distinction between household and society and can to a part explain the dualism, which has influenced the view of the subject in Home Economics education.

Turning to the liberal movement, this party was more engaged in using scientific results from the growing natural science into the household area in order to assist the families in getting a better, healthier life; but they also wanted to further female education as such. They stressed the need of being educated formally as a need not only for boys but also for girls. Within this liberal group many frontiers in Home Economics were established, for example, woman founded private female schools and also teacher training colleges. One of these women, Nathalie Zahle, founded one of the first school kitchens, which could be used for female education in a period of the girls' lives when they were in 'bodily' growth and needed to do some practical work as she formulated this.

The last faction was the socialists. In Denmark, this faction was against Home Economics as part of the compulsory education, as they did not want the women to be bound to the kitchen and they found or thought that more institutionalized community kitchens in the future would take care of domestic work. This was quite opposite to the American situation, as described by Doris Badir, where socialist feminists were thinking that 'Home Economics education provided solutions to the nation's social problems and represented a practical choice of study for women.'(Badir, 1993 p. 208)

Another influence for Home Economics at this time was found within the pedagogical and psychological theories which promoted the introduction of Home Economics. Among these was the thesis of Dewey of "learning by doing" and his laboratory school. Kerchensteiner's thoughts of the need for practical work in education were essential, too, and finally developmental theories of more psychological sort had an impact (Dewey, 1998, Kerschensteiner in Husen, 1980/1912). Taken together the arguments for Home Economics were feministic, pedagogical, psychological, educational, and social. The title of the subject became female domestic work or housework more directly. The textbook title of the most used material from 1912 to the 1970s was however Home Economics.

1920s–1960s

After the first introductory period of Home Economics concerned with defining the subject and describing the aims, the Home Economics teachers were engaged in describing teaching methods, making textbooks and core curricula. A definite format of the lessons was developed, which has had an impact on thinking regarding Home Economics teaching. John Dewey inspired the teachers to install laboratory kitchens (Dewey, 1912/1998) and teaching was transformed in a way that every single pupil made her own task standing beside one another. This was then used as an introductory method followed by working in big kitchen divided into small family kitchens, where tasks were divided between '*the family members*', who were guided by textbooks describing how to work and containing the recipes of cooking or you may say the recipes of the good life so to speak. Both ways to design the school room are still seen all over the world, and so is the way to plan the teaching. The school kitchen has had and still has a very huge impact on thinking and conducting Home Economics in both positive and negative ways. Seen in a Home Economics history light, this period from 1910 to 1960s was focused on methods practical and educational. The theory of the subject, mainly natural scientific, was taught isolated from the practical part (Benn, 2000).

The word women was deleted from the title of the subject in 1938, but still the subject was only for girls, apart from the Copenhagen community, where boys were taught from the 1940s.

1970s–1990s

In the late 1960s, women's liberation was gathering support, and house work was not considered to be so essential any more, at the same time as boys in the whole country were enrolled in the education. But women should earn their own money, be educated but not necessarily within Home Economics. Home Economics was downgraded both in the general opinion and also in the school system. Lessons were shorter, cut down. The way to regard the subject was found more within creativity and as a break in the school day. This resulted in more focus on the practical issues, cooking and baking. In Denmark the subject was also grouped together with other practical-creative subjects, and therefore considered as such a subject. Group work and gender equality was however on the agenda, and from the aims the following can be seen:

- knowledge and experiences within consumer issues, planning and maintenance of work in the home
- skills in techniques and working processes, in rationalising the work in the home
- understanding of the meaning of proper composition of food
- aesthetical attitude regarding hygiene and organisation and maintenance of the home

In 1971 the inspector of Home Economics formulated the subject as follows:

> "The subject encompasses in all classes theoretical, technical and practical work. It is ethical, aesthetical and pragmatic. Weight is put upon hygiene and economy…In Denmark we still work in such a way, that we link knowledge and skills, which the pupils have from other subjects together with the more general practical and technical tasks… The motto from the first year of education is: Simplicity, clarity and to go into depth (according to J.Fr. Herbart). Every pupil prepares and arranges her own portion."(Sivertsen, 1971)

Regarding the last point — "simplicity, clarity and to go into depth" was not the full truth of Home Economics education, as time was diminished and problems regarding foods and food production had become more and more complex and difficult to understand. It was not possible just to recommend eating herrings for health reasons, if you did not know where they had been caught.

The subject title was changed to Home Economics or more directly translated home knowledge as it was called in Sweden and Norway, but still the focus was on cooking, food and nutrition and not home as such.

1990s

In 1995 a new curriculum was developed by a group of Home Economics specialists, the work was inspired by both national and international Home Economics work and also by general educational theories of the state and problems within home, society and institutions. The work of Patricia Thompson (), Buboltz ()) and Sontag () and Vaines () had a great impact on the formulation and description of the curriculum and also on the understanding of the home as *oikos* surrounded by *polis* or society (see Benn,), and of the role of the teacher as an eco-centrered person. In the words of Karsten Schnack we were in a period of challenges for education and didactics (Schnack, 1993). The challenges could and can be seen as both global and local, or as key problems which another philosophical pedagogue named Klafki has described (Klafki, 1994). These key problems must also have an impact in the Home Economics curriculum and syllabus, which the working group implemented in the aim (Ministry

of Education, 1996). From the aim of Home Economics the following principles can be derived:
- responsibility and care for the activities in the home
- practical, experimental and sensorial tasks
- development of self-esteem and joy of life
- take critical stand and act
- understanding of one's own culture and the culture of others as expressed in the act of housework
- understanding of the meaning of use of resources considering the environment

Home Economics at present

The tendency for a new school subject is in general, that firstly it has to promote itself, through encircling aims and visions. Thereafter it needs to stabilise and refine its content and methods. After that a period of stagnation often occurs and finally an evaluation is needed. This was clearly seen in a Danish analysis of school subjects in 1995 (this study is in Danish language only).

The period limits cannot be given as fixed time terms, it must be seen more as trends and tendencies. Historical characteristics from each period will more or less be carried on to the next period and also up until today's education, Figure 5.2. The introduction period was going on from 1890s to 1910s, the stabilising period from 1920s to 1960s, the stagnation or (re)creative period from 1960 to 1980s, and we have the (re)evaluation period from the 1990s.

Home Economics after 2000

What can be said of Home Economics today? In many countries the subject is compulsory for both boys and girls. The name and curricula differ from one country to another, the education in primary or secondary school or both, the name and the teachers. In

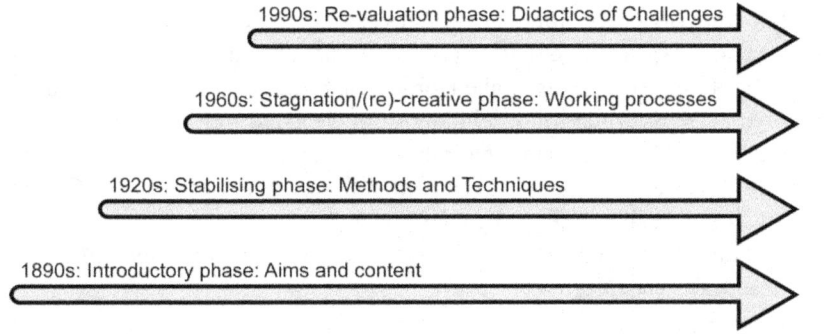

Figure 5.2

Focus in different periods (Benn, 1996)

Denmark the name Home Economics is seen as outdated, and the suggestion for a name from the Home Economics association is food and health as in the Norwegian title. Other groups wish the title to be food literacy (Bildung). The problem concerning the subject in the school is still resources, resources concerning time for the subject both within a year as over more years, it concerns economy in order to have materials for the teaching both text books, artefacts and food. Last resources are to be found as competencies of the teacher within the area of Home Economics, as teacher education has lesser time for the subject, and also further education of teachers.

The name signalises the content and focus of a subject, but still the Home Economics classroom is the school kitchen. The room defines part of what can be taught in the room, but it could be broadened and the 'laboratory' thought from Dewey could be taken seriously, so that pupils should 'labore' or experiment and experience in a lot of ways, sensory, scientific, and take theory and practice in together.

Perspectives for Home Economics in the future

What does it imply to be a "home economizer" in the new millennium or to be educated in the 21st century?

I think 3 scenarios are possible as regarding Home Economics in the school system or perhaps I should mention the fourth also: *"Now is the time to take it apart for good "*as Gena Attar said in her evaluation of Home Economics in England. The reason was that Attar had experienced in her survey that teachers did not take up relevant issues in education, but educated on behalf of their problems and their own middle-class lives. They were not considering what the pupils needed to be able to manage in their roles as:

- Householders and educators
- Workers and producers
- Citizens (Kristensen, 1987)

What Attar really criticizes, is, that teachers do not understand society and culture as e.g. related to different life forms, different conditions in society, different individuals and human beings. But they teach Home Economics as a-cultural and a-historical. So this scenario where Home Economics is out of school is one possibility, which I will reject and instead argue that Home Economics education must be changed and teachers should be educated to make Home Economics a part of pupils' 'Bildung' as empowered citizens, prudent householders and creative producers for the benefit of their own life and that of others. That means that teachers have to consider their role in a way as described by Vaines as eco-centered taking into consideration that they should teach to live a life in a caring relationship.

But turning to the first mentioned 3 scenarios, I could see school and especially Home Economics classroom as:

- a cultural centre
- a survival centre or a centre for sustainability
- a laboratory for developing and challenges

Home Economics is or should be a subject for all human beings in a developmental perspective and in order to be able to live together. It should be a subject for educating citizens (global and local) to assist the lay perspective, which is a precondition for democracy, and educating householders to be able to act ecologically and economize. Finally, Home Economics has to educate caregivers that mean to care for the other and for the surroundings.

In the introduction it was mentioned, that Home Economics is a subject in a conflict between science (theory) and everyday life experiences (practice), but this is an issue which can be explored and researched in order to be able to teach in a way which combine theory and practice. It could be an issue for a common research project.

The gender issue is within Home Economics; but is a theme to deal with in Home Economics education offered for both boys and girls and conducted by both male and female teachers taking up gender themes in lessons concerning cooperation, gender perspectives on different household tasks and so forth.

Home Economics is culturally dependant, society determined, individually featured, I claimed in the introduction. This means that you have to see Home Economics in the cultural context you are part of. It does not imply that there is a national or regional culture to consider alone, but also the culture connected to different life forms, their values and priorities and differentiations among these. The society sets the rules for schooling and defines the curricula, but within these the teacher has her action room based on her/his view of education, learning and subject in cooperation with the pupils and sometimes with the parents. The individual both the teacher herself and all the single pupils are part of different groups and families, who have to be respected as human beings and have a role to play in the learning environment.

As it can be seen in the chapter, Home Economics holds potentials, possibilities, and also difficulties. The difficulties in teaching Home Economics can both be of external character and internal, the external is to be dealt with politically both at local level and national and perhaps international level. The internal problems and difficulties are partly within the subject, also inherited from history, but also within the single teacher and her understanding of the subject, of teaching and of the situation for the subject and the pupils in the 21st century. This understanding must be drawn to the surface and discussed within the profession, within teacher education and at the school level.

The possibilities and potentials are multifaceted and should be developed, as I have tried to reveal in the chapter. Parts from history are valuable to preserve and perhaps reconsider in new ways. Taken all together a home economist engaged in the subject for more than forty years must say in the wordings of the Norwegian philosopher Erling Lars Dale

> 'The school subject home economics is important, for example, for fostering positive attitudes towards carrying out tasks and taking care of obligations in everyday life…. Home Economics can be seen as a basic element in the students' ethical language, which encompasses care, responsibility and equal values in human interrelations.' (Dale, 2000, p. 34, translation Benn)

Summary

This chapter presents a brief historical overview of Home Economics, discuss the future possibilities for Home Economics in schools, as a tool for change and to develop literacy and 'Bildung'
- home economics history
- characteristics of the subject
- problems and challenges
- possibilities

Discussion Prompts

- Consider how teachers in Home Economics could develop the classroom for further learning in a broader sense?
- How is your own Home Economics understanding?
- What does your understanding mean for teaching concerning goal, content, methods, materials?
- Compare curriculum from a couple of selected countries. Discuss the differences related to culture, content and the aimed competencies

References

Attar, Gena (1993): *Wasting Girls' Time. The history and politics of home economics.* The Education Series

Badir, Doris (1993): The Marginalization or Ghettoziation of Home Economics: In Particular its Ghettoization within Academe. I: Kettschau, Irmhild, Methfessel, Barbara and Schmidt-Waldherr, Hiltraud, ed.: *Youth Family and Household.* Global Perspectives on Development and Quality of Life: 203–218

Badir, Doris(1988): *Home Economics and feminism.* I: People and Practice. International Issues for Home Economists. *Vol. 1,* No. 3

Benn, Jette (1999a): Home Economics Teachers, Their Past and Present Roles and Valuations and Implications for the Future. In: *Hauswirtschaft und Wissenschaft; 4*: 157–164

Benn, Jette (1999b): Home Economics — Standpoints and Experiences in Danish School Settings. *Arbejdspapirer no. 13*

Benn Jette (2000a): Home Economics in 100 years. Home Economics in the 21st century. *History — Perspectives — Challenges.* In: Benn, Jette, ed.: *Home Economics in 100 Years. History, Perspectives and Challenges.* The Royal Danish School of Education: 13–29

Buboltz, M.M., Sonntag, M.S.(1993): *Human Ecology Theory.*In:Boss, Pauline G. et al., ed.: *Sourcebook of Family Theories and Methods. A Contextual Approach.* Plenum Press: New York and London: 419–447.

Dewey, John(1998/1938): *Experience and Education.* Kappa Delta, Indianapolis Engberg, Lila E.(1994): *Towards Reflective Problem Solving.*I: D'Oyly, Vincent, Adrian Blunt, Ray Barnhardt (eds):Education and Development — Lessons from the Third World. N.Y.:Detseling Enterpises Ltd.:215–233

Helgesen, Helga (1900): Huslig Ökonomie som obligatorisk Fag for Folkeskolens *Piger.*(Home Economics as compulsory subject for the girls in primary and secondary school). In: Vor Ungdom: 771–786 (In Norwegian)

Husen, Michael (1978) Arbejdsbegrebet I den pædagogiske filosofi. Georg Kerchensteiners Dannelsesteori. Odense Universitetsforlag, Odense (The work concept in the educational philosophy. The 'Bildung' theory of Georg Kerschensteiner — this work is a comprehensive study of all Kerschensteiner's works 1910–1933)

Klafki, Wolfgang(1994a): Schlüsselprobleme als inhaltlicher Kern internationaler Erziehung.I:Seibert, N., Serve, H.J.: Bildung und Erziehung an der Schnelle zum dritten Jahrtausend. Multidiziplinäre Aspekte, Analysen, Positionen, Perspektiven. München:135–161

Klafki, Wolfgang(1994b): Zum Verhältnis von allgemeiner Didaktik und Fachdidaktik — *Fünf Thesen.* I: Meyer, Meinert A, Plöger, Wilfried: *Allgemeine Didaktik,* Fachdidaktik und Fachunterricht: 42–65

Ministry of Education ( ): Ministry of Education(1996):Aims and Central Knowledge and Proficiency Areas. The Danish Primary and Lower Secondary School

Schnack, Karsten (1993): *Fagdidaktik og almendidaktik. Didaktiske studier, Bidrag til didaktikkens teori og historie.* Bd.5 , DLH, Copenhagen

Schön, Donald A. (1983): *The reflective practitioner : how professionals think in action* New York: Basic Books

Sivertsen, Lilly (1971): Husgerning. I: Petersen, K. Helweg, ed.: *Uddannelse i Danmark* (Education in Denmark): 247–255.

Thompson, Patricia(1993): *A Feminist Theory for Everyday Life.* I: Kettschau, Irmhild, Methfessel, Barbara, Schmidt-Waldherr, Hiltraud, ed.: *Youth, Family and Household.* Global Perspectives on Development and Quality of Life:166–177

Thompson, Patricia(1992): Bringing Feminism Home. Home Economics and the Hestian *Connection.* Home Economics Publishing Collective, UPEI

Vaines, Eleanore(1990): *Philosophical Orientations and Home Economics: An Introduction.*I:Revue Canadienne dèconomie familiale;40(1)Hiver:6–11

Vaines, Elanore, Badir, Doris, Kieren Dianne(1988): *Introducing the Reflective Home Economics Professional.*I:People and Practice: *International Issues for Home Economists. Vol 1.no 1*

CHAPTER

6

History and Potential of Home Economics in the People's Republic of China

Peng Chen

This chapter focuses on the development of Home Economics in the People's Republic of China (P.R.C). Home Economics in China has experienced different stages of development from its introduction, from cancelation to its reconstruction. Home Economics' history is closely related to the nation's modernization process and with the evolution of women's social status. This chapter is organized chronologically into four sections: the predecessor of Home Economics in China, women's education in China; the introduction of Western Home Economics to China; the cancellation of Home Economics after the P.R.C. was established; and the reconstruction of Home Economics since 1978. The chapter concludes with an assessment of the potential of Home Economics in China through three lenses: education, research and extension.

To gain deeper, contextual understandings about the development of Home Economics, its history in China is also analyzed using both the critical theory of daily life (Yi, 2005a) and social gender theory (Zhou, 2011). Using the critical theory of daily life, we can understand the significance and value of the discipline in China: the modernization of the human. Using social gender theory, we can view the development of Home Economics within the different contexts, including gendered education, gender-neutral education and gender-sensitive education. Home Economics, which is closely connected with femininity, needs to go beyond the social gendered bias and make great contributions to the modernization of the human in China. Figure 6.1 provides a brief overview of the history of Home Economics in China, with more details provided in the following text.

Feudal Times	Introduction of Western, modern Home Economics	Cancellation of Home Economics in All Levels of Education	Reconstruction of Home Economics
1046BC-1840s	1840s-1949	1949-1977	1978-ongoing
For more than 2000 years, philosophers valued families as the foundation of social stability

Women's education was informed by the Confucian Classics and prepared women to be "an understanding wife and a loving mother" | 1840s foreign missionaries taught female students about caring for the home

1907 China's last feudal dynasty (Qing) established women's normal schools (teacher's college)

1914 Feudal system over; new **Republic of China** government sent women overseas to be trained in Home Economics

1919-1920 Home Economics was included in Women's Higher Normal School and missionary universities trained Chinese Home Economics professionals

1938 Minister of Education began promoting Home Economics in elementary and secondary schools

Concurrently, during 1930s-40s, new social movements in China led to female university students rejecting Home Economics | 1949 **People's Republic of China (PRC)** was established under the leadership of the Chinese Communist Party

1950s Home Economics was cancelled in all levels of education because it did not meet the needs of the times

1950s Home Economics departments at universities were dismantled and merged into related disciplines (e.g., medicine, education and art) | 1978 the PRC implemented reform policy and welcomed Western modernization

1994 the PRC began establishing a socialist market system

Modernization and a socialist market system are transforming China

Home Economics is reappearing in a few higher education institutions but it is taught by non-home economists from related disciplines; it does not have a separate entry in the Chinese Clasification of Instructional Programs (under Sociology) and it is viewed as experimental and not formal

The future of Home Economics in China is threatened by the strong push for technical career paths/success and narrow understanding of its mission and potential; many Chinese women are still wary of its perceived focus on women |

| Gendered education | Gendered education | Gender neutral education | From Gender neutral to Gender sensitive education |

| Pre-modernization | Semi-modernization | | Modernization |

Figure 6.1

A brief overview of the history of Home Economics in China

The predecessor of Home Economics: Women's education in China (221BC — 1840s)

Viewed through the macroscopic lens of a feudal society, China has attached great importance to the family since ancient times. Several philosophers pointed out that families were the foundation of social stability. Famous thinkers, like Menci (about 372 B.C-289 B.C), put forward: "The foundation of the world is countries, foundation of country is families, and foundation of family is oneself" (Mencius Liloushang, 2001). This famous saying greatly influenced the governing ideas of Chinese feudal rulers. An important book on the institutional system in ancient China, *The Book of Rites* (about Warring States to Qin Dynasty)[1], outlined the relationship among individuals, society and the nation. "To put the world in order, we must first put the nation in order; to put the nation in order, we must put the family in order; to put the family in order, we must cultivate our personal life; and to cultivate our personal life, we must first set our heart right" (Daxue, 2001). *The Book of Rites* had a great impact on the Chinese culture. Ancient kings in successive dynasties all thought highly of the relationship among the individual, the family and the state, so they placed it at all levels of the official agenda, bringing it to the attention of all levels of people.

Viewed through the microscopic lens of a feudal society, it can be said the family played an important role in regulating the relationship between the sexes. There were very detailed rules about the relationship among family members. More specifically, men ruling women was seen to be an effective tool. In the "Liwei Hanwenjia" (n.d.) (about 25 A.D.-220A.D.), the following rules were articulated: "the ruler guides the subject, the father guides the son, and the husband guides the wife." Under these rules, ancient women's education emerged as the times required. Women were asked to stay at home and learn their legal duty systematically, which was the requirement of the patriarchal society. Women were isolated from the public domain, accepting different education than that provided for men. Women's ideal role was to be an understanding wife and a loving mother.

The contents of women's education included sericulture and silk reeling, weaving, cooking, sweeping, the festival rite, how to conduct oneself for all occasions, et cetera. The core of women's education was three obediences and four virtues. Regarding the former, a single woman obeys her father, a married woman obeys her husband, and a widowed woman obeys the deceased husband's son (Yili Snagfu, 1996). The four virtues included the females' virtue, females' verbalism, females' visages, and females' handicrafts (Zhouli Tiangong Jiubin, 1996).

In the Chinese feudal society, education for women was gendered; women were separated from the men. The content of women's education was all about effective knowledge and skills accumulated by the ancestors under the guidance of Confucianism. Women were attached to men, and what they learned was much less valuable than what men learned. Although all levels of people paid much attention to the family, men were asked to be far removed from household activities, considered to be the domain of women.

Western modern Home Economics introduced to China (1840s–1949)

After the opium war in the 1840s, China was forced into the modernization process due to constant invasions of Western powers. During the past one hundred-plus years, China, under the impact of modernization, has undergone its most significant changes in the past 5000 years. China experienced exogenous modernization, meaning that it was responding to external forces instead of initiating change voluntarily, from within. For this reason, the traditional culture was still influential during China's modernization process (rather than being left behind or replaced with new traditions, as is often the case with endogenous modernization).

Starting in the 1840s, foreign missionaries began to establish missionary schools and to recruit female students, teaching them the knowledge and abilities of housekeeping and of character formation. More importantly, the missionaries intended for female students to have careers and to live independently in society. What with Western cultural influences and the growing awakening of people's consciousness, several Chinese reformers, at the end of 19th century, started female schools and advocated for women to attend. Under pressure from the Chinese society at the time, the Qing government (China's last feudal dynasty), in 1907, established the women's normal school around the goal of creating an understanding wife and a loving mother. Consequently, women's education was formally incorporated into the school system. Although the contents of women's education did not essentially change, the normal school (teacher's college) altered the home school pattern.

After the 1911 Revolution overthrew the feudal monarchy, the Republic of China was established. The new government continued the women's education policy of the Qing dynasty. In order to solve the problem of a lack of teachers, the government, on the one hand, sent some excellent girls overseas to learn Home Economics, beginning this practice in 1914. On the other hand, it began to offer women's higher education (university level). In 1919, the Ministry of Education released the *Women's Higher Normal School Regulations*. The curriculum in the Regulations included a division for Home Economics, providing for sewing, craftwork and housekeeping, et cetera (Wang, 2006). In 1920, the Beijing Women's Higher Normal School began to offer Home Economics education. Following this initiative, some missionary universities introduced Home Economics from the U.S., training many professionals for China, such as dieticians and early childhood teachers.

During the same period, several social movements broke out in China, including the New Culture Movement in 1915 and the May 4th Movement in 1919. Democracy and science spirits began to be transmitted amongst the Chinese intellectual elite. The leaders of these movements opposed the traditional virtues mentioned earlier and advocated equity between women and men. Many educated women became supporters of this idea, going out of their family and throwing themselves into the battle against the old, oppressed culture. Not surprisingly, traditional female roles began to change.

In 1938, the Ministry of Education formulated the *Home Economics Education Extension Methods Below the Secondary Education*, which promoted the spread of Home Economics education in many elementary and secondary schools. At this time, there was also a noticeable phenomenon: many young ladies who accepted these progressive ideas refused to take Home Economics at universities. This boycott reflected their resolute rupture from traditions.

The ancient state in China was filled with war and social movements. The exogenous cultural crisis increased the number of critics and accelerated their doubts about traditional culture. Modern rational spirits began to brew in China. Chinese women started to challenge traditional gender roles and called for gender equity. But, this kind of rebellion only occurred in the small, intellectually elite group. Meanwhile, the lives of the masses were still greatly influenced by traditional culture. Therefore, although the government introduced foreign-informed Home Economics, the discipline looked quite different in China. The enlightenment spirits originating in Western Home Economics did not grow in China.

During the war era, the core of Home Economics was maternalism, which emphasized the relationship between women and children, the nation and the country. Although gender equity thought began to spread, the ideal model of women's education, "an understanding wife and a loving mother," did not, in essence, change. The dual-track, gendered approach to education between the sexes still existed. But, this kind of gendered education did not receive general recognition and implementation, and even suffered resistance from some female students in universities.

With the deepening of national crises, more and more female students threw themselves into the social movement for liberation. Most women considered learning Home Economics as a sign of backward thinking and began to learn from men as their role model. Gender differences diminished, even disappeared. Many women believed they would not get true equity until they had rushed out of the fencing-in of the family. Although this kind of understanding was very radical, it became an inevitable process in women's liberation all over the world, not just in China. Home Economics, everywhere, was affected by the women's movement.

The cancellation of Home Economics after the PRC was established (1949–1977)

In 1949, the People's Republic of China (PRC) was established under the leadership of the Chinese Communist Party. They obeyed Marxism's women's liberation principle, incorporating the gender equity principle into the system's construction and into social practices. Gender equity became a basic national policy. The government advocated that women go outside of the family and take part in all kinds of activities, just like the men. Like in other countries, besides working outside of the home, most women undertook household duties after work when they returned home.

In that context, gendered education, such as Home Economics, was criticised. Also, with the political tension between socialism and the capitalism coalition, Home Economics education was considered to be rotten, hedonic, adhering to capitalism. It was seen as not meeting the needs of the times in China, in the middle of the 20th century. As a result, in the 1950s, it was cancelled in all levels of education when the government adjusted all national colleges and universities. The teachers and the equipment in Home Economics departments were merged into the related apartments. For example, food and nutrition was incorporated into the medical college, early childhood into the education college, and textile and interior design into the art college (Jin, 2006).

During this period, the typical outstanding women were "iron girls" who could do anything as well as men in the smelting, machinery, chemical, construction, transportation and other industries (Jin, 2006). Its essence was to deny the different physical fitness levels between the two sexes. This idea was rooted in women's education in the national liberation practices in the 1940s. The emotional characteristics and the life styles related to the private area (family and home) were denied and decried as humanism and as small bourgeois emotional appeal. This masculinism trend in women's education resulted from the national crises and from class struggles (Jin, 2006).

Women's education during this time was called gender-neutral education (Zhou, 2011). Women and men accepted non-gendered education in the schools. Government officials thought it was an effective way to liberate women; hence, they cancelled gendered education, which was considered a hindrance to the growth of female students (Zhou, 2011). In this context, learning Home Economics was equated to being housewives at home; such women were seen as lagging behind the times. Even today, this idea influences numerous women in China, remaining an important obstacle to rebuilding Home Economics.

The reconstruction of Home Economics since 1978

In 1978, China implemented reform policy and opened up and welcomed the Western culture, objectively and dialectically. In1994, China began working towards establishing a socialist market economy system, succeeding at the end of the 20th century. China has witnessed unprecedented rapid economic development during the last 30 years, which has attracted attention from the entire world. So far, this vibrant economy has experienced, more or less, all of the developmental trends in the Western post-industrial society: aging, globalization, technological development, prosperity, humanization, commercialization, health and environment, acceleration, network organizing, and urbanization (the megatrends mentioned in the Stimulus chapter).

However, the Chinese people's experiences are quite different from those of the Western world. China is in a drastic social transition from an agricultural society to an industrial society, still in the process of comprehensive modernization. Modernization always refers to the transition of a traditional society to the modern society. There are many symbols of modernization, the first being the powerful transition from an agricultural society to an industrial society (Yi, 2005b).

The second key symbol of modernization is the modernization of the human, which refers to the fundamental transition of one *way of being* or behaviour pattern to another. In the traditional society, most people are accustomed to living in a limited space governed by the habits, traditions, customs, experiences, unrestrained regulations, conventions, common sense and emotions et cetera that are natural cultural components. The modernization of China means Chinese citizens have to be convinced to change from the natural, traditional conditions to free, conscious conditions. Each citizen will have to become a creative individual who can adapt to the needs of science, technology and socialized mass production. Such people have the advantage of subjective consciousness, critical consciousness and a technical, rational, humanistic spirit (Yi, 2005b).

The third symbol of human modernization is cultural transition, which means being critical of the traditional daily life world. Daily life refers to: (a) daily consumption activities, such as food clothing, shelter and means of travelling; (b) daily communicating activities, such as miscellaneous chatting; and, (c) daily concept activities, which feature in repeated and non-creative, emerging in the daily consumption and communicating activities (Yi, 2005a). Therefore, human modernization is a process of stepping out of the daily life world (Yi, 2005b). It does not mean we can live without the daily life; rather, we must pursue getting rid of the old way of being so we can transition to the new.

China's traditional culture is still so very powerful. It is the most ancient, longest-living civilization in the world and the only one without interruption since its origination in the world. Although the Chinese people have begun to welcome the cultural spirit of reason and the contract, and to appreciate subjectivity, personality, freedom, self-awareness, creativeness, social participation awareness, critical spirit et cetera, the leading cultural type in China is still used to living by experiences and worldly wisdom rather than reason, legal systems and contracts. This situation is mainly reflected in two aspects. First, in the institutional dimension, China is farthest from modernity. Second, in the spiritual dimension, the rational spirit is not rooted in human survival, public life, social operation or system arrangement as essential mechanisms and regularity in China. As well, the intrinsic mechanism in the society, or the cultural spirit of the life world, is still in the pre-modernization stage (Yi, 2005a). There is still great tension between the exogenous modernization culture and the traditional culture.

Under this cultural context, people in China resisted the utopian idealism doctrine under the planned economy from 1950s to 1970s, and embraced the commercialization wave and utilitarianism thinking (Yi, 2005a). People gave up their traditional, ideal, elite culture of reasoning, the value of life and the ultimate concern for history and they regressed to the basic necessities of daily living and the natural instincts of man, and accepted the mass and consumerism culture, consciously or unconsciously.

With the enhancement of living standards, Chinese people now pay more attention to their daily life and to individuals' well-being, which are the key focus of Home Economics. Normally, Home Economics should attract attention from all kinds of communities. But, it is a pity it is severely despised, that it merely equals the nanny service now (to be discussed in the next section). Although some scholars are calling for the reestablishment of Home Economics, their weak voices have not been brought to the forefront. Why does this happen? On the one hand, the historical factors noted in the previous discussion make it hard to re-establish Home Economics in China. Home Economics as gendered education has depreciated under severe attacks over the last 30 years, and is seen as a stumbling block to women's development. On the other hand, although people have begun to enjoy the material life now, they have not internalized the spirit of reason in their daily life. They rely on the habits, traditions, customs, experiences, unrestrained regulations, conventions, common sense and emotions in their daily life, which was not considered worthy of formal study. Therefore, by association, as a discipline that focuses on daily life, the development of Home Economics in China still encounters great difficulties.

The potential of Home Economics in China (education, research and extension)

The potential of Home Economics in China is of special relevance to the process of human modernization, especially in the rural area. China has a very typical structure of urban and rural systems. Together, each of rural urbanization, the industrialization of agriculture, and farmers have almost become the core of modern modernization. On the one hand, the city economy features in big, modern, industrial production, the development of urban roads, communication, health and education and other infrastructures. On the other hand, the rural area is typical of a small-scale peasant economy and the infrastructures are falling behind those of the city.

The rural social security level is low; the rural living conditions and the living environment have deteriorated; the population quality generally lags behind that of the city. All of these factors are key barriers to modernization in China. Rural education is needed. What can Home Economics do in this process? The enlightenments from Home Economics in the United States showed that it could contribute to modernization through an integrated system of education, research and extension service. Home Economics could be like seeds rooted in the daily life of China. It could help the rational spirits (reason, contracts, law and the modernization paradigm) grow in the daily life of citizens, which could deepen the modernization process, moving it from the grand narrative structure into the microscopic world of family life. Modernization could come true if only we could get humans used to the new life style and to live it unconsciously.

The value and significance of Home Economics is greatly overlooked by Chinese mainstream thinkers. The current situation and developmental possibilities of Home Economics in China will now be analyzed from three perspectives: education, scientific research and extension.

Education

Home Economics education is not appropriately positioned in the Chinese education system. In the Chinese Classification of Instructional Programs, within the university system, Home Economics does not have its own separate entry; instead, it is under Sociology, marked with an asterisk, behind which it is characterized as experimental in nature rather than formal. This classification means it is not readily visible and is not considered legitimate as a discipline on its own.

Although Home Economics as an experimental major has reappeared in a few colleges and universities in China (especially since the advent of the family service industry, to be discussed shortly), the original reason for re-introducing it was to strengthen the economy (increase economic demand) and to relieve employment pressure. Currently, career-oriented programs are welcomed and valued in higher education settings, because they are seen as guaranteeing that students get a satisfying job after graduation. A powerful example affecting the future of Home Economics in China is the family service industry (the nanny example used above). As people's living standards rise, the family service industry has expanded rapidly, because both parents are working. For clarification, this service involves training people to be nannies and home workers. Family service refers to the family as the main object of service, run by a business operator providing for-profit, family-related activities (e.g., cleaning, washing clothes, cooking, home care, infant care).

The gap between the supply and demand of family service providers is huge in large cities, so large that in 2010, the Chinese State Council released a policy regarding accelerating the family services industry (Wenjiabao, 2010). The policy recognized that the family services industry has an important role to play in creating more jobs, improving people's livelihood, expanding domestic consumer demand and adjusting the industrial structure. Some scholars consider it a good opportunity for the Home Economics discipline. But, the policy only focuses on the family services industry, rather than the full scope of Home Economics as a discipline. This policy may be an opportunity to expand training and employment-related work with Home Economics extension service, but the effect seems so limited. What is worse, given the lack of theoretical clarification around the mission of Home Economics in China, more people will regard Home Economics as a component of the family services industry, which may confuse their understandings about Home Economics. Indeed, some college administrative staff members think Home Economics programs may be a good way to relieve college employment pressure and meet the huge demand of the family service industry.

Although Home Economics is a new term in elementary and secondary education, it has great potential in the on-going educational reform in China, unfolding since the end of 20th century. The educational reform is called *Quality Education*, and it emphasizes students' moral quality (character), human ability and physical and mental health. It reflects humanistic thought and pays special attention to the students' daily-life experiences. Home Economics could find exciting opportunities in primary schools. Home Economics could be the best source of applied life knowledge, either as an independent subject or incorporated into other subjects to help students make close links between education and their daily life.

As well, Home Economics has much to offer adolescents in secondary education. In this phase of their lives, students' physical and psychological development is undergoing huge changes, and they need various kinds of correct guidance about life and career. In secondary education, big college-entrance pressure, exam-oriented education is in vogue. Because many schools consider graduation rates (intimating a successful career) to be the only standard of success, it is challenging to spread Home Economics education in middle schools and high schools. Home Economics is focused on the home, the individual, family well-being and quality of life, which includes, but is not limited to, success in one's career. China needs more insights into how to integrate the full spectrum of Home Economics content and processes into the secondary curriculum, because its inclusion would be so valuable.

Research

Research on Home Economics and by home economists is still in the initial stages in China. First, Home Economics research lacks social recognition or legitimacy. Home Economics bears so many prejudices, and it is often classified into skills training rather than academic research. Second, Home Economics research forces are scattered. The different dimensions or aspects of Home Economics (e.g., clothing, food, housing, consumer, and family) are no longer together in one department, but are spread over several departments. This fragmentation makes it difficult for Home Economics to be whole again, even to see itself as a whole. Third, existing Home Economics research lacks deep analysis. Strictly speaking, there are few professional home economists in China; the scholars who are interested in the discipline mostly put forward suggestions based on their own disciplinary background, such as sociology, economics, education and history, rather than the conventional interdisciplinary approach associated with Home Economics.

Fourth, the research resources are limited and repeated, mainly focusing on the present situation in China and achievements overseas, which has less value for revelation. Fifth, the research forces are less powerful. Home Economics researchers and institutions are mostly from open university or vocational and technical college. There are few first-class universities paying attention to Home Economics in China. Sixth, research achievements are poor. There are few published Home Economics papers, monographs et cetera and those that are published are featured in low level, poor quality and marginalized venues. Above all, Home Economics research in China does not have *the right* position within the academy, which hinders its professional development. The current, awkward position (fragmented and spread over many departments) does not reflect the importance and the value of Home Economics in China.

Extension service

Home Economics in China has not become a well-recognized discipline, so extension services are not carried out in large scale in the name of Home Economics. Recently, some governmental departments and non-governmental sections have launched several rural extension projects on women's literacy, practical technical training and other aspects of rural education. But, these are far from enough. We need a perfect Home Economics social extension system like that which is well established in the United States. Home Economics extension training could be an effective way to further human modernization, especially in the rural area.

Under the impact of urbanization, many Chinese peasants moved out of the countryside to the urban area. A large percentage of members of the rural labour force (most of whom are men) go to non-agricultural industries (including long-term and seasonal), leaving women to do the agricultural work. In 2010, the number of Chinese migrant workers in the big cities totalled more than 240 million (Wuguo, 2011). They are engaged in all kinds of jobs and make great contributions to the modernization movement. The agricultural tasks in the countryside become the main work of rural women staying in the hometown. However, women in the rural area are poorly educated. They are relatively conservative and their lack of technology, concepts, operation ability and decision-making skills in the market economy has serious impacts on the rural modernization process in China.

Home Economics extension, closely linked with daily life, could contribute to the modernization process, especially in the rural area. The mission of rural Home Economics extension is to (a) introduce new knowledge, new skills and new ideas about family life and production to the peasants (especially the women staying in the rural area); (b) make them fully understand and accept the new ideas; and, (c) change the old way of daily life and production style so they can make family management, production and child-rearing more effective and scientific. Rural Home Economics extension, as an important part of agricultural extension, could play an important role in modern agriculture and rural development. The ultimate goal of Home Economics extension would be the development of all individuals (especially rural women), helping them gain higher self-esteem, self-confidence, self-reliance and self-improvement, thereby further promoting the modernization of Chinese citizens. Home Economics' contributions would promote the comprehensive modernization of China.

Summary

In the feudal society, women's education, as the predecessor of Home Economics in China, was about accumulated life and production knowledge and skills of the ancestors, which was gender-biased and separate from men's. This kind of education confined women to the private area and made the woman become a subsidiary to the man in the family.

With the exogenous cultural influence, China has been changing greatly since the middle of the 19th century. The imperialist war and the civil war awakened the Chinese people. Under the illuminating spirit from the West, Chinese women began to get out of the family and contribute to the nation's liberation. In this period, Western Home Economics was introduced into China, but it did not grow because of cultural differences and the affairs of war.

In 1949, the P.R.C. established the idea of "the women are the same as the men," and women were asked to do all kinds of jobs, same as the men. Within the context of gender-neutral education, Home Economics was cancelled as a decadent culture, behind the age.

After 1978, China implemented the reform policy and opened up. With high economic growth and improved life quality, Home Economics reappeared again, albeit in a very narrow and fragmented form. In the process of modernization, Home Economics will be one of the indispensable parts of the process of human modernization, especially in the rural area.

The premise of the development of Home Economics in China is to realize the significance and the value of the discipline. In contemporary China, it plays an important role in human modernization, especially in rural people's modernization. Home Economics could help optimize people's living environments, and improve the quality of people's lives. Home Economics is required so that the modern citizen can accept the spirit of reason in daily life, not just rely on experience and common sense.

We must study the complex relationship between Home Economics and social, gendered roles. Being perceived as gendered, and focused on keeping women at home, is the key barrier to the advancement of the discipline of Home Economics in China. At present, many women still have serious misunderstandings of Home Economics. They erroneously equate learning Home Economics to doing housework and to being housewives. People need to be taught that Home Economics does *not* confine the female into the family. It can help all people learn how to live better lives within their near environments.

The discipline needs to be formally and intentionally developed. The reappearance of Home Economics education happened in the context of the expansion of the family service industry. The latter is but one of the basic aspects of Home Economics. We should develop a professional academic team, set up formal communication mechanisms, expand the academic institutional exchange platform and cultivate more professional talents. Currently, there are no shared concepts and theories in China. Home economists only have a faint voice in academic circles, let alone garnering official government support. It lacks a clear mission, purpose, body of knowledge and research paradigm. In China, Home Economics as a discipline should base its legitimacy on the modernization progress.

Home Economics in China needs to establish an integrated, cooperative system of education, scientific research and social extension. In the wave of educational reform, Home Economics has great potential in all levels of the education system, especially elementary, secondary and higher education.

Home Economics research could find an appropriate place in interdisciplinary research. For example, it could unite with educational research, women's studies, nutritional studies and rural studies. Home Economics extension services could play a significant role *in* the modernization process, especially in the construction of a new socialist countryside in China.

China is experiencing great cultural conflict. It is difficult for us to establish a relatively strong, uniform cultural value and spirit at present. Each of traditional culture, the modern rational spirit, and the post-modern cultural spirit influences our thoughts and our daily lives. Home Economics, as a daily-life-focused discipline, can greatly contribute to the progress of modernization and cultural transitions. It can help people overcome and move beyond the barriers of a traditional culture and learn the core spirit of reason, while regarding the malpractice and the crisis of the post-industrial society, rationally and critically. Although introduced from the U.S. at the beginning of the 1900s, it was interrupted for half a century. The reconstruction of Home Economics is still in its infancy. To aid this process, Home Economics needs to remain connected with the world.

Endnotes

1. There were multiple authors of The Book of Rites. The time of writing is uncertain. Most of the chapters may be from Confucius' seventy-two disciples and some ancient books and records in the Pre Qin Dynasty (about 5700 B.C to 221 B.C).
2. A note about referencing the Chinese Classics. Many Chinese books have been lost in the long history of China. For example, the Western Zhou Dynasty (about 1046B.C.–771B.C) was more than 3000 years ago. Nonetheless, copies of many documents still exist, but their authors are often unknown or estimated by historians. When this sort of material is cited in China, we just list the name of the old source, the name of the book it came from (if relevant), and the most recent modern publisher and publishing date. Each Chinese reference is this chapter is presented in this order: Pin Yin (the official system to transcribe Chinese characters into the Roman alphabet), the English translation and then Chinese.

References[2]

Daxue 大学. (2001). In Z. Yuan (Ed.), Sishu wujing (The Four Books and Five Classics)四书五经. Beijing: Xianzhuang shuju 线装书局.

Jin, Y. (2006). Tieguniang zai sikao-zhongguo wenhua da geming de shehui xingbie yu laodong (The rethinking of the Iron Girls: The social gender and labour during the cultural revolution in China) 铁姑娘"再思考——中国文化大革命期间的社会性别与劳动, Shehuixue yanjiu 社会学研究 1, 130-170.

Liwei Hanwenjia礼纬•含文嘉 [Embodied eminence and blessings in apocryphal interpretation of the Book of Rites]. (n. d.). No publisher.

Mencius Liloushang 孟子•离娄上. (2001). In Z. Yuan (Ed.), Sishu wujing (The Four Books and Five Classics)四书五经. Beijing: Xianzhuang shuju 线装书局.

Wang, H. (2006). Er shi shiji qianji liumei nvsheng yu zhongguo jiazhengxue de fazhan (1910s-1930s) (Overseas female students in the early 20th century and the development of home economics in China (1910s-1930s))廿世纪前期留美女生与中国家政学的发展. Zhongzheng lishi xuekan中正历史学刊, 8, 33.

Wenjiabao zhuchi zhaokai guowuyuan changwu huiyi shishi wuda cuoshi fazhan jiating fuwuye (Wen Jiabao chaired a State Council executive meeting to implement the five steps to develop the domestic service (family service industry))温家宝主持召开国务院常务会议 实施五大措施发展家庭服务业. (2010, September 1). News CN. Retrieved from http://news.xinhuanet.com/politics/2010-09/01/c_12508415.htm.

Woguo nongmingong da 2.4 yi xinshengdai nongmingong suqiu bianhua mingxian (The Number of Chinese Migrant Workers Reached 240 Million, the Appeal of The New Generation Migrant Workers Changes Greatly) 我国农民工达2.4亿 新生代农民工诉求变化明显. (2011, March 23). China News. Retrieved from http://www.chinanews.com/cj/2011/03-23/2924455.shtml

Yi, J. (2005a). Xiandaihua yu richang shenghuo pipan (The Modernization and Daily Life Critique) 现代化与日常生活批判. Beijing: Renmin chubanshe 人民出版社.

Yi, J. (2005b). Xiandaihua yu wenhua zuzhili (The Modernization and The Blocking Force)现代化与文化阻滞力. Beijing: Renmin chubanshe人民出版社.

Yili Sangfu 仪礼•丧服. (1996). In Ruxue shisanjing (The Thirteen Confucian Classics) 儒学十三经 Beijing: Beifang wenyi chubanshe北方文艺出版社.

Zhou, X. (2011). Shehui xingbie shijiao xia de jiaoyu chuantong jiqi chaoyue (Transcending the Educational Traditions from the Perspective of the Social Gender) 社会性别视角下的教育传统及其超越. Beijing: Jiaoyu kexue chubanshe教育科学出版社.

Zhouli Tiangong Jiubin 周礼•天官•九嫔. (1996). In Ruxue shisanjing (the Thirteen Confucian Classics)儒学十三经. Beijing: Beifang wenyi chubanshe北方文艺出版社.

CHAPTER
7

Deaths, Disasters and Tasty Treats: Challenging Public Perceptions of Home Economics

Jay R. Deagon

The purpose of this chapter is to propose ways the Home Economics profession can harness the power of existing and emerging Internet technology to reinforce positive public perceptions, mitigate the effects of negative media and legitimize the role of Home Economics now and in the future. Three strategies are suggested 1) citizen and participatory journalism; 2) creating content with public appeal; and 3) consistent use of key terms when tagging articles on the Internet. Supporting these strategies is a snapshot of online news headlines to benchmark current patterns of reporting on global Home Economics events available for public access on the worldwide web.

Ending the silent revolution

> 'Until critical situations arise, people and empires often remain reticent and slow to respond to the obvious clarion call for alterations in the status quo' (Agnello, White, & Fryer, 2006, p. 312)

The American radio program *Talk of the Nation* recently interviewed a history professor from Michigan State University. She advocated to 'bring back Home Economics' but in the same interview announced that 'the name Home Economics is dead'. This story caused me serious concern because I research in the field of Home Economics and therefore know that the name and the profession are far from dead ... agreed that we need renewal but not resurrection. Most disturbingly, this announcement was globally accessible to an English-speaking audience via a podcast on the Internet. To my deep satisfaction, the majority of the comments left on the *Talk of the Nation* website gave a resounding "aye" to the clarion call to "bring back Home Economics". There were nineteen comments ... can you image the power of nineteen thousand comments? One key to success is participation.

Despite diverse attempts to "keep up with the times", Home Economics has remained a marginalized profession and subject for study (Pendergast, 2003). The role played by the media and journalism has afflicted Home Economics for over a century, hindering efforts to attain credibility and standing in communities. A passage from the 1901 Lake Placid conference papers may be directly quoted today and still hold relevance. Editor of the Boston Cooking School Magazine, Mrs Janet Hill wrote,

> The chief concern of thoughtful men and women today is for the physical, practical and economic welfare of the community. In the attainment of these results journalism in the past has played a conspicuous part, but the science of home economics has not yet been considered seriously; the latest thought is looked on as food for a reporter's 'story' or the filling of so much space (Hill, 1901, p. 103)

Janet Hill knew that Home Economics in its infancy was in a transition period; however she possibly did not realise the depths of her truism 'all true growth is slow'. Despite desperate pleas for urgent action from leading practitioners, Home Economics still struggles for legitimacy and recognition. We are in new times; new times require new actions.

There is no doubt that the Internet has inevitably changed the way that we work, live and play. Our world is constantly evolving and is a radically different place compared with one hundred years ago. In her keynote address at the 20th World Congress of the International Federation for Home Economics in Japan, Donna Pendergast (2004) provided a compelling argument that in 'the digital age' we have an opportunity to reconsider the impact and influence of Home Economics on modern society through developments in communication technologies. An increasingly globalised world has the capacity to communicate by multimodal means (text, visual images and audio) via a single medium — the Internet.

Using the Internet

ICTs have diverse formats — the Internet is the focus of this chapter. DiMaggio, Hargittai, Neuman and Robinson (2005) define the "Internet" as 'the electronic network of networks that links people and information through computers and other digital devices allowing person-to-person communication and information retrieval' (p. 307). At the end of the industrialised age, newspapers were simply text on paper; whereas, in our current information age, news can be spread in "real-time" without mediation by journalists and newspapers. This is cause for optimism because we can bypass "the middle man mediator".

The Internet has evolved at an exponential rate. Uptake or diffusion of social networking sites such as *Facebook* and *Twitter* have enabled instant information sharing on a global scale. Multimedia channels are converging. Convergence means that you are now able to connect to different mediums (online newspapers, You Tube, streamed television, *Facebook*, *Skype*, radio, podcasts and web-surfing) through one device such as television or mobile phone. All of these are Internet capable.

In recent times we have, through the media, witnessed extraordinary instances of social and political change. To set the scene for comparison, it was once not uncommon to see photographs in a newspaper days or weeks after the event, such as a lone protestor chained to a tree in an attempt to stop a bulldozer from demolishing a patch of rainforest. Now it is common to see mass protests occurring in "real-time" (peaceful and violent) often resulting in exposure of corrupt individuals or corporations and even instrumental in overthrowing governments. Astoundingly, these protests are being supported by public displays of solidarity, simultaneously organised around the globe ... coordinated with a few button taps on a mobile phone or keyboard.

Crowds creating content

This collaborative social phenomena using humans as agents of change enabled through Internet technology has implication for *crowdsourcing*. One purpose of crowdsourcing is to 'put a call out' to a particular community (a crowd) to solve a problem (Wexler, 2011). *Wikipedia* and *wikileaks* are good examples of crowd sourcing — brainstorming sessions on a mass scale. For the Home Economics community, solving problems can mean targeting health interventions (such as obesity) or collecting knowledge for a community to share (teaching resources or lesson inspiration) or ways to make Home Economics relevant for the 21st Century.

The follow-on movement to crowd sourcing is *crowdserving* which Davis (2011, p. 94) predicts

> ...has the potential to effectively harness the machine's enormous raw power and the crowd's genius ... and can assist us in tapping into the vast, unused capacity in the deep recesses of the collective human brain for societal benefit.

Virtual communities of practice are becoming significant online places to share research, ideas, resources, find collegial support and participate in two-way mass communication projects for the benefit of the community or communities they serve (Bessette, 2004; Cook-Craig & Sabah, 2009; Wegner, 2001). In futuristic terms, this means using the human brain multiplied by the number of participants facilitated through the use of the Internet is capable of solving problems on a mass scale. This may seem farfetched, but we are already seeing the effects of social networking, crowdsourcing and crowdserving within virtual communities of practice as demonstrations of 'people power' instantaneously accessible and effective, without the need to be physically present. Importantly for the Home Economics community, is participation without mediated journalistic intervention. The online Home Economics community has an opportunity to create their own content and influence the profession's Internet presence and thereby, its image or brand. We now face an issue of responsibility. If we do not participate (Bessette, 2004), we will achieve very little headway.

Power, knowledge and the Internet

The "digital divide" is of real concern (Organisation for Economic Co-Operation and Development, 2001 (OECD); Pendergast, 2004). Lima and Brown (2007) remind us that while the Internet is generally celebrated for its potential to facilitate social change and develop informed global citizens, access to the Internet and its content is not equally distributed locally or globally. We now have seven billion earth inhabitants and Pendergast (2004, p. 6) affirms that the Internet 'serves particular interests and by its very nature reinforces the positioning of marginalised groups in society, be they women, people of colour, people with little education, people living in poverty'. Privileged societies such as Denmark, Australia, Canada and America enjoy open access or moderate Internet censorship; however, China, Saudi Arabia and North Korea for example, have very strict and highly censored access to the Internet (Warf, 2011). Many governments view the Internet with caution and attempt to maintain some control over information flow. Similar control is exerted by marketing agencies, media moguls and journalists who dictate what we are "allowed" to see, hear, read and think.

Mediated and unmediated content have their benefits and drawbacks. Mediated content is regulated by governing agencies and is bound by specific laws to provide as accurate reports as possible. The drawback is that individual reporters and their editors make the decisions on biasing stories in ways that suit employers and may not always act in the best interests of the subject area or people involved. Unmediated content has undesirable elements also, such as misinformation, gender bias, racism, or malicious information being perpetuated across the Internet, sometimes maintaining or reinforcing negative aspects of the status quo. Unmediated content is also a powerful community communication and participation tool (Bessette, 2004; Cook-Craig & Sabah, 2009).

There is a growing mistrust of the Internet and, as a result, information control is present in many institutionalised settings. See Pendergast, 2004, p. 8 for misuses of ICTs in school settings. Both incoming and outgoing information is controlled, monitored and regulated. There are also rising economic, policy, legal, ethical and safety concerns about the release of information and images on the Internet (DiMaggio, Hargittai, Neuman, & Robinson, 2001; Knobel, 2006). Warf (2011, p. 4) cites reasons for censorship interventions ranging from matters of national security (terrorism, control of dissidents, social stability), religious reasons (contraventions to sacred texts), undesirable activities (anti-social behaviour, crime, pornography, gambling), control over minority groups (failure to provide language translations) and protection of intellectual property (music, movies). Despite censorship and restrictions, the Internet has enabled borderless information sharing on an immense scale and facilitated uninhibited announcements of "public" opinion in many countries. As indicated in the opening paragraphs, Home Economics is a feature of these public conversations. Some conversations are positive; others are unhelpful to the advancement of the profession. How do we change negative public beliefs, perceptions and attitudes toward Home Economics?

Reciprocal Determination

The 'venturesome' or 'early adopters' will see an opportunity and seize it, immediately recognising the benefits contained in media messages. At the other end of the spectrum, 'laggards' will hold back, not participate and 'see what happens' before they commit to action. User uptake of Facebook is a useful example. Not everyone was eager to create a profile and upload personal information onto Facebook. Since its launch in 2004, eight years later, there are now 800 million active users with 50% of those users engaging with this Internet platform every day (Wikipedia, 2012).

A pioneering theory of behavior change using mass communication techniques and psychosocial means is Albert Bandura's Social Cognitive Theory (SCT). Applying SCT means that we may be able to understand how attitudes and behaviors can be changed by managing environmental conditions (Bandura, 2001). In this context, environmental conditions refer to the Internet environment for Home Economics. Although there is no 'fixed pathway' to changing an individual's behavior, Bandura (2001, p. 283) believes that 'media influences create personal attributes as well as alter pre-existing ones'. The way people feel towards technology and Home Economics will have some impact on internal and external effectiveness.

Public perceptions mean the way people "outside" the profession perceive the purpose and effectiveness of Home Economics. Working effectively in mass communication media (the Internet) would have a twofold effect on public perceptions of Home Economics. Reciprocal determination means that an individual's behavior is affected by their environment and also an individual's environment affects their behavior (Nutbeam & Harris, 2005). Bessette (2004) recognizes that it may take some time for participants to become familiar with new forms of communication technology, but is worth the effort to obtain positive outcomes. We just need to apply some thought and preparation to a focused intervention on public perceptions about Home Economics. A good place to start with any intervention is to start with an inventory of the current situation. Therefore, I investigated how Home Economics is currently portrayed on a day-to-day basis on the Internet.

Snapshot of the Home Economics brand as folksonomy

Despite some debate as to whether or not the term is accurate (Golder & Huberman, 2005), Thomas Vander Wal (2007) coined *folksonomy* (folk taxonomy) to mean

> the result of personal free-tagging of information and objects (anything with a URL) for one's own retrieval. The tagging is done in a social environment (usually shared and open to others). Folksonomy is created from the act of tagging by the person consuming the information. The value in this external tagging is derived from people using their own vocabulary and adding explicit meaning, which may come from inferred understanding of the information/object. People are not so much categorizing, as providing a means to connect items (placing hooks) to provide their meaning in their own understanding.

Tagging is an 'Internet-based information retrieval methodology' so that web-resources can be categorised and labelled (Noruzi, 2006, p. 1). Like any system of filing, it is important to have consistency for ease of retrieval. To benchmark the current status of the Home Economics online filing system, I monitored *Google Alerts* from 1 January 2011 to 31 December 2011. Table 7.1 next page represents the number of Google Alerts delivered to my email inbox as a weekly report of news, blogs and web material that had been tagged "Home Economics"[1] within that week.

By examining the names of publications, web addresses or specific mentions, I was able to determine that twenty four countries were represented. The top countries

Table 7.1
Google Alerts

Google Alerts from 1 January to 31 December 2011	Total number of multimedia items that "the people" have tagged "Home Economics"	Number of items that contain specific information or news about topics that would be considered "Home Economics" practice
News	386	110
Blogs	49	18
Web	227	97

producing Internet material, in order, were Australia (71), USA (45), Pakistan (16), United Kingdom (11), Ireland (11) and the Philippines (10). It was interesting to note that from a total of seventy one items from Australia, twenty (20) were advertisements for "Teaching Jobs". To provide a snapshot of the current online Home Economics folksonomy, the next section has been categorised into negative, neutral and positive. These categories are constructed from the content of the Google Alerts.

Negative

Death, disasters, cutbacks & closures
One devastating event in the Philippines linked Home Economics with death of students. A food poisoning incident where a Home Economics teacher prepared a contaminated local rice dish resulted in the death of 2 students and the hospitalisation of 42 others (http://www.mb.com.ph/articles/322951/luistro-visits-bad-food-victims). A follow-up story 20 days later reported that all Home Economics teachers in the Philippines were to undertake a safe-food-handling course (http://www.pia.gov.ph/?m=7&r=R02&id=42131&y=2011&mo=07). In the twelve-month observation period, this was the only report that connected Home Economics practice with death. There were no other incidents or accidents of this nature reported from any other countries. However, I found "liability reasons" due to potential danger of equipment and budget cuts as the main rationales for the closure of Home Economics departments in various parts of the world. Additionally, there were four accidental fires in or near Home Economics rooms resulting in temporary school closures, one account of arson on a Home Economics building, two gas leaks, and one closure initiated by parents because the Home Economics building had constant flooding from leaking pipes and exposed electrical outlets.

Not exclusive rights
I found that the term "Home Economics" is not exclusively reserved for the Home Economics profession. To illustrate, Amy Hoak, a journalist who writes the "Home Economics" column for the MarketWatch (www.marketwatch.com), a section of The Wall Street Journal, has tagged "Home Economics" to everything financial or real estate related in America. Instances like this may have disastrous effects on the future of the profession in terms of brand name protection.

Neutral

Passing of a silent generation

A service or 'missionary' focused 'silent generation' (Pendergast, 2009, p. 510) of home economists are passing away ... but not so silently. On a weekly basis, memorials, funeral notices and tributes are reported from the United States (40 in total). These tributes celebrate the lives of women who started their careers with a degree in Home Economics and either became loved wives, mothers and active community members and/or continued as leaders of the Home Economics profession making a wide variety of impacts at local, national and international levels.

Tasty Treats

The most frequently reported Home Economics activities were cooking and sewing followed by financial skills and household tips. Many of these references to skills were not from recognised, trusted or official Home Economics sources or resources. Hospitality and Catering was most commonly reported as a "Home Economics" activity and students regularly participated in culinary competitions, exhibitions, fairs and shows — often winning prizes for their efforts. Alternatively students and their teachers provided catering services for local functions and events. Unfortunately, it seemed that the importance of food literacy for "fighting" obesity and other lifestyle diseases was only a small portion of news -very little emphasis was placed on lifelong learning, or the essential skills provided by Home Economics education. A few fashion parades were also reported to have taken place in Colorado, the Philippines and Pakistan.

War on Obesity and Revival of Home Economics

One news event that enjoyed a brief global exchange was about the role of Home Economics in "fighting" childhood obesity. The lead article is the same that appeared in the opening paragraphs of this Chapter. I have categorised this as neutral because the public conversations surrounding this article raised both helpful and harmful perceptions of Home Economics. Table 7.2 is the online news article that enjoyed brief global recognition. After this media event, there were several follow-up stories, blogs, radio podcasts and public comments made on various websites. The reason I have placed this event as neutral is because of the evenness in negative perceptions stemming from biased and misinformed reporting and public opinions versus positive effects of awareness about obesity and the role of Home Economics. Many Home Economics and Family and Consumer Science Teachers in America and Canada made their voices heard by participating in public website comments.

Positive

Hooked on Home Economics

Do not underestimate the impact Home Economics has in shaping the future careers and personalities of students. There were fourteen articles about high-profile Chefs, Restaurateurs, Teachers, Business People and a Chocolatier who were first "hooked"

> "Time to Revive Home Ec" written by Helen Zoe Veit on 5 September 2011 in The Opinion Pages of the New York Times. The opening line was "NOBODY likes home economics. For most people, the phrase evokes bland food, bad sewing and self righteous fussiness"
>
> http://www.nytimes.com/2011/09/06/opinion/revive-home-economics-classes-to-fight-obesity.html

Table 7.2
News headline that enjoyed brief global recognition

on their passion during their high school Home Economics classes. It was interesting to note that considering the perception that Home Economics usually slants towards female participation, a high proportion of men were represented in these articles. Table 7.3 shows excerpts and is indicative of these news reports.

Inspirational
The news stories in Table 7.4 affected me as positive inspiration, proud to be home economist.

Summary of observations

Many of these articles would not be recognized as "hard-hitting" news. This investigation confirms the role of journalism in spreading messages about Home Economics has been, at best, just "media filling" or "feel good" news. We are considered an oddity and often a relic. With the exceptions of obesity and the inspirational stories, very few of the articles captured the essence of Home Economics in any real way. Where is Home Economics? Are we a strong or weak online community? It will be fascinating to revisit this chapter in 5, 10 or 20 years' time to see how far we have come. The purpose of this book is to help shape a desirable future for Home Economics. I now suggest a few simple strategies to bring the name Home Economics into the 21st Century as a celebrated and mainstreamed profession and subject for study. I propose three strategies:

- Citizen and participatory journalism
- Content with maximum effect/affect
- Consistency in tagging.

Citizen and Participatory Journalism

In the past decade, there have been rapid changes in accessing "news". Quinn and Lamble (2007, p. 10) suggest that a rise of 'citizen or participatory journalism' has made a significant impact on news gathering and reporting. Converging multimedia are now used at different times of the day and have become the preferred method for under-30 year olds to engage actively with a continuous 24 hour news cycle (Quinn & Lamble, 2007). Mediated reporting through "official" journalistic pathways has meant that reporting on Home Economics "news" has been somewhat outside our control.

Citizen or participatory journalism has the potential to turn the tide on legitimising the field. The global Home Economics community of professionals, teachers, students, past students and clients need to be 'expert novices' (Pendergast, 2008, p. 9) and capable of gathering and reporting news through the latest multimedia tools available (television, radio, internet, mobile phones and the yet unknown). Our

---

Harold Dieterle: Owner of two restaurants in New York City

Platelist: 'Top Chef' Harold Dieterle Exudes Confidence in the Kitchen:

Growing up on Long Island, Dieterle said he became hooked on cooking at age 15 when he took a home economics class in high school. "I wasn't terribly popular in high school either so I kind of took to cooking with the scheme that if I took a home economics class, it would definitely help me meet girls," he said. "That's kind of how the cooking started."

http://abcnews.go.com/Nightline/platelist-chef-harold-dieterle-exudes-confidence-kitchen/story?id=12971538

Gary Goldie: Scotland's Chef of the Year 2011

Irvine man is Scotland's Chef of the Year: Home Economics probably wasn't every teenage schoolboy's favourite subject — but it set Gary Goldie on the road to becoming Scotland's Chef of the Year

http://www.irvineherald.co.uk/ayrshire-news/local-news-ayrshire/local-news-irvine/2011/04/08/irvine-man-is-scotland-s-chef-of-the-year-75485-28466568/

Eamon Sullivan: Australian Olympic Swimmer, Winner of Australian Celebrity MasterChef, Cleo 2011 Bachelor of the Year, cookbook writer and restaurant owner

Like a fish to water in Subiaco: Home Economics saved him from certain starvation and left an indelible impression. "I was quite a fussy eater and home economics sort of forced me to try different things."

http://au.news.yahoo.com/thewest/lifestyle/a/-/food/10419773

Phillip Lim: World famous fashion designer

Phillip Lim — *Leading The Current Wave of Asian American Designers:* So strong was Lim's 'double life', so to speak, that while studying home economics throughout university, his own mother believed he was studying business. It was only until he received his degree in home economics and had a job that he finally broke the news to his mother, who had always expected him to go into business.

http://www.schemamag.ca/archive2/2011/01/phillip_lim_-_leading_the_curr.php

---

Table 7.3

Online news headlines about high achieving personalities who attribute Home Economics as making an impact on their lives and careers.

Six Home Economics teachers were reported as receiving state or national teaching awards for leadership, Teacher of the Year awards, or recognised for excellence in their education programs

Students in an America school used recycled T-shirt material to sew clothes for orphans in Kenya

http://www.abc27.com/Global/story.asp?S=14052204)

Ada Ruth Stovall (1913-2008), a high profile Home Economist, was inducted into the Alabama Women's Hall of Fame

http://www.awhf.org/stovall.html

An Australian year nine textiles class, guided by their Home Economics teacher, made soft toys and donated them to Project: Love and Care, which provides "Care Kits" for children and teenagers being placed in foster care

http://www.bne.catholic.edu.au/news/Pages/care.aspx

Lee Chin-yen, a teacher at Nantou County's Tung Der Home Economics and Commerce Vocational High School in Taiwan competed in an ultra-marathon across the Sahara Desert to inspire his students because they kept saying "Teacher, I can't"

http://www.taiwantoday.tw/ct.asp?xitem=143436&ctnode=413&mp=9

A newly-qualified home economics teacher in Scotland received an award for her project "The Growing Greener Company" which involved many departments to help "youngsters set up their own firm to grow vegetables, which were turned into soup during Home Economics classes and sold to pupils at lunch"

http://www.paisleydailyexpress.co.uk/renfrewshire-news/local-news-in-renfrewshire/paisley-news/2011/07/04/vanessa-cooks-up-award-winning-project-87085-28978747/)

In Suva, Fiji, a qualified home economics teacher who could easily get a paid job has chosen to teach lifeskills (such as cooking, sewing, kesakesa (stencilling), how to sew pillow cases and other home economics subjects) to physical and hearing impaired students on a voluntary basis

http://www.fijitimes.com/story.aspx?id=176360

Table 7.4
Inspirational news reports that involve exceptional people doing their everyday jobs

capacity to "keep up with the times" (especially with ICTs) will play an important role in the future of Home Economics. However, we need to be aware of a need to mitigate the effects of undesirable news reports and quality control of information.

Content with maximum effect/affect

We would be expressing our content and communications (Bessette, 2004) using one or a combination of three forms of media:
- mass and converging media (news, radio, television)
- traditional media (storytelling, theatres, songs)
- group or community media (video, photographs, posters)

To provide the reader with practical ideas about content of articles with maximum effect within these three forms of media, I have observed that inspiring articles contain the following four elements: (a) vulnerability and courage — stories of personal success and failure; (b) service to humanity — regardless of the size of contribution (high impact or local impact) — stories that contain information about service evoke emotion and connect the reader; (c) care and stewardship — stories about how Home Economics contributes to the care of community and also sustainability practices for humanity as a whole and the environment; (d) transcendence — stories that move beyond the individuals involved and connect to larger realities. I suggest that a future-oriented approach would be to make full use of these four elements. Capture the elements through photography, digital recordings, reflective journals and essays that can then be distributed through multimedia channels such as social networking sites, media releases, school websites, personal, school or professional blogs or vehicles yet unknown.

Consistency in tagging memes

Congruency is important (Coker, 2011) and regardless of our feeling towards the name, Home Economics is a known brand name and is recognised in many countries around the world. We need to apply consistency in our tagging. Collaborative tagging has many benefits. Golder and Huberman (2005) identify the kinds of tags as identifying 1) what (or who) an article is about; 2) identifying what it is; 3) who owns it; 4) refining categories; 5) identifying qualities or characteristics (adjectives like funny, inspirational, scary according to the tagger's opinion); 6) self reference; and 7) task organizing. To ensure that "stable patterns" of tagging occur, it would be advantageous if we applied some congruency to tagging Home Economics content on the Internet.

Enduring packets of cultural knowledge about Home Economics that have survived through generations can be called memes (pronounced meems). According to Knobel (2006) memes are 'contagious patterns of cultural information that are passed from mind to mind and which directly shape and propagate key actions and mindsets of a social group'. Each of the above online media excerpts highlight current Home Economics memes. The challenge we face is bringing "Home Economics" back to the status within the hierarchy as the central, enduring and celebrated meme. Then bring "health and well-being", "essential skills", "families", "relevant", "rich history", "pioneers", "community leaders" into the second tier of public consciousness juxtaposed with "life-skills", "food literacy", "financial literacy", "technology", "consumer science", "nutrition & food", "textiles and clothing" and finally, push "cook'n 'n' sew'n", "do you remember when", "formally known as", "scone cutters" and "chief bottle washers" as far down the meme list as possible, until derogatory and negative memes fade from our collective cultural knowledge.

Conclusion

To recycle Janet Hill's 1901 message to home economists quoting Napoléon, "four hostile newspapers are more to be feared than a thousand bayonets" (p. 102). Instead of silently "feeding" the media monster more bayonets, let us satisfy its appetite and feed it more positive, peaceful and practical Home Economics solutions.

For the sake of congruency, I strongly advise against using any other term than "Home Economics" in the public arena as it may give "outsiders" the impression that we are confused about our own profession and its history. If we are to rebrand Home Economics, we need to present Home Economics as a branded and marketable "package" which brings together our unique perspective of the family, our specialized and consolidated knowledge, and communicates obvious, proud and coherent collegial solidarity.

My preferred future vision of Home Economics is that we no longer hear, read and see the public or journalists referring to Home Economics as an antiquated subject still hampered by department closures, gender debate, legitimisation and relevance; rather I envisage the Home Economics brand maturing as a gender-neutral and publically accepted tool for emancipatory change and individual, family and community empowerment. Engaging in citizen and participatory journalism, social networking, blogging and digital media outlets of the future may provide opportunities to influence positively the future of Home Economics. We may achieve this through the proliferation of achievement-oriented publicly accessible news items and digital media proudly tagged with our main meme "Home Economics".

Discussion Prompts

- Something to share? Citizen and participatory journalism.
- Participation in online Home Economics communities.
- Teaching and learning about the trustworthiness of information and multiliteracy skills.
- Proud to be a home economist?
- Pros and cons of gaining permission: the release of student, teacher and school information for the purpose of posting worthwhile articles on the Internet.

Endnotes

1   The name 'Home Economics' is the preferred name as defined by the International Federation of Home Economics Position Statement 2008 and was selected as the primary focus of this investigation. A search of "Home Ec", "homeec", 'Family and Consumer Studies' or 'Domestic Science', as examples, may have produced different results.

References

Agnello, M. F., White, D. R., & Fryer, W. (2006). Toward Twenty-First Century Global Citizenship: A Teacher Education Curriculum. *Social Studies Research and Practice, 1*(3), pp. 312-326.

Bandura, A. (2001). Social Cognitive Theory of Mass Communication. *Media Psychology, 3*(3), 265-299. doi: 10.1207/s1532785xmep0303_03

Bessette, G. (2004). Involving the community: A Guide to Participatory Development Communication Retrieved from http://www.idrc.ca/openebooks/066-7/

Coker, B. (2011). What makes a 30 second movie go viral? Retrieved 18 January 2011, from http://www.webreep.com/blog/post/2011/11/14/What-makes-a-30-second-movie-go-viral.aspx

Cook-Craig, P., & Sabah, Y. (2009). The role of virtual communities of practice in supporting collabrative learning among social workers. *British Journal of Social Work, 39*, 725-739.

Davis, J. G. (2011). From Crowdsourcing to Crowdservicing. *Internet Computing, IEEE, 15*(3), 92-94.

DiMaggio, P., Hargittai, E., Neuman, W. R., & Robinson, J. P. (2001). Social Implications of the Internet. *Annual Review of Sociology, 27*(1), 307-336. doi: doi:10.1146/annurev.soc.27.1.307

Facebook. (2012). Wikipedia, The Free Encyclopedia. Retrieved from http://en.wikipedia.org/w/index.php?title=Facebook&oldid=470975579

Golder, S. A., & Huberman, B. A. (2005). The Structure of Collaborative Tagging Systems. *Cornell University Library*. Retrieved from http://arxiv.org/abs/cs/0508082v1

Hill, J. M. (1901). Journalism in Relation to Home Economics. In American Home Economics Association (Ed.), *Lake Placid Conference Proceedings*, (Vol. 1-3). Ithaca, New York: Cornell University, Mann Library.

Knobel, M. (2006). Memes and Affinity Spaces: some implications for policy and digital divides in education. *E–Learning, 3*(3).

Lima, C. O., & Brown, S. W. (2007). Global citizenship and new literacies providing new ways for social inclusion. *Psicologia Escolar e Educacional, 11*, 13-20.

Noruzi, A. (2006). Folksonomies: (Un)Controlled Vocabulary? *Knowledge Organization, 33*(4), 199–203.

Nutbeam, D., & Harris, E. (2005). *Theory in a nutshell: a practical guide to health promotion theories*. Sydney: McGraw-Hill Australia Pty Ltd.

Organisation for Economic Co-Operation and Development. (2001). E-Learning: the partnership challenge: education and skills. France: OECD Publications Service.

Pendergast, D. (2003). From the margins: globalization with(out) home economics. [Article]. *International Journal of Consumer Studies, 27*(4), 331-334. doi: 10.1046/j.1470-6431.2003.00326.x

Pendergast, D. (2004). Nu Xs: Is it 2 L8 4 family? [Keynote address at the 20th World Congress of the International Federation for Home Economics, Japan, August 2004]. *Journal of the HEIA, 11*(2), 11.

Pendergast, D. (2008). Sustaining the Home Economics profession in contemporary, convergent times M. O'Donoghue (Ed.) *E-Book — Global Sustainable Development: A Challenge for Consumer Citizens*. Retrieved from http://www.educationforsustainabledevelopment.org/introduction.html

Pendergast, D. (2009). Generational Theory and Home Economics1: Future Proofing the Profession. *Family and Consumer Sciences Research Journal, 37*(4), 504-522. doi: 10.1177/1077727x09333186

Quinn, S., & Lamble, S. (2007). Online Newsgathering : Research and Reporting for Journalism

Vander Wal, T. (2007). Folksonomy Coinage and Definition, from http://vanderwal.net/folksonomy.html

Warf, B. (2011). Geographies of global Internet censorship. *GeoJournal, 76*(1), 1-23. doi: 10.1007/s10708-010-9393-3

Wegner, E. (2001). Supporting communities of practice: a survey of community-oriented technologies (Version 1.3 ed.).

Wexler, M. N. (2011). Reconfiguring the sociology of the crowd: exploring crowdsourcing. *The International Journal of Sociology and Social Policy, 31*(1/2), 6-20. doi: 10.1108/01443331111104779

CHAPTER

8

Clothing and Crafting: A Proposal for Home Economics Under the Perspective of Solidarity and Creative Economy

Rita de Cássia Pereira Farias

In 2003, the United Nations (UN) launched the *Millennium Development Goals*, aiming to reduce world hunger and poverty and generate income from sustainable actions which may promote culture and equality in terms of race and gender. Among these goals, four are directly related to clothing and crafting in the perspective of Home Economics: Eradicating extreme hunger and poverty; promoting gender equality and empowering women; establishing a worldly partnership for development; ensuring environmental sustainability. Therefore, this article is a proposal of actions for home economists to get engaged in social projects and programs, focusing on clothing and crafting, under the perspective of Solidarity and Creative Economy. Crafting activities reassure ethnical identities and group history, besides proportioning work and income for several families and communities, including *Quilombolas* (group of descendants of fugitive black slaves in Brazil in the 17th and 18th centuries) and indigenous ones. Due to the fact that the home economist has been capacitated for acting in the social promotion of families and groups, this professional may foster community development and favor access to citizenship, credit and income. He/she may disseminate knowledge and qualify workers, motivating the development of competences, leadership and autonomy. He/she may also develop the commercial potential of cooperatives and associations, strengthening competition, proportioning access to markets and investments with no middleman, besides elaborating strategies for incorporating into the products the culture and history of the group which produced them.

Home economist professionals have been involved in rural and urban extension projects since the primordium of this profession, facilitating community development, better use of resources, income generation, promotion of well-being and improvement of life-quality of groups and families. In this process, clothing has been one of the focuses, as its production includes studies of fiber, adequacy of cloth for specific uses, textile conservation, modeling and making of clothing articles, as well as the relationship between clothing, sustainability and social development.

The Home Economy course provides professionals with multidisciplinary and humanistic views. They are encouraged to acquire critical perceptions about social, economical, cultural, political and environmental phenomena which affect individuals, families and groups. In this process, they ought to identify problems, potentialities and interests and motivate sustainable actions which generate income and promote improvement in life-quality of families and social groups.

The elaboration and accompaniment of communitarian development projects founded on the principles of Solidarity and Creative Economy achieves relevance nowadays, mainly after the UN launched *the Millennium Development Goals,* aiming to reduce hunger, world poverty and generate income from sustainable actions which might promote culture and reduce racial and gender inequality.

As we live in a post industrial period (BELL, 1974), in which the services sector is the major employer, *the Millennium Development Goals* favor the promotion of public policies and government actions in several countries, occasioning a fertile terrain for home economists acting in the implantation and accompaniment of projects and social programs focusing on clothing and crafts. Therefore, motivating minor groups to seek its development and autonomy — based on the triad economy, sustainability and society — becomes a relevant proposal for home economists, who might look for partnership with public and private organizations, nongovernmental organizations and programs of social responsibilities in business enterprises.

However, before approaching the projects and programs focusing on clothing and crafts it is necessary to verify the degrading face of fashion which affects life quality of individuals and groups and to lead home economists to actions which aim to reduce poverty and social differences.

Degrading face of fashion

Fashion is a powerful instrument which promotes status and ensures class distinctions. To keep social distinctions, the fashion industry activates a large market that moves a significant parcel of the world economy. Marketing strategies emphasize a disdain for old products and a passion for new ones. To incorporate fetish into fashion, fashion shows are structured as mega events that call for a dream world in which pain, sadness, misery and anguish do not exist (ROCHA, 2010). Billboards, magazines, store windows and advertisements promise enchantment, power, acceptance and integration to this dream world at the time of purchasing and possessing new products for which the appeal may be understood as: "I consume, therefore, I live".

In line with this world of dreams and fetish, fashion has another face which is of extreme human degradation. Globalization has made possible clothes production at prices lower and lower, the so-called *fast fashion*, that also leads consumers to consider clothes as disposable objects. However, clothes are produced at low prices at the cost of a lot of human sacrifice, and serious environmental damages.

One of the pillars for cheap production is child labor, illegally utilized in clothing factories in several developing countries such as Pakistan, India, China, Taiwan, Jordan, Malaysia, Cambodia, Argentina and Brazil. Despite the efforts of the International Program for Elimination of Child Labor (IPEC) developed by the International Organization of Work (IOW), several industries and enterprises have not committed themselves to these programs yet.

In the clothing factory center of Agreste Pernambucano, one of the poorest regions of Brazil, for example, for decades the exploration of child labor has affected the lives of many children. In 2007, there were 440,000 children and teenagers working not only in the clothing factories, but also in farms, open markets, homes and streets. On the streets, they make a living by means of the sales of candies or prostitution.

For families in an extreme poverty situation, child labor in such activities represent a possibility for generating income, in spite of the low payment and very bad working conditions (Sobreira; Oliveira, 2001). Also in clothing factories in Dhaka and Bangladesh, under owner coercion, some children work up to 10 hours a day for a dollar payment, besides being threatened by the owner of the clothing factories (Claudio, 2007).

To this degrading setting, we may add the cotton industry, since several countries such as China, India, Pakistan, Argentina, Paraguay, Brazil, Azerbaijan, Benin, Burkina, Egypt, Kazakhstan, Kyrgyzstan, Pakistan, Tadzhikistan, Turkmenistan, Uzbekistan, Zambia and Turkey exploit child labor in cotton fields. Those children let go of their studies, health, and childhood to work in an extremely tiresome job, which may involve physical, verbal and sexual abuse. To worsen this situation, during the cultivation of the cotton plants, more insecticide is used than in any other crop. Sometimes, children spray pesticides without any body protection, which represents serious risk to their health (Claudio, 2007).

Global competition in the clothing industry requires more and more reduction in production costs, even if this means lower salaries and degrading working condition. To ensure their participation in the global market, clothing factories of several developing countries such as China, Guatemala, Cambodia and Brazil use slave work, under very bad conditions. Cláudio (2007) mentions that China, one of the largest jeans producers in the world, in order to answer the daily demand of 10,000 pairs of jeans, have operators who work all night long making and pressing jeans to make them present a shabby look. These workers receive from 12 to 18 cents an hour in precarious work situations. In addition to that, the blue dust of jeans irritates their lungs severely.

In Brazil, from 2009 to 2011, the Parliamentary Inquiry Commission (Comissão Parlamentar de Inquérito — CPI) from the Ministry of Work sued more than 30 clothing factories for using slave labor. Famous enterprises and brand names such as C&A, Pernambucanas, Marisa, Riachuello, Collins, Leader, Zara, Ecko and Cobra

D'Água were fined. In the capital of São Paulo an operation was established to investigate Zara enterprise and set free 15 Bolivians, including a 14-year-old teenage girl.

Although Brazil has launched the National Pact to Eradicate Slave labor, coordinated by the Ethos Institute, many clothing factories has not agreed to sign it yet. Therefore, this scenario is marked by illegal contracts, degrading working conditions, lack of safety equipment, child labor work, working daily shifts of 16 hours, low remuneration (average of R$2, 00 per piece or US$1.18), illegal charging of debts to salaries and restrictions on leaving the working place, since the authorization is permitted just in case a parent has to take a sick child to the hospital.

Another problem of the *fast fashion* industry relates to environmental questions. Studies indicate that even in developed countries, just a small proportion of unwanted textiles are recycled or re-used. What is not used ends up in incinerators or trash cans, which may cause problems for the environment and for human health. For example, in 2005, in the United Kingdom, 1.9 tons of textiles were purchased, 1.2 tons were disposed of and only 0.3 tons were sold or recycled (Morley et al, 2006).

In Brazil, some clothing factories located in São Paulo produce around ten tons of cloth daily and residues are discharged on the streets, close to the clothing factories. When it rains, these residues are spread by the water and clog the water drains, causing floods which destroy houses and transmit illnesses. Even when rags and unused clothes are discharged in dumps, their decomposition process may contaminate the environment (soil, water and air). Lixiviation of ammonia and methane gas, besides being toxic, contributes to the greenhouse effect and global warming[1]. In addition to that, textile residues which are not incinerated may release organic compounds such as dioxins, heavy metals, acid gases and dust particles which are highly harmful to human beings and the environment (Caulfield, 2009).

Adding to this scenario, there is the craftsman's invisibility factor, which means that they frequently sell their products to middleman and famous brand names without the appropriate recognition. When they enter into the sphere of large scale fashion, the artisan is left out from the authorship of his work and the history of the group which produced it is erased as if by magic, once in fetish fashion just the brand for which the artisans sold their work will appear.

Karl Marx maintained that the product fetish erases the marks of work and expropriates the worker from the authorship of his art. In fetish products, the worker, the marks of the work and the means of production do not appear in order to leave only the product fetishist to enchant and seduce with promises of happiness and power.

Anthropologists and sociologists, such as Bourdieu, Marshall Sahlins and Daniel Miller, who studied the social world construction by means of material goods, support the understanding that the product did not appear as in magic. The process of production involves hard work, often permeated by privation and exploitation. Daniel Müller (2007) proposes that we reflect about our responsibilities as consumers, through the analysis of the capitalist goods chain. He recommends that we recognize the corporification of human work in the products we consume and in the working relations which are established, in order to understand the effects of capitalism in social process and everyday practice.

Considering that industry and marketers seek daily to generate new "needs", fetish and wishes, the home economist may provide visibility to the ways in which the fashion industry reaches individuals, families and social groups. In opposition to the fetish world of dreams that fashion promises, home economists may act against an uncertain scenario, marked by several kinds of human exploitation, fears, anguishes and menaces, besides the consequent environmental degradation. Therefore this professional may look for alternatives to transform such scenarios into sustainable actions which bring human dignity, citizenship, empowerment, autonomy, and life quality and self-realization.

Social policies which subsidize the action of home economist professionals

For appropriate action, it is necessary that home economists are conscious of public policies which underpin their professional actuation, once they direct finance, projects and actions. Each year the UN promotes reunions, conferences and encounters over subjects which have global impact. Besides this, several publications and reports which subsidize public policies of countries are launched. In 2003: *the Millennium Development Goals*; in 2009: *the International year of Natural fibers*; in 2010: *the International year of Afro descendent*; and, in 2012: *the International year of Cooperatives*.

In terms of the eight *Millennium Development Goals*[2], four of them have direct relation with clothing from the perspective of home economists: Eradicating hunger and extreme power; Promoting gender equality and women's autonomy; Establishing a world partnership for development; and Warranting environmental sustainability.

Concerns with aspects linked to the promotion of work and income are due to the high index of unemployment which is a result of the Fordism crisis in the post-industrial society and the industrial and state incapacity to promote employment (Harvey, 1992). The adoption of new technologies and replacement of salary work by wedged work (flexible model), occasioned a precarious work and unemployment which weakened worker movement, once the work has been concentrated in the sector of services (Bell, 1974).

Aiming to establish a world partnership for development, one of the goals proposed for the millennium is the reduction of social inequality. To reach this goal, countries have been trying to build a more just commercial and financial system, equitable and larger which integrates sustainable development, safety and human rights, by means of familiar agriculture and food safety, sustainable development, and Solidarity Economy.

Public policies based on the millennium goals proposed not only reduce poverty and hunger, but also promote gender equality and women's autonomy. It is considered that thousands of people in the world suffer with famine and live in absolute poverty[3], that the major index of social inequality occurs in Sub-Saharan Africa, Latin America, Caribbean and also in East Asia. Besides that, most of the economies do not supply job opportunities for youth, thus there is a probability of three unemployed young people for each unemployed adult (UN, 2007).

Searching for equitable gender promotion and women's autonomy is justified in terms of gender construction, once the need to conciliate domestic activity and paid jobs which place women in inequitable situations and reflects in the unemployment rate. It is important that unemployment rate reports reflect gender and social class components. In Brazil, for example, in 2005, from the unemployed population, 6.3% was composed by white men; 8.1% by African American men; 10.7% by white women and 14.1% by African American women.

In order to accomplish this goal, countries involved in the *Millennium Objectives* have implanted specific policies for women, aiming to overcome the social inequality that affects them. Actions proposed include women's validation and respect for cultural, ethnical, and racial factors, promoting their professional capacity, favoring social and economical interaction, in order to let them interact dynamically in politics and the economy, besides enlarging their power to decide about their lives and bodies. For this purpose, governors have created programs to warrant gender and race equity, besides measures to face violence against women.

In relation to warranting environmental sustainability, countries committed to the *Millennium Goals* propose to accomplish the commitment of 1992, when the Agenda 21 was for sustainable development. On that occasion, it was verified that from 1970 to 1995 we have lost more than thirty percent of natural resources which sustain life in the planet. For minimizing resource loss and integrating principles of sustainable development to policies and national programs, governors propose the adoption of techniques for environmentally clean technologies which brings respect to the environment and improve life quality of families and groups.

For reaching this goal in relation to the textile and clothing-making sector, in 2009 the UN has launched *the International Year of Natural Fibers*, aiming to motivate sustainable strategies for generating work and income. This initiative is due to the fact that rising production of artificial fibers, since 1960, has brought several environmental implications, in particular, not being biodegradable. Besides that, this production excludes the smaller producer linked to the family economy. The proposal of the UN is that the countries get back to the production and consumption of natural fibers as a strategy to overcome hunger and poverty, besides collaborating for an ecologically conscious society. Thus, natural fibers, besides being biodegradable, may be produced in smaller scale, including the smaller agriculturalist.

Another action of the UN, aiming to reduce social inequality, was the International Year of Afro Descendant, in 2011. When this year was declared, the UN considered that slave traffic constituted disrespect to human dignity which still generates racial discrimination to people of African origin who are the ones who most suffer with racism. With the declaration of the year, it was looking to promote respect for diversity, rescuing cultural inheritance and integrating Afro-Americans into society.

In the Brazilian case, due to forces of globalization and considering the great religious syncretism of society, the government has looked at ways to finance public projects and programs for racial equality and divulgation of culture. The program Live Culture encourages visibility for several cultural manifestations present in society, promoting the development of *Quilombolas*' work, as a way to restitute the dignity which was confiscated from them (Santos, 2008). Besides that, it assures citizenship and social inclusion. Governors have created several programs for generating work, income and professional qualifications, as well as for eradication of child labor and slave work.

At a time when the government and industry have not been able to create sufficient employment for the population, facilitating social development within associations and cooperatives becomes a promising strategy. Therefore the UN recognizes that the Solidarity Economy, by means of articulation between State and Civilian society, is a promising alternative for social inclusion of workers who are at the margin of the capitalist production system and who do not have financial resources enough for private investment, as much as those who "believe it is possible the creation of a fairer and equitable society in which the ideal of solidarity is actually seriously considered" (Araujo 2007).

The term Solidarity Economy presupposes the idea of worker organization in interactive and cooperative networks, with mutual help and sharing material resources and experiences, aiming for mutual development. Centered in the valorization of human beings, cooperatives presuppose the work as a means of freedom, once they create possibilities for exercising citizenship, empowerment and the economical, social and cultural development of beneficiaries. In the cooperatives, the owner-workers participate in the choice of actions, strategies and priorities, besides having more economical incentives for dedicating their time and effort to work (Santos, 2002).

Recognizing that worker's cooperatives are alternatives for efficiently responding to global markets, once they are more productive, when associations are more voluntary, common property exists and the management is democratic, the UN has declared the year 2012 as *The International Year of Cooperatives*.

In the clothing and textile sector, there are several cooperatives for production and commercialization of clothing and craft, in relation to recycling of textile products. In Brazil, an initiative which deserves recognition is COOPA-ROCA, cooperative of sewing and craftwork, which is located in the Favela da Rocinha, a slum in Rio de Janeiro. The formation of this cooperative was a way to foster the potential of tenants, besides delivering autonomy, empowerment and income (Moura, 2011). There the craftswomen produce pieces for the fashion and design market, in partnership with brands such as Osklen, Lacoste, Ann Taylor, Paul Smith and Christian Lacroix. The stylists of these enterprises draw pieces and the artisans of COOPA-ROCA give their final touch of craft in the products that are exported to countries such as United States, France, Germany, England and Holland. This project propitiates a positive look over Rocinha, and grants potential for local development, increased life quality of craftswomen, besides contributing to them being considered innovative and creative. The positive experience of craftswomen at Rocinha has stimulated craft workers throughout Brazil.

Another promising initiative for recycling fabric leftovers in Brazil has been developed by Ecosimple enterprise, in partnership with cooperatives. By means of a contract established with great textile companies, clothing factories and the community, Ecosimple collects leftover cloth and takes it to the small cooperatives, where it is separated by color. When they are returned to Ecosimple, the fabric leftovers are passed into machines where they are dismantled, returning to the condition of fibers. Afterwards, they are passed by a process of cleaning, then transformed into thread, woven and made into fabric. Once those fabric leftovers are separated by color, it is not necessary to add paint or colorant. For the sustainability and differentiation that they provide, the Ecosimple fabrics are used by great brands in Brazil and abroad, avoiding that millions of tons of fabric residues are discharged monthly into litter and sanitary landfill, besides generating several working positions, as in Brazil millions of people live under the poverty line (ECOSIMPLE, 2011).

An initiative which has currently been adopted by several cooperatives, NGs and enterprises of several countries is the recycling of PET bottles (polyethylene tereftalate). Due to the high consumption of soft drinks in the world, tons of bottles would be put annually in the landfill, unless recycled. Besides avoiding accumulation of litter and pollution of rivers, recycling make possible income for pickers, economic use of material in industries, reduction of production costs, besides bringing a marketing opportunity for enterprises, when it attracts the sympathy of ecology-minded consumers. According to this tendency, several brands and marks, in partnership with cooperatives, NGOs, city halls and groups of litter pickers, are dedicated to the production of recycled jeans, developed from the mix of recycled PET with recycled cotton (Alves, 2002). Although several stylists and enterprises have committed to the project which benefits several families, in 2010, Brazil recycled only 55.8% of the resin of PET produced, demonstrating that there is still lot of work to be done. In Finland, which is on the top in international comparisons, the rate of reused bottles return is 98%.

To be effective in this scenario that demands knowledge and abilities to reinvent sustainable strategies of production, it is necessary to incorporate the principles of Creative Economy, embraced in several countries such as Sweden, Finland, Spain, Holland, England, United States, Colombia and Brazil, and which motivates the development of creativity as part of the economic and cultural policy.[4]

This economic sector, which involves industrial sectors, service industry and cultural companies, is classified as the third greatest in the world, just behind petrol and weapons, and is responsible for 7% of the world GDP. In Brazil it gets even higher proportions, once it moves around R$ 380 annual billion, it means 16.4% of GDP (Rodrigues, 2011).

The Term *Solidarity Economy* results from the union between the economy, culture and technology, which refers to the junction between symbolic universe and concrete world, valorizing the capacity to go beyond creating the new, but also of reinventing, diluting traditional paradigms, uniting apparently disconnected points and with that, "entering the equation of solutions for new and old problems". Creative Economy attracts and stimulates the action of new producers, creating opportunity to promote social insertion and rescuing the citizen, "through an activity which emanates from its own formation, culture and roots", transmutation of creativity in a catalyst of economic value (Reis, 2008, p. 15).

Creative Economy has produced important transformations in the economic sphere. Rodrigues (2011) mentions that Creative Economy is a way to stimulate generation of work and income from the valorization of regional specificities and cultural diversity in detriment to mass production, in such a way as to reinforce civilian society and smaller producers and still favor the process of transformation of communities and promote development.

Possibilities of home economists actions in government programs

In considering the capacity of home economists to act in the social promotion of families and groups, in such a way as to improve life quality, social programs created by several countries offer great opportunity for professional action.

One strategy of action refers to maintaining cultural identity. Considering that capital perspective makes instable the ways of living and erases the culture, home economists may develop projects which may rescue ways of living of groups, in order to valorize and transmit cultural identities, mainly via craft production. Thus, craft activities proportionate work and income for several families and communities, including *Quilombolas*' and indigenous ones. Techniques employed, besides being ecological, are passed from generation to generation, preserving cultural roots, reassuring ethnical identities and supplying the history of group.

However, many craft producers do not know how to innovate their products, besides having difficulties in commercializing them. Many times, techniques are transmitted among generations without innovation, although the differentiation of design is a relevant factor in competition and value aggregation to the products. Hence, in the process of communitarian development, the creative potential of groups should be exploited in order to let producers generate new ideas and innovative products. For products to be renewed, it is interesting to incorporate elements of the fashion, such as color cart, patterns, mesh together traditional materials with contemporizing elements.

Researches prove that the creative potential of human beings is bound to decline during life due to mental blockades created. However, creative processes may be restored by the use of techniques which make possible that part of creative abilities is retained, minimizing the process of robotizing. Besides several techniques for liberating creativity which might be used, the contact with other realities might enlarge inspiration sources. Many times, groups get isolated and do not have opportunity to live other reality and know what other people produce. Therefore, when working with a community, the home economist may place craft workers in contact with market events in order to enlarge their cultural repertory and creative sense, besides exposing their products to other locals, enlarging their market potential

For supplying visibility to artifacts produced, besides motivating the work and processes ecologically correct, it is necessary to invest for divulgation products in the Internet, fairs and events. For this, it is interesting to elaborate folders, *tags* and portfolio which identify products and incorporate the culture of craft workers and group history. Also relevant is elaborating projects for obtaining financing aiming to promote craftwork and local potentialities.

For increasing potential of communitarian development and favor access to work market, citizenship, credit and income, it is necessary that the home economist disseminate technical knowledge and qualify workers in order to have autonomy for facing problems and proposing sustainable alternatives. For this it is necessary to motivate the development of competences, potentialities and creativities, incentivizing the exercise of leadership and multiplications of knowledge, based on the participative and solidarity work.

In the process of professional capacitating, it is important to take information to the craft workers about themes such as textile fibers, sustainability, cooperatives, associations, besides technical subjects inherent to each modality of service offered.

One problem which generally accompanies craft workers is the absence of knowledge about the manner in which prices are derived. Many times, when pricing a product, there is no consideration of inputs such as electricity, water or equipment wear. Therefore, the home economist may help groups in the determination of fair and competitive prices. Besides that, for reinforcing competition and developing the commercial potential of associations, it is necessary to proportion producers access to market and investments, free from middleman, besides looking for partnership together with city halls, NGOs, enterprises, clothing factories and designers.

A partnership which deserves emphasis in Brazil is the establishment between the designer Ronaldo Fraga and women knitters from Paraiba. In his collections that are launched in São Paulo Fashion Week, one of the greatest fashion fairs in the world, Fraga plans his pieces together with women knitters and divulgates in his fashion shows the history of the group which produced them. The stylist has been highlighted by the social project *Talents of Brazil*, which has benefitted 400 people in several points of the country.

Another project that deserves acknowledgement in Brazil is being developed by the stylist and plastic artist Cocco Barçante. His project *Feelings of Rio*, has as main characteristic portraying in panels and crafting object the beauty of Rio de Janeiro. Reusing fabric leftovers in the process of creation and use of PET packaging for conditioning products, aggregate conceits of responsibility and sustainability to the work. When he began his work with craftswomen and knitters in the slums of Rio de Janeiro, these women had low self esteem and did not believe in their creative potential. Cocco Barçante motivated them to believe in their potential and today the work of these women is been divulgated in several famous events, besides being sold on the Internet.

Other highlighted work is being developed in China, one of the world's major fabricants of textiles, by Jin Yuanshan, a popular artist from the northeast of China, in partnership with old women. With his talent and patience, he collaborates with these women to transform fabric leftovers which would be dumped into clothes, accessories, and works of art for house decoration. One of his works took seven years to be concluded, when presented in a fair in Xangai, the artist received an offer of Five thousand dollars from an Italian collector.[5]

Besides designers and artists, with whom the home economist may look for partnership for communitarian development, it is worth mentioning the name of some home economists who conjugated communitarian development, sustainability, creativity and generation of income. One of them is Débora Teixeira, who, mediated by the Technological Incubator of Popular Cooperatives (ITCP), develops activities with *Grupo Retalharte*, in association with descendants of the *Quilombolas* from Ponte Nova, Minas Gerais, Brazil. Using fabric leftovers donated by clothing factories, women develop craftworks such as cushion covers, bed covers and couch covers. In search of preserving cultural identity of the *Quilombolas*, after rising the group history by the group itself and the *Quilombolas* in Brazil data were conjugated to techniques for unblocking creativity proportioning building inspiration diaries containing elements of afro identity, which were incorporated into their products. By means of color combination and development of features and using homemade process, new products were elaborated, such as notebook covers, diary covers, aprons and home decorative utensils. Besides reusing textile residue, the work involves transmission of cultural inheritance, generation of income, socializing crafts techniques, besides proportioning sociability to women.

Other highlighted work is developed by the home economist Fátima Singulano, working at EMATER-MG. One of her projects, developed in the Metropolitan Region of Belo Horizonte, capital of Minas Gerais, with women mobilized by local associations, mothers affiliated to Parents and Friends of Handicapped Association (APAE) and interns from a female presidium, involve capacitating in modeling, cut, sewing and crafts. A partnership established between city hall, enterprises of private sector, district associations, churches and parliamentary men, made it possible to structure a project with acquisition of machinery and financing for participation of producers in fairs and events. This initiative which generates resources for low income women with use of fabric leftovers and donated materials has stimulated the creativity and ability of the participants, besides incentivizing environmental responsibility.

Once qualification do no restrain in mere techniques, it is necessary sensibility for comprehending the group need, so that the intervention in the promotion of bettering life quality of families and group becomes a pleasant and enriching act, permeate by great learning.

Final considerations

In the global capitalist system, the dissociation between ownership of capital goods and the work, as much as valorization of profit in detriment of the human being, creates a great social exclusion. In times when the government and enterprises cannot supply the need of jobs and the economy concentrates in the service sector, it is necessary to look for entrepreneurial alternatives which unite economy and culture, for proper valorization of creativity.

Therefore, Solidarity Economy and Creative Economy associated to the principles of sustainability, is an alternative to the capitalist system. As mentioned by Araújo (2007), this indicates that it is possible a relation of work in which the human being is put in the center, differently from the capitalist accumulation.

Within this scenario, the importance of a qualified professional for subsidizing minoritarian groups in search of innovation is clear. For an appropriate action, it is important that the home economist has knowledge about the actions which have been developed in the sectors of clothing and textiles, as much as public policies which direct action of communitarian development, searching alternatives and partnerships which conjugate the pillars of sustainability: ecologically correct, economically viable and socially just.

As professionals who guide consumers, home economists might inform them about several human and material factors involved in the production and commercialization of textile products, stimulating them to demand responsibility of retailers for warranting their products are produced ethically and sustainably.

Appropriating of the knowledge acquired during their course, and renewing their information during participation in fairs and events, the home economist may act as a facilitator in the organization of the process of creating groups involved with clothing, such as associations and cooperatives, focused in generation of income, maintaining cultural identity and environmental preservation.

Therefore, the great challenge which is placed in the professional actuation of home economists is that they seek for acting into projects and social programs, for providing visibility to identities and ways of life of groups in which the clothing and the craftworks are produced, in such a way that they may find sustainable measures for generating income and reduce social inequity.

The ways have been indicated and are ready to be followed. After all choosing the way may make all the difference. As Mahatma Gandhi said: "You must be the change you want to see in the world".

Endnotes

1. Emissions of carbon dioxide may contribute to changes in global climate, and have increased from 23,000 million tons in 1990 to 29 billion tons in 2004, (UNITED NATIONS, 2007). In recognition of economical and social impacts, several countries have been seeking alternatives for minimizing environmental problems. In 2007, for example, the European Unit promulgated the European Community Regulation (REACH), which demands that importers and clothes manufacturers identify, quantify and inform consumers about potentially dangerous chemical substances used in their textile products. These regulations, added to the increasing consciousness of consumers regarding less toxic products and more sustainable actions, may motivate the search for solutions for problems generated by textile and clothing.
2. The Millennium Cupola was an event promoted by the United Nations (UN), held in its Headquarters, in September 2000. On that occasion, 191 leaders of Member-States of the United Nations signed the Millennium Declaration, in which they committed to eliminate hunger and extreme poverty all round the planet. From this document was elaborated The Millennium Development Goals of the United Nations (MDG), a proposal for mobilizing government and society to look for alternatives to overcome hunger and poverty, and the establishment of eight goals to be reached by 2015.
3. The poverty line is based on the consumption of goods and services. Just for international comparison, the World Bank established this line as 1 US dollar daily, per person. In Brazil, it is considered that the poverty line is monthly income of 1/2 minimum salary, per capita and extreme poverty as monthly income of 1/4 of minimum salary.
4. In Finland, for example, in 2006, more than 102,000 people worked in the cultural industry which represents 4.19 per cent of all the workers employed in this country. The support for the reinforcement of the creative economy and cultural enterprising in rural areas happens by financing via the Program for Development of Business and Internalization of Creative Industry, which is

inserted into the Cultural Program for Promoting Exportation, implemented by Ministry of Work and Economy, Ministry of Foreign Business and Ministry of Education (FINLAND, 2010).
5   CHINA. Patch up fabric leftovers into fine arts. 2010. <http://www.china.org.cn/video/2010-10/22/content_21178115.htm>.

References

Alves, A. C. N. (2002) A reciclagem de PET na fabricação de jeans: o caso da parceria Rhodia-ster, Santista, M.Officer e Coopa-Roca. *XXII Encontro Nacional de Engenharia de Produção ENEGEP/ABEPRO*. Curitiba.

Bell, D. (1974) *O Advento da Sociedade Pós-Industrial*. São Paulo. Cultrix.

Caulfield, K. (2009) *Sources of Textile Waste in Australia*. January. Apical International Pty Ltd.

Claudio, L. (2007). *Waste Couture: Environmental Impact of the Clothing Industry*. Environ Health Perspect 115: A449-A454. <http://dx.doi.org/10.1289/ehp. 115-a449>

Ecosimple (2011). *Sustentabilidade prêt-à-porter! Tecidos renováveis, reciclados e 100% sustentáveis para o mercado de moda e decoração*. Disponível em: <http://www.ecosimple.com.br/>. Acesso em 29/11/2011.

Finland, Ministry of Education. (2010) *Creative Economy and Culture in the Innovation Policy*, 2010. <http://www.minedu.fi/export/sites/default/OPM/Julkaisut/2010/liitteet/OPM13.pdf?lang=en>

Harvey, D. (1992) Condição pós-moderna. São Paulo: Edições Loyola,.

Morley, N. Slater, S.; Russell, S.; Tipper, M.; Ward, G. (2006) *Recycling of low grade clothing waste*, Oakdene Hollins, Salvation Army Trading Company and Nonwovens Innovation & Research Institute. <http://www.oakdenehollins.co.uk/pdf/defr01_058_low _grade_clothing-public_v2.pdf >

Moura, R. M. (2001) *Recortes da moda: Coopa-Roca um conceito de arte*. Dissertação (Mestrado em Artes Visuais). Rio de Janeiro: Universidade Federal do Rio de Janeiro, 2001.

Recyclable Plastic Bottles In Finland (2008). *Scandina Vianbre Wers' Review*. vol .65 N.1,. <http://www.scandbrewrev.dk/User_files/812155675bd5976df4040b3e2dcee9cf.pdf>

Reis, A. C. F. (org) (2008). *Economia criativa como estratégia de desenvolvimento: uma visão dos países em desenvolvimento*. São Paulo: Itaú Cultural.

Rocha, E. (2010). *Magia e capitalismo*. São Paulo: Brasiliense.

Rodrigues, C. (2011). Menos transpiração e mais inspiração. In: *Revista FAPESP. Edição Impressa 187*. Setembro 2011.

Santos, B. de Souza (2002). *Produzir para viver: os caminhos da produção não capitalista*. São Paulo: Civilização Brasileira.

Santos, E. G. dos (2008). *Formulação de políticas culturais: as leis de incentivo e o programa cultura viva*. Escola de Administração de Empresas de São Paulo. São Paulo: Fundação Getulio Vargas.

Sobreira, J. L.; Oliveira, R. V. de (2011). A invisibilidade da infância: o trabalho infantil na cadeia produtiva do jeans em Toritama — PE. *VIII Congresso de Iniciação Científica da Universidade Federal de Campina Grande*, 2011. <http://pesquisa.ufcg.edu.br/anais/2011/ content/humanas_sociais_aplicadas/SOCIOLOGIA/Jessica%20Lobo%20Sobreira%20-%20CH.doc>

United Nations (*2007). The Millennium Development Goals — Report 2007*. United Nations: New York, 2007. <http://www.un.org/millenniumgoals/pdf/mdg2007.pdf>

CHAPTER

9

Writing New Maps — Considering the Phenomenological Attitude as a Theoretical Framework for the Future-Orientated Field of Home Economics

Henna Heinilä

"Life is understood backwards but must be lived forwards". These are the words of Danish philosopher Søren Kierkegaard (1813–1855). How true and confusing as well. Does this mean that people are bound to be wise after the fact? No, I do not think that Kierkegaard's words should be interpreted this way. But how should the aphorism be interpreted then? This question has inspired me, more or less, during the process of writing this chapter. With this aphorism in mind, I am going to consider one possibility which I view as a fruitful potential for a future-orientated Home Economics. My intention in this chapter is to draft a picture of phenomenology and the potential it holds for the science of Home Economics. I will introduce the *phenomenological attitude* as a theoretical possibility for the future-orientated field of Home Economics. Toward this end, I use 'the map' metaphor, which I have picked up from the recent history of the science of Home Economics, but which, at the same time, represents the early history of my personal theoretical thinking. The understanding grows from the past, but at the same time, in this moment, the possible futures are simultaneously enveloped in it. Several possibilities are conceivable, but I have decided to nurture one of them with the phenomenological attitude. My contribution is one intervention to advance the home economists' journey towards a living and affective Home Economics culture and academic discipline. The argumentation is based on the results of my study *Domestic skills as the art of everyday life* (Heinilä, 2007) and loosely based on my new material collected in the ongoing study, *The domestic heartbeat — joint and divergent rhythms in the lives of adult students and their families* (Heinilä, 2012).

The chapter includes two separate parts. Firstly, I describe the nature of phenomenology, the phenomenological attitude, and the lived experience intertwined in it. Secondly, I do some new map writing in the context of the phenomenological attitude. My focus is on Home Economics as an academic discipline. The content of the chapter connects especially on the themes of conducting research, knowledge creating and creating new ways of thinking. These themes are important for all home economists around the world now and in the future, as long as we aim at the coherent multidimensional, living and affective Home Economics culture.

Phenomenological attitude and new map writing

Fourteen years ago, in 1998, The International Household and Family Research Conference was held in Helsinki. The conference theme was 'New Approaches to the Study of Everyday Life'. One of the keynote speakers was Professor Eleanore Vaines. In her speech, Vaines introduced new maps as a way of grasping the complex nature of the Family Perspective on Everyday Life (Vaines, 1998). She introduced the idea of maps as metaphors, which were meant to help professionals find their way in the changing sphere of everyday life and the field of Home Economics. Map metaphors were enlightening because they explained one phenomenon by way of another, and because they could be used to discover relationships between different phenomena. Vaines' contribution was significant because metaphors produce meanings using analogies, and meanings are central in constructing the human-related field of science.

One of the maps Vaines introduced was named *The Many Ways of Knowing Map*. Vaines (1998) argued that this map was needed because the world had become complex and a broader view over it was needed. Vaines described how to combine different ways of knowing in the sphere of Home Economics. *The Many Ways of Knowing Map* was the metaphor that was meant to help professionals to ground their reflections in their experiences, and to encourage them to live in the first-hand reality of their practice. *The Many Ways of Knowing Map* also helps professionals to combine scientific methods of understanding with the life world and narrative methods. When different ways of knowing are integrated, a Home Economics pattern of knowing is created. Vaines argued that home economists must step "in the middle of the map" and make their dialogue visible and heard. home economists should find new ways to announce their thesis and mission. This is how the complex, interrelated and invisible webs of life become honored and lived. The map helps the professionals find their way and provide the means whereby they can see the rich and enriching meanings of the science of Home Economics. With this map, Vaines characterized Home Economics as part of a wide web of knowledge and knowing and as a multidisciplinary field of study (Vaines, 1998). The map metaphor also revealed the theoretical inheritance adapted by Vaines. Many ways of knowing basically identifies the human being as a bodily being, and from this point of view Vaines' theoretical insight can be considered phenomenological. In her view, Vaines included an idea of Home Economics as a science and practice with deep moral and ethical dimensions. The idea nicely refers to the phenomenological attitude where the scientific intention is to remain as close as possible to lived experience.

We are now living in the 21st century and serious questions about the future of Home Economics still remain and, obviously, are increasing as well. Donna Pendergast (2006) points out that there is a need to identify what the major trends affecting individuals and families are at present and in the future and, after that, to develop Home Economics as a living and affective culture. Pendergast argues that home economists are constantly struggling from the repeated failure of attempts to establish a legitimate identity. There are problems, for example, with the splintering of specializations and knowledge in the profession, and with the impact and cohesive potentialities within the research. The IFHE position statement (2008) pays attention to one current trend, namely global interaction and interdependency, which increases the mutual intertwining of individuals, families and communities. It could be fairly assumed that there is also a trend in the society that increases the common space between public and private: one's paid work can be performed at home, the shopping malls can serve as "living rooms", and personal private life can be introduced to strangers on the Internet and so on. It is not misleading to say that homes are becoming "open spaces" both interacting with and modifying themselves in active process with their environment.

Vaines mentioned in her keynote speech: "We do our research, develop maps, and as information and circumstances change, updates and replacements of these maps are made." (Vaines, 1998, p. 22). Now fourteen years after the Helsinki conference I am going to reflect upon the idea of the map metaphor and try to update and rewrite the maps for today's navigators. By introducing the phenomenological attitude as a theoretical frame and a new map I am calling for a philosophical conversation, and the deep philosophical study of Home Economics as a phenomenon, discipline and science. In spite of all diversity and complexity in the world, my argument is that there is always a universal unifying mode in family life; such as, togetherness, shelter, care, collective rhythms and other profound being-in-the-world related features (Heinilä, 2007). That is why there is a need and possibility to share some common maps among Home Economics professionals around the world.

Phenomenology as an attitude

If an academic discipline wants to be proactive and remain alive there has to be, as a foundation, a strong scientific and academic identity and a suitable and credible frame of reference for theoretical insights. My contribution to this discussion is phenomenological philosophy as one possible theoretical and methodological frame of reference for the research, and as the paradigm for the philosophy of Home Economics. The philosophy of Home Economics is mostly needed in establishing the identity of the discipline. Phenomenology offers theoretical constructions, concepts and a practical method too, but most of all it offers an ideal as to how to carry out the inquiry. Phenomenology is founded upon certain essential arguments. Firstly, it is always a question of the phenomenon, not of theories or concepts. Secondly, the inquiry begins from real life, from concrete experience. These essential arguments, basic phenomena and experience ensure that phenomenological inquiry entitles the phenomenon to be revealed in its whole richness without minimizing it, for example, through the external definitions set by the discipline. When the essential elements appear, the fruitful ground for the phenomenological attitude is set.

The phenomenological attitude invites the phenomenon to show itself as it is (Heidegger, 1996). The Greek expression *fainómenon* forms the root for the noun phenomenon, which means 'to show itself' or 'appearances'. The phenomenological interpretation of the expression 'lógos' covers all the ways the meanings may be brought out. Phenomenology itself is therefore like the manifestation of a phenomenon (Heinilä, 2008). Edmund Husserl (1859–1938), Martin Heidegger (1889–1976) and Morice Merleau-Ponty (1908–1961) are well-known European philosophers in the field of phenomenology. Their philosophical study has been significant for the further development of phenomenology in the twentieth century. Husserl created an idea of strict phenomenology, returned philosophy from its abstract and separate theoretical constructions back to its origins, back to experience and life itself. Husserl also created the phenomenological reduction as a scientific method (Husserl, 1995). Heidegger took his departure point from Husserl, but directed his philosophical interest towards the being of beings. Heidegger pointed out that the most important question is the question of the meaning of being. The question must be formulated because the meaning of being is always included in every other question, in every research question too. That is why it must be made transparent and conscious. Being-in-the-world should not be taken for granted. Merleau-Ponty's phenomenology, like Heidegger's, concentrates on being-in-the-world too, but he raises the question of the body as well. Indeed, the engagement with the world is not purely cognitive. People are in and with the world, and the experience of the world is, among others, emotional, practical, aesthetic and imaginative. Merleau-Ponty argues that bodily perceiving is prior to conscious reflecting. The body is the "ground" which is the natural subject of perception. According to Merleau-Ponty (2002) we are our body. There is a remarkable contact between the body and the world. The body is not an object but rather a lived relation with the world. The body is the subject of perception, and we shall rediscover ourselves, our being-in-the-world, when examining perceiving as we do with our body. Sensations enter the body and light up the experience of being. After that conscious thinking emerges and the different perspectives about meanings. Bodily being-in-the-world is reversible. The idea of reversibility becomes real, for example, when shaking hands. The hand that is touched turns to the hand touching. Both modes of being, being touched and touching are present simultaneously. The reversible nature of being, or chiasm as Merleau-Ponty also calls this entity, is the perspective from which the phenomenological research attitude should be regarded. Chiasm is the focal point where the researcher turns towards the impersonal point of view and towards shared scientific understanding (Heinilä, 2008).

There are two important elements in the phenomenological research process: an immediate experience and methodologically- ruled scientific description. The phenomenological method uses a reduction which means that all assumptions and beliefs are put into 'brackets' so the 'essences' of the phenomenon inquired upon could be considered more effectively, and the meanings of the phenomenon could be uncovered (Husserl, 1995; Matthew, 2006). In the phenomenological reduction, immediate experience, which from now on, I will call *lived experience* according to Max van Manen (1990), is deconstructed with a description so the essential features of it can form the reflecting surface for lived experience. If the phenomenological description is carried out, and the lived experience of mine and yours are resonating, something essential and meaningful is uncovered and shared. With reduction, phenomenological inquiry can drill down to the core of the phenomenon — this means 'to the things themselves', to the lived experience of the human being (Husserl, 1995; van Manen, 1990).

When the phenomenological reduction is used as a strict method which is put into practice, the phenomenological attitude is more like a general view over the whole research process. The phenomenological attitude, altogether, is much more than a collection of theoretical tools. It is a profound philosophical way of thinking, providing a holistic position in the world for both the human being and scientist as well. Phenomenological research may be seen, for example, as a dynamic interplay among several research activities:

- investigating lived experience,
- reflecting essential themes,
- describing through writing and rewriting,
- maintaining close contact to the phenomenon and lived experience,
- consideration of the parts and the wholes during the description process.

These are examples of intertwined phenomenological research activities. The interpretive examination of the phenomenological research attitude has a methodical feature of relating the particular to the universal, part to whole and episode to totality (van Manen, 1990). The phenomenological attitude enables the researcher to approach the core questions and the essence of the field of study in a fruitful way, and helps to reveal an essential experience of what it is like to be a culturally, socially, locally and globally situated person (Heinilä, 2009). The phenomenological attitude enables the researcher to stay close to lived experience.

Lived experience

Husserl attempted to develop phenomenological theory into an ideal of rigorous science. He criticized philosophy for being like a 'dead letter'. Philosophy was dealing with concepts for concepts' sake and philosophers for philosophers' sake. Philosophy was separated from its essence (Husserl, 1965). According to Husserl (1995), phenomenology's mission is to stay close to its essence and in his thesis he called for turning back to experience. Husserl reconstructed the meaning and the position of experience in the context of a rigorous science, and the concept of the lifeworld became central. Basically, objects and experiences can not be separated from each other. The phenomenological reduction remains on the absolute ground of philosophical study, which is lived experience. But inevitably there are contradictions in the argumentation of the phenomenological reduction and lived experience, which are both subjective. There is a need to study carefully the delicate moment, the chiasm, when lived experience becomes observed and reflected on and stops being lived and immediate.

"Lived experience is the starting point and end point of phenomenological research," as van Manen (1990, p. 36) clearly describes the nature of lived experience. He argues that the aim of phenomenology is to transform lived experience into a textual expression of its essence. The textual expression must resonate with a reader's own lived experience. The effect of the text should be a reflexive re-living and reflective attaching into something meaningful. The nature of lived experience is enveloped in the reversibility of our being-in-the-world. First, people have their taken-for-granted relation to their own body, and are immediately and naturally involved in the activity. Second, this taken-for-granted relation can be disturbed when others start to look at you, for example in front of a class or other audience, and you get the "feeling of being looked at". Being looked at and being involved in an activity are both manifestations of being-in-the-world, but lived experience, the actual moment of experience, has a temporal structure. It can never be grasped in its immediate manifestation. This ontological fact forces the phenomenological researcher to admit that the full richness of lived experience will never be reached. The meanings it manifests will always be something past. But the intention of the researcher is to stay *as close as possible* to lived experience.

New map writing: from many ways of knowing to expanded experiencing

According to Vaines, *The Many Ways of Knowing Map* helps professionals to combine scientific methods of understanding with the lifeworld and narrative methods. She argued that when different ways of knowing are integrated, a Home Economics way of knowing is created. But how do professionals find their way in this splintered world of enormous possibilities, and how can they still confirm the identity and theoretical coherence of the discipline? What would be the uniting force that confirms the coherence of the whole research procedure when different ways of knowing is used in analysis? I myself needed another map, a new map for finding the suitable way to integrate the different perspectives and different ways of knowing. My map was delineated from out of the phenomenological attitude and I am calling it in this chapter *Expanded Experiencing Map*. The map highlights that, if many ways of knowing is preferred in the context of Home Economics research, there must also be an understanding of those many dimensions the human being is experiencing in the world, and also the strict theoretical frame to conduct these dimensions. The new map can be seen as interplay between four essential waypoints for the navigator. These waypoints are:

- the phenomenological attitude as an anchor for research activity,

- being-in-the-world as bodily beings,
- lived experience which is reversible and bodily by nature, and
- interplay among phenomenological research activities in following the attitude.

Around these essential waypoints the shared sphere of meanings and knowledge becomes enveloped.

My first inquiry with the phenomenological attitude was located in the field of domestic skills (Heinilä, 2007) and the second inquiry in the sphere of the rhythms of everyday life of families (Heinilä, 2012). In both cases, my interest is in how the phenomenon, domestic skills and the rhythm of everyday life manifest themselves in people's experience, and this explains why I turned my researcher's gaze towards lived experience and not towards action observed. My new map has guided me not to gather empirical data about the phenomenon. Instead of this I read and reread phenomenological literature, scientific writings about everyday life and, of course, research material from the area of the science of Home Economics. I also ask myself: how do I reach and stay close to lived experience? I have my own experience of the phenomenon as a Home Economics professional and as a mother and family member, but I have to create the sphere where my own experience and experiences of others could come into dialogue. In both cases I decided to use conversations. I made notes on different conversations in which I was involved during the research process. I made recordings too. The conversations dealt with household activity, domestic skills, organizing family life and discussions about the meaning of everyday life and its dimensions. In addition I decided to use literature, like prose, short stories and poems, where there were descriptions about living everyday life. Van Manen (1990) argues that in phenomenological research it is natural to make use of the works of poets, authors, artists and cinematographers because it is in this material that the human being can be found as a situated person, and it is in this work that the variety and possibility of human experience may be found in condensed and transcended form. During the textual process (writing and rewriting) I used some citations from conversations and literature along with my theoretical argumentation. My target was not to make a theoretical interpretation of the material. But the citations settled into the dialogue with me and my theoretical thinking. The citations and theory are the realisation of the reversible nature of being: the personal and impersonal sides of experience.

The Expanded Experiencing Map allows me to listen to and see the richness of lived experience. As a researcher I have my lived experience of the phenomenon, I share it with others. My purpose is to stay close to shared experience, because *knowledge about the meaning of the phenomenon comes from this experience*. So in the phenomenological research the researcher is involved with the phenomenon she/he is studying. She/he is like an anthropologist who lives along with others without any intention to make interventions during the process. The phenomenological attitude includes the idea of the researcher both as active and passive, as regards experiencing and acting. The researcher is not an observer but a companion. From this position, after being involved, the researcher is reaching an impersonal picture of the phenomenon. She/he must step outside her/his individual point of view and look at the phenomenon in a more impersonal way, make descriptions, uncover major themes embedded in the phenomenon and deconstruct meanings. The purpose is not to count the number of all the things we happen to experience, but to describe *how we experience* that reality. This impersonal perspective is what the researcher can share in a scientific way.

Traditionally, scientific knowledge is considered as being logical and objective. These are characteristics which are still important and desirable. But *the Expanded Experiencing Map* introduces another aspect to scientific knowledge. Knowledge which accompanies lived experience, which not only explains or analyses the world, but describes it and enables meanings to pop up and resonate with a reader's or listener's understanding. The new map challenges the researcher to become a perceiver instead of remaining an observer (Heinilä, 2009). This kind of knowledge honours the richly complex Home Economics phenomenon and allows us to understand it more deeply.

One potential course to go — aesthetic experiencing

Because phenomenologically- orientated study dives deep into lived experience, it brings to the surface a considerable amount of feelings and emotional experiences too. Feelings are usually seen to be problematic in the sphere of science. Especially in the role of perceiver, feelings increase the amount of uncertainty and confusion into the argumentation. That is why they are usually swept under the rug. But the new map takes the whole experience seriously. It counts all the ways the human being perceives, so the emotional extension cannot be denied. In my inquiry of domestic skills, I found that emotional experiencing serves as one essential extension of domestic skills, and of household activity as well. The extension of emotional experiencing is one essential element of Home Economics as a phenomenon. (See more on ontological extensions of domestic skill in Heinilä 2007 and 2009.) People are searching for happiness, safety, beauty and the feeling of fulfilment in the course of everyday life. Emotional experiencing is an element that we can share with each other, no matter which part of the world we live in or what kind of cultural tradition we belong to. Discussion about the *meaning* of emotional experience in the context of Home Economics can be a unifying process, even more than discussion about pure and "cold" cognitive knowledge about the human being as an emotional being. Home Economics as an academic discipline needs traditional scientific knowledge, of course, but my point is that because Home Economics practice is deeply involved with lived experience, and constitutes an emotional extension within it, it reveals what is obscure and should therefore also be studied as something complex and obscure. The phenomenological attitude is one possibility for entering the phenomenon without reducing it and without turning it into something unrecognizable.

In my inquiries so far (Heinilä, 2007; 2012) I have discovered that the most meaningful moments of everyday life are connected to the feelings of fulfilment. On the one hand, the feeling of fulfilment no doubt forms one theme of the phenomenological description of my study. The feeling of fulfilment is hard to describe and reconstruct but, on the other hand, its meaning can be easily brought out. In the process of phenomenological description the feeling of fulfilment has theoretical form: the idea of aesthetic experience. The aesthetic experience differs from other experiences because it remains whole, enriching and ends with the feeling of fulfilment. The aesthetic experience acts like a unifying element for the human being's inner world. It unites the actor and the act, reveals the meanings of things, acts and moments, and opens the logic of the everyday activity. The aesthetic experience is mostly considered in the context of art and has often been thought of as the experience of something beautiful. Any vivid experience can even be considered as an aesthetic experience. Postmodernism has broken the "walls" between art and other spheres of life. In the 21st century the aesthetic experience is being seriously investigated within many fields of study, for example, education and learning. Beauty, goodness and truth, perennial dimensions of aesthetics, are not only a matter of art, but are connected to the whole sphere of the human-related world. There is little knowledge about Home Economics' aesthetic experience. Thus I propose that home economists should carefully examine what the issue is and what the meaning of the aesthetic experience would be, both the science and practice for Home Economics, and finally what the criteria for the Home Economics' aesthetic experience would be. From the phenomenological perspective (referring to the lived experience), aesthetic experiencing is significant for all dimensions of Home Economics practise: academic field, school subject, policy and society issue and everyday life in families (Turkki, 2004, p. 57).

Summary

I started this chapter with the quotation of Kierkegaard: "Life is understood backwards but must be lived forwards." I do believe that it is possible to construct new maps for a future-orientated discipline using the current understanding, many ways of knowing and expanded experiencing. History should be taken as a set of resources, should be reflected upon and viewed as an essential part of the future. Understanding the past enables present living as well as a means to prepare for the future. Vaines introduced the map metaphor in 1998 and it became a memorable start of my personal development as a Home Economics professional.

The key message can be summarised into four issues which I have localized in this chapter:

- There should be more philosophical discussion, reflection and inquiry in the field of Home Economics. Professionals are invited to investigate the essence of Home Economics alongside other important questions. The philosophical ground of Home Economics should be strengthened.
- Bodily being-in-the-world as an ontological entity should be more consciously reflected in the context of research practise.
- Phenomenology as a research attitude enables us to reach the phenomenon as it is. Phenomenology also offers a suitable frame for researching lived experience which is the source of knowledge.
- The vivid experience can become an aesthetic experience and Home Economics is a unique sphere for this to emerge.

Discussion Prompts

- Are the universal and unifying essential elements of Home Economics phenomena probable, possible or preferable to define?
- How should the ontological notion of bodily being-in-the-world influence the research practice of Home Economics?
- How should the meaning of the aesthetic experience of Home Economics be studied?
- What would be the main questions of the philosophy of Home Economics?

References

Heidegger, M. (1996). *Being and Time.* Oxford UK & Cambridge USA: Blackwell. (Orig. Sein und Zeit 1926).

Heinilä, H. (2007). Domestic Skills as the Art of Everyday Life — An inquiry about domestic skills as a way of being-in-the-world in the light of existentialist-hermeneutics phenomenology. Kotitalous- ja käsityötieteen laitoksen julkaisuja 16. (In Finnish, abstract in English).

Heinilä, H. (2008). The Art of Everyday Life within the Domestics Sphere — Phenomenological Inquiry of Domestic Skills as a Way of Being-in-the-world. In Tuomi-Gröhn, T. (Ed), *Reinventing Art of Everyday Making.* Frankfurt am Main: Peter Lang.

Heinilä, H. (2009). How Domestic Skills turn out to be the Art of Everyday Life — Phenomenological Attitude as a Research Method in the Field of Home Economics. *Family and Consumer Sciences Research Journal,* 38(2), 158-174.

Heinilä, H. (2012). The Domestic Heartbeat — Joint or Divergent Rhythms in the Lives of Adult Students and Their Families. (Unpublished paper).

Husserl, E. (1965). Philosophy as Rigorous Science. In Q. Lauer (ed.), *Phenomenology and the Crisis of Philosophy,* New York: Harper. (Orig. Philosophie als strenge Wissenschaft 1910).

Husserl, E. (1995). *Fenomenologian idea. Viisi luentoa.* Helsinki: Loki Kirjat. (Orig. Die Idee der Phänomenologie 1907).

International Federation for Home Economics. (2008). *IFHE Position Statement — Home Economics in the Century.* Bonn: IFHE.

Matthews, E. (2006). *Merleau-Ponty: A Quide for the Perplexed.* London New York: Continuum.

Merleau-Ponty, M. (2002). *Phenomenology of Perception.* London and New York: Routledge.

Pendergast, D. (2006). Sustaining the home economics profession in the new times — A convergent moment. In Rauma, A-L., Pöllänen, S. & Seitamaa-Hakkarainen, P. (Eds), *Human Perspectives on Sustainable Future.* Joensuu: University of Joensuu.

Turkki, K. (2004). The Influence of Eleanore Vaines on Home Economics in Finland. In Smith, M.G., Peterat, L. & de Zwart, M.L. (Eds.) *Home Economics Now. Transformative Practice, Ecology, and Everyday Life.* Vancouver, Canada: Pacific Educational Press.

Vaines, E. (1998). A family perspective on everyday life: the heart of reflective practice. In Turkki, K. (Ed) *"New Approaches to the Study of Everyday Life"* Part I. Helsinki: University of Helsinki, Department of Home Economics and Craft Science. Publication 3.

van Manen, M. (1990). *Researching Lived Experience.* London: State University of New York Press.

CHAPTER
10

Considering an Alternative Route for Home Economics — Education for a Sustainable Future

Karin Hjälmeskog

Consumption is an important part of our lives in the twenty-first century and consumption can be seen as 'framing' the ways we are in the world. The way in which today's society forms its members seems most of all to be dictated by the need of people playing the role of consumers, and thus the norm which the society holds for it's members becomes the capacity and will to play that role (Bauman, 1998). This means that in our time consumption is important for individuals, for identity formation, for prosperity etc., but also for the society. When difficulties appear in our societies, from terror attacks to economic crises, the citizens are asked to do their duty — to shop — that is why sometimes the label consumer society is used. A consumer society is built on continuous economic growth and a vision of rising prosperity with economic growth, and this is, according to Jackson (2009), a "modern construction". It is a construction that has come under considerable criticism. Critics of ever-increasing economic growth claim that its material implications lead to depletion of natural resources and the degradation of the environment, impoverishing present as well as future generations. To mention some material concerns: climate change, water scarcity, loss of biodiversity and depletion of fossil oil. Further, beyond these ecological concerns lie social ones, as both the benefits and the costs of economic growth are unevenly distributed. Disparities between rich and poor individuals within a nation and between nations generate rising social tensions. Finally, the critics argue that economic growth does not appear to advance human happiness, maybe even the contrary.

The overall aim for Home Economics is a good or prosperous life for individuals and families as well as sustainable development. In this paper, I discuss ideas on Home Economics education in relation to the above critique of economic growth. We

111

live in a world of finite resources, constrained by strict environmental limits. A world characterized by 'islands of prosperity' within 'oceans of poverty'. Are ever-increasing incomes and consumption of goods for the already rich really a legitimate focus for our continued hopes and expectations? Or is there some other path towards a more sustainable, a more equitable form of prosperity (Jackson, 2009)? If so, what can the consequences for Home Economics education be?

Confronting the taken for granted

The demands on the consumers to continue and even increase their consumption is by many taken for granted. In this chapter I will confront this idea. The main source of inspiration is a report by Tim Jackson, *Prosperity without growth? The transition to a sustainable economy* (2009; 2012). Jackson is Economics Commissioner in the Sustainable Development Commission for the British government. In the report he deals with the obsession for growth in our time. He presents a vision on how we can live prosperous and happy lives and still reduce our material impact on the environment. Further, his ideas for transition towards a more sustainable economy concern governmental level, but he states that this process must start by developing financial and ecological prudence at home. This is why the micro level also needs to be addressed and Home Economics education becomes relevant.

Prosperity

Prosperity is said to be a megatrend (see chapter one in this book) as the majority of the population of OECD countries and large groups in formerly developing countries are now growing more prosperous. As I understand it, this trend is based on a prediction of economic growth. Growing Gross National Product (GNP) is usually used to measure and compare wealth of nations. I argue that it is possible to question such an assumption, and ask questions like: What is prosperity? Is it something that only can be measured in economic terms?

To define prosperity is not easy, but I will present three ideas on prosperity (see Jackson 2009; 2012 drawing on Amartya Sen). *Prosperity as opulence*, which corresponds to a conventional understanding that prosperity is about material satisfaction. The concept opulence refers to the ready availability and steady throughput of material commodities. If the volume flow of commodities increases, so does prosperity. This idea is based on the need to provide material commodities to meet the necessities of life, but, as Jackson (2009; 2012) argues, it is clear that this simple equation of quantity with quality, of more with better, is false in general. Thus, he means that the sense that more sometimes can be less provides the beginnings of an understanding of the dissatisfactions of the consumer society.

The second idea on *prosperity — as utility —* recognizes that opulence is not the same thing as satisfaction. Rather, this idea relates prosperity to the satisfaction that the commodities provide. This relation is complex, especially as consumer goods and services increasingly provide identity, experience, a sense of belonging and maybe meaning of living and a sense of hope. GNP is the sum of all market exchanges. "Broadly speaking, it measures the total spending across the nation on all commodities that flow through the economy" (Jackson, 2012). So in this perspective total spending is taken as a proxy for utility, a ground for believing that GNP is a useful measure for well-being. This measuring has been criticized on several grounds. I will here mention the so-called happiness or life-satisfaction paradox, meaning that there is no simple relationship between self-reported happiness/life-satisfaction and increased GNP. On the other hand, this measuring has been criticized. It has been argued that prosperity is about balancing between short-term arousal and long-term security, and neither GNP nor self-reported measures of happiness reflect an accurate reflection of this balance.

As an alternative, a third idea of prosperity is presented, based on the *capabilities* people have *to flourish*. This has to do with how well people are able to function in any given context — it is about functions such as living a long life, having a meaningful job and taking part in society. One aspect is the possibility of freedom to choose whether to take part in society, to work in paid employment or even to live a healthy lifestyle. It is the capability to flourish that is important. There are reasons to not take the focus on freedom too far, argues Jackson (2009; 2012). First, what value freedom of choice has is due not only to the choice itself but to the function. Second, in a world of limits, certain choices are impossible or immoral. To buy endless amounts of goods or to achieve certain social recognition at the expense of a collapse in biodiversity or by using child labour are examples of that. So it is rather a "'bounded capabilities' to live well — within certain defined limits" (Jackson 2012, p. 34). And two critical factors, ending ecological resources and the global population, can be mentioned in relation to these limits. A prosperous society can only be conceived as one in which all people everywhere have the capability to flourish in certain basic ways, without risking natural and human life on earth.

Central human capabilities

An alternative to the idea that GNP is the way to measure and compare the level of wealth and prosperity in a country, implying that growth is a way to prosperity, is actually already in use. The United Nations Development Program produces a Human Development Report each year that ranks nations in accordance with, not GNP, but using a human development approach based on theoretical work by Amartya Sen (see http://hdr.undp.org/en/humandev/). Martha Nussbaum has used the same approach and developed "central human capabilities" as a way to illuminate what it means for humans to flourish. She presents a list of ten capabilities, keys to a truly flourishing human life. Nussbaum invites negotiation in open dialogue and for different specification due to differences in histories and traditions. Her list incorporates:

Life. Being able to live to the end of a human life of normal length.

Bodily Health. Being able to have good health, including reproductive health; to be adequately nourished; to have adequate shelter.

Bodily Integrity. Being able to move freely from place to place; to be secure against violent assault.

Senses Imagination and Thought. Being able to use the senses, to imagine and to think.

Emotions. Being able to have attachments to things and people outside ourselves.

Practical Reason. Being able to form a conception of the good and to engage in critical reflection about the planning of one's life.

Affiliation. A/ Being able to live with and towards others; B/ having the social bases of self-respect and non-humiliation.

Other Species and the World of Nature. Being able to live with concern for and in relation to animal, plants and the world of nature.

Play. Being able to laugh, to play and to enjoy recreational activities.

Control over One's Environment. A/ Political: being able to participate effectively in political choices that govern one's life; B/ Material: being able to hold property and having property rights on equal basis with others; having the right's to seek employment on an equal basis with others (Nussbaum, 2007, p24).

As Mary Robinson, chair in "Realizing Rights, The Ethical Globalization Initiative" and former president of Ireland states in one foreword in Jackson (2012): "as remarkable progress the contrasts remain strong in the world today. In a time of prosperity for some, 54 countries are now poorer that they were a decade ago. The number of people living in chronic poverty and daily insecurity has not changed for the last decade or so, and women and children are disproportionately hard affected". So the way the economy works today, including increased consumption, does not seem to offer prosperity for all or social justice. The challenge is not new: how can we reach a state in the world where central human capacities for all becomes a reality?

The "iron cage of consumerism"

Thus, it is of great importance to recognize differences between individuals and between nations when discussing consumption. The striking fact is that one billion people across the world live on less than one US dollar a day. At the same time, we need to recognize that prosperity is not synonymous with increased income. Jackson (2009; 2012) discusses the role material artefacts play, and the fact that material commodities continue to be so important for us, long past the point at which material needs, such as food and shelter, are met. Consumer goods provide a symbolic language in which we communicate with each other continually. This communication is not only about the commodity itself; it is about identity, status, friendship, and a sense of belonging, meaning, purpose of life etc. It is tempting to believe that it is so only in the western part of the world, but it has been proven to be true in every society for which records exist. Novelty plays an important role in this communicative play; novelty has always carried information about social status. The American economist Veblen said more than a hundred years ago that "the consumption of luxuries, in the true sense, is a consumption directed to the comfort of the consumer himself, and is, therefore, a mark of the master" (Veblen, 1899, p. 49). Further, he argues that the consumption of latest appliances, food and fashions are accessible first only to the rich, and thus becomes a mark of status. Veblen names this conspicuous consumption. In this perspective, the individual is "at the mercy of social comparison" (Jackson, 2009, p. 65). Such social comparison is driven by an anxiety not to be left behind on the social ladder. In the long run, this social logic of consumerism, i.e. anxiety and the run for novelty can undermine well-being.

If we take for granted that material goods are of great social importance, there is a problem because we can never say that we have enough. The baseline for the comparison is always the current level of commodities. And this will continue to drive the material demand forward endlessly. The consumer is kept in the "iron cage of consumerism". Soper (2007; 2008) offers an alternative view on the role of consumption and of the consumer. She argues that so far the consumer almost always has been conceived as pursuing their private desires, either as more freely chosen or created or as systematically distorted or semiotically brought into being through the consumer society. What is lacking is a theorizing of the consumer as reflecting and responsible agents who can act responsibly in the world beyond their private interests. With the notion of *alternative hedonism* she highlights that this responsibility is not taken with self-restraint, but with the pleasure of breaking with the growth-driven, "shopping mall culture". In the concept of alternative hedonism lies an assumption that the motives for changing consumption practice derive from the negative aspects of consumption such as anxiety, run for novelty, in other words, the high-speed, work-dominated, materialistic lifestyle. It is the sense that important pleasures and sources of gratification are lost or unrealized as a consequence of such a lifestyle. The concept points to the fact that consumers can revise their conception of the good life as a result of the less enjoyable consequences of conspicuous consumption.

Home Economics education

Home Economics education has always had a relationship to social justice, as its aim is individuals and families well-being. I have argued elsewhere that the school subject in itself can be regarded as an anomaly, due to its aim. This because the school system, as we know it today, can be regarded as a result of the societal process leading to men leaving home to work in industry or other public domains. As Nicholson (1994) puts it: "As these two realms became distinguished in terms of both practices and norms, what arose was a need for an institution to socialize young people, primarily young boys, out of the family into the public world" (p78). Thus, it can be difficult to recognize a subject aiming towards home and family life and the well-being of individuals and families.

Swedish Home Economics education will here serve as an example. When the school subject was introduced in comprehensive school at the end of the 19th century, the main reason was to educate working- class women so that they could provide a healthy home for their family, even though salaries were low and living conditions often poor. Home Economics education could also be a start of a career, a way to earn one's own living while working, as maid in someone else's house or for women of middle and upper classes as for example a teacher. By studying Home Economics a girl could either become a good housewife or make a career in areas that at that time were considered suitable for women (see Johansson, 1987 & Hjälmeskog, 2000).

Many years and two world wars later, in 1962, through a school reform the whole Swedish school system changed. The aim was to give every child the same chance, independent of sex and socio-economic background. A National curriculum and National syllabus for Home Economics (and all other school subjects) was introduced. One important change concerning the subject was that it became compulsory for boys as well as girls. One way to meet this change was to highlight the consumer issues — the aim was to educate consumers, not housewives or housemaids, as had been the most important task before. It is emphasized in the syllabus from 1962 that every part of Home Economics education is 'consumer education'.

Also in the present syllabus for the subject, now named Home and Consumer Studies, consumer issues are highlighted. In the syllabi it is stated that knowledge of consumer issues as well as of housework gives the students important tools to make everyday life function, and the ability to make conscious choices as consumers (Lgr11). Further, I would argue that the revision of the National curriculum in 2011 has strengthened the vocational policy framework, for example by emphasizing the fostering of entrepreneurial spirit linked to the idea of ever-increasing GNP. This is in line with what has been put forward in the revised syllabus in Home Economics, such as issues concerning consumption and personal finances, such as saving, borrowing money, buying over the Internet and budget. At the same time, the focus has been narrowed from including the various activities in the household, covering food and meals and consumer economics as well as housing and intimate relationships/sense of community, to emphasizing food and meals. The core content is now grouped into three parts: food, meals and health; consumption and personal finance; and environment and lifestyle. Subject areas, for example concerning what makes a house a home, co-operation, communication and gender, have been reduced or rejected. What is kept is a care for the body, while what goes on in the mind, expressed for example in the syllabus from 2000 in terms of pleasure in domestic work, ethical views and living together in a diverse society, has been removed.

Considering alternative routes

In education today, at every level and subject, young people are encouraged to develop social justice and democratic ethics and thus reflect on social ends and values. At the same time, they are prepared for a labour market where competitive self-interest and a rather uncritical commitment to profit win the highest rewards. Soper (2008) argues that when education increasingly is subject to purely vocational policy frameworks, as it seems to be now, it holds back the variety of teaching content that would help to strengthen human capabilities, satisfaction and self-realisation in a less work-driven society. Education should, in her perspective, be a preparation for life rather than merely as an adjunct of industry.

Focusing on consumer education could mean an acknowledgement that increased consumption and the need for economic growth is a social construct — one way of interpreting the world and its future development. There are other options. Jackson (2012) presents a series of steps that are needed to effect the transition towards a sustainable economy. These steps fall into three categories: Building a sustainable macro-economy; protecting capabilities to flourishing, and respecting ecological limits. These are steps that need to be taken by governments, but it is a process also influencing, or even starting, at home. The second category, which concerns freeing people from the powerful social logic that locks them into materialistic consumerism, is the one step with direct bearing on Home Economics education.

One aspect is the importance of making explicit the desires that are implicit in the current expressions of consumer anxiety, and follow up with pointing out possible alternative structures of pleasure and satisfaction to which they refer (Soper, 2007). In this perspective, the materialistic consumerism is seen as *compromised* by its negative by-products such as stress, pollution, congestion, noise, ill health, loss of community and personal forms of contact etc., this is included in much Home Economics education today. It can be about making conscious consumer choices with regard to health, finance and the natural environment, locally and globally. But materialistic consumerism is also seen as *pre-emptive* of other enjoyments. For example a person living in a city is to a large extent denied the experience of silence or of full darkness or of the feeling and fresh fragrance of air-dried sheets; a person eating in conventional restaurants and living in accordance with "always get the best bargain" may never have tasted a sun-ripe tomato. And this is, I believe, not explicit in Home Economics education to any large extent. And is the satisfaction of consuming differently dealt with, i.e. are different conceptions of what a good life can be, and the role of work, domestic work, family and friends within it, included in Home Economics education?

There are already people around the world that resist the demand to "go out shopping", and instead spend their time on less materialistic pursuits such as gardening, walking, enjoying music or reading or to care for others. Some have even accepted lower income to achieve these goals (Jackson, 2012). Further, beyond this silent revolution there is a series of more radical initiatives aimed at living a less materialistic and more sustainable life. "Voluntary simplicity" is at one level an entire philosophy for life, drawing on the ideas of the Indian cultural leader Mahatma Gandhi. We can find examples in our time of initiatives in line with simplicity. More substantial examples such as Findhorn Community in Scotland and the Plum Village in France can be mentioned. The Simplicity forum and Downshifting Downunder are examples of networking. To what extent is that kind of living expressed and experienced within Home Economics education?

Many people trying to live more sustainably experience conflicts, not least due to the fact that in most societies pro-environmental behaviors are penalised, and thus it makes it nearly impossible even for highly-motivated individuals to act according to their own choice without great personal sacrifices. This highlights the boundaries of voluntariness. Simplified requests to consume less are bound to fail as long as the urge for consumption points in the opposite direction. Is this relationship between, on the one hand, the individual and the family, and politics and the societal structures on the other, dealt with in Home Economics education?

My aim with this chapter is not to present answers, but rather to highlight the importance of teachers being aware that they always have a choice when it comes to plan their teaching in Home Economics. I have discussed some of the present discussions on prosperity and ideas of the good and prosperous life and thereby illuminated what can be seen as alternative to ideas often taken for granted. Have I been discussing only Home Economics education in rich countries? No, I argue that this idea of an alternative, ecologically, economically and socially-sustainable conception of prosperity and good life can also "figure as an ideal thorough which less-developed countries can consider critically the conversations and goals of 'development' itself — and thereby understand the worst consequences of north-west 'over-development' and how to avoid them" (Soper, 2007, p223). I hope that this chapter can be an inspiration for home economists in any country.

Summary

When presenting views on prosperity as based on the capabilities people have to flourish, and on 'central human capabilities, as keys to enhance a flourishing life, I have tried to provide some tools to handle the task to educate for sustainable development. I urge critical consideration on Home Economics education in relation to:

- issues concerning what constitutes "good life", human flourishing and personal fulfilment,
- several views on consumption, for example hedonistic as well as 'alternative hedonism',
- consumption as compromised by its negative by-products, but also as pre-emptive of other enjoyments,
- visions of a future consumption built on less ecologically, economically and socially destructive production and consumption, and examples of different lifestyle choices,
- possibilities for individuals and families in relation to political and societal structures.

References

Bauman, Z. (1998). *Arbete, konsumtion och den nya fattigdomen.* Göteborg: Daidalos. (Original title: Work, Consumerism and the New Poor)

Hjälmeskog, K. (2000). *"Democracy begins at home". Utbildning om och för hemmet som medborgarfostran.* (English title: "Democracy begins at home". Education about and for Home and Family Life as Citizenship Education). Uppsala University: Department of Education.

Johansson, U. (1987). *Att skolas för hemmet. Trädgårdsskötsel, slöjd, huslig ekonomi och nykterhetsundervisning I den svenska folkskolan 1842–1919 med exempel från Sköns församling.* (English title: Schooling for the Home. Gardening, Handicraft, Domestic Science and Temperance instruction in

Swedish Elementary School 1842-1919. With an Example from the Parish of Skön). University of Umeå: Department of Education.

Jackson, T. (2009). *Prosperity without growth? The transition to a sustainable economy.* United Kingdom: Sustainable Development Commission. http://www.sd-commission.org.uk/

Jackson, T. (2012). *Välfärd utan tillväxt. Så skapar vi ett hållbart samhälle.* Stockholm: Ordfront Förlag.

Lgr62 (1962). *Läroplan för grundskolan* (National Curriculum for Comprehensive School). Skolöverstyrelsens skriftserie 60. Stockholm: SÖ-förlaget.

Lgr11 (2011). *National Curriculum for the Compulsory School, Preschool Class and the Leisure Time Centre.* Stockholm: Fritzes http://www.skolverket.com

Nicholson, L. (1994). Women and Schooling. In Lynda Stone (ed) *The Education Feminist Reader.* New York: Routhledge.

Nussbaum, M. (2007). Human Rights and Human Capabilities. *Harvard Human Rights Journal,* Vol. 20 pp21-24

Soper, K. (2007). Re-thinking the 'Good Life': The citizenship dimension of consumer disaffection with consumerism. *Journal of Consumer Culture,* Vol. 7, no 2, pp205-229

Soper, K. (2008). Exploring the relationship between growth and wellbeing. Think piece for the SDC Seminar: Living Well — within Limits, February 2008. London: Sustainable Development Commission. http://www.sd-commission.org.uk/pages/redefining-prosperity.html

Veblen, T. (1899). *The theory of the leisure class.* http://www.elegant-technology.com/TVwrite.html.

CHAPTER

11

From Ice Boxes to Smart Grids: Technology in the Homes of the Future

Gwendolyn Hustvedt, Christiane Pakula, Hester Steyn, Mira Ahn, and Rainer Stamminger

While the Copenhagen Institute for Future Studies (CIFS), which developed the 10 megatrends being considered in this book, suggests that these megatrends will have "different meanings for different companies, organizations and individuals, because we react, consciously or not, differently to trends…" the identified megatrends are much like waves sweeping the earth (CIFS, 2012). How we react to the trend is more important than debating the reach of the trend. The megatrend of "technological development" is one that has particular significance for home economists who are involved in work related to household technology. To better explore the impact of this particular trend on our field, this chapter examines how the megatrend of technological development intersects or encapsulates each of the other nine megatrends.

"The past century of invention and development…" that the introduction speaks of was a wellspring of technology that profoundly impacted the home. Refrigeration, cleaner and more efficient cook stoves, laundry equipment, safe water heating, heating and cooling … these technologies contribute to the improvement of the health of our families and the liberation of countless men and women from lives of service. It has freed our hands and minds for "higher activity". While eliminating many forms of employment related to the home, technology has also created new jobs that force us to learn new things. While many disciplines might consider the impact of this trend on larger organizations or levels in society, the home economist is required to envision and prepare for how the changes created by technological developments of the future (e.g. smart grid or the clean cook stove) will assist families to learn, change and adapt.

Research on the effects of technical devices and consumer behavior on private households is necessary to identify the Best Practice for doing a household job. The Programme Committee "Household Technology & Sustainability" (PC HT&S)

within IFHE is taking on this task; since its foundation in 2008, numerous international scientists have worked to collect and exchange data of global relevance and disseminate Best Practices for sustainable solutions for daily household work.

Technological Development

For more than a decade the reduction of greenhouse gas (GHG) emission has been the focus of many governments, policy makers and other stakeholders. Initially adopted in 1997, the Kyoto Protocol, aimed at fighting global warming, has been signed and ratified by 191 nations, 37 of which have committed themselves to reduce GHG emissions by 5.2% relative to their annual emissions in the base year 1990. During the world climate conference in Durban 2011, the majority of participating countries have reinforced the goal of restricting the global temperature increase to 1.5–2 °C in relation to the pre-industrial situation.

At the same time, the United Nations has declared the year 2012 to be the "Year of Sustainable Energy for All". Energy access is seen to be crucial for human well-being and economic development for all nations. The United Nations goal is therefore to provide universal modern energy access by 2030. The World Energy Outlook (WEO) 2011, published by the Organization for Economic Co-operation and Development (OECD) and the International Energy Agency, estimates that in 2009, 1.3 billion people (20% of the world population) lived without access to electricity and 2.7 billion people (40% of the world population) did not have clean cooking facilities (OECD, 2011). The WEO New Policies Scenario estimates an increase of the world primary energy demand of 36% by 2035, still leaving 1 billion people without access to electricity and 2.7 billion people without clean cooking facilities. Providing modern energy access for all would require a 2.5% increase in electricity generation. The demand for fossil fuels would rise by 0.8% causing an undesirable increase of GHG emissions by 0.7% compared to the estimates in the WEO New Policies Scenario.

As of yet, there is no universally agreed definition of modern energy access that could be used to measure progress towards this goal. The WEO defines it as "a household having reliable and affordable access to clean cooking facilities, a first connection to electricity and then an increasing level of electricity consumption over time to reach the regional average". The initial threshold level of electricity consumption for rural households is assumed to be 250 kWh per year. This could provide the use of two compact fluorescent light bulbs for about five hours per day, a mobile phone and a floor fan. For urban households, the initial level of electricity consumption is assumed to be 500 kWh per year (OECD, 2011).

Achieving universal access to energy while reducing GHG emissions will not be possible without renewable energy technologies. In general, providing electricity on grid is cheaper than mini-grid or off-grid supply. However, in remote areas the extension of the grid might be expensive and difficult. As more than 95% of people without access to electricity live in either sub-Saharan Africa or developing Asia and 84% live in rural areas, off-grid and mini-grid solutions are of high relevance in terms of providing access to electricity. In addition, simulations included in the "Energy for

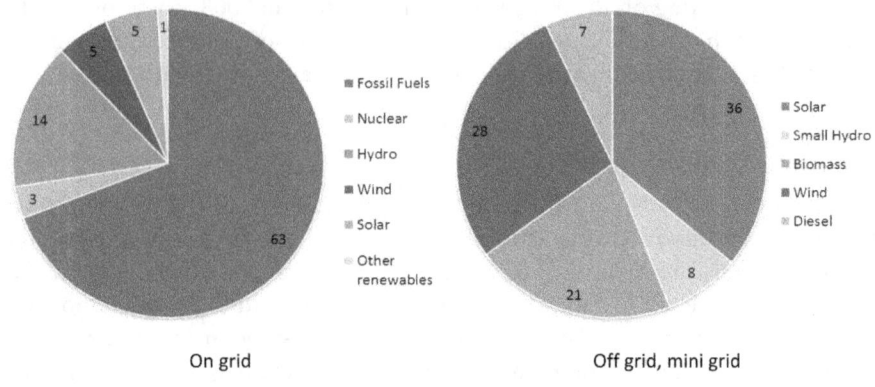

Figure 11.1

Sources for electricity generation from the World Energy Outlook 2011 (OECD, 2011).

All Case — 2030" (OECD, 2011) show that more than 60% of the additional on-grid generation will come from fossil fuels. In the case of mini-grid and off-grid generation, more than 90% can be provided by renewable energies (see Figure 11.1).

Lack of access to energy goes hand in hand with a lack of provision of clean water. Hydropower would thus play an important role in achieving universal energy access because the resulting water basins can provide two essential enablers for development: energy and water. The global technical potential for hydropower is estimated to be 14500 TWh, more than four-times current electricity production, with most of the undeveloped potential being in Africa and Asia. Of course, hydropower may have adverse environmental and social impacts, if not designed carefully.

The barriers to achieve universal modern energy access are surmountable, as many countries already have proven. Latin America expects universal access to energy by 2030 with renewables playing an important role. The project *Luz para Todos* (light for all) promotes renewable energy as the most practical solution in remote areas, with the government of Brazil providing financial support for renewable energy projects (OECD, 2011). However, reinforced efforts are still necessary to provide access to sustainable energy for all, particularly in remote areas of sub-Saharan Africa and developing Asia. The prize will be a great contribution to human well-being and long-lasting social and economic development.

Aging

According to the U.S. National Institute on Aging (NIA), the increased lifespan of consumers in almost all countries around the world, with the exception of some parts of Latin America and Africa, means that between 2005 and 2030 there will be a 104% increase in the number of people over the age of 65 (NIA, 2007). In developing countries this increase will be even more rapid as the number of people over 65 will increase by 140% by 2030 (NIA, 2007). Although the strong desire of many older persons is to grow old and possibly even die in their current home, and "aging in place" is not a new or unusual phenomenon, it has only recently become an emerging issue among researchers, policy-makers and designers, based on concerns about older peoples ability to function and live independently. From a societal perspective, aging in place is a cost-effective approach to support older adults' housing preference. However, numerous challenges exist to age in place, such as safety issues that result from the design and layout of the home without consideration of the aging process.

Recently, technology has had a tremendous impact on our daily lives, but the role of technology for assisting older persons to live independently has not been fully considered. The growing number of older people, together with the increasing societal costs of public health care and assistance, may lead to the need for housing that is accessible and equipped with assistive technology for helping elderly people live in their homes while maintaining a high quality of life. Independent living refers to the ability to live and function outside of an institutional setting; this is highly dependent on a person's ability to manipulate the designed environment. Most researchers agree that an elderly person's ability to function in activities of daily living is related to a person-environment problem. This is especially true for the home environment of elderly persons, because the amount of discretionary time spent inside the home increases with age.

Age-related losses in function and decline in cognitive abilities make older people susceptible to certain types of injuries such as burns, falls and poisoning from various home-related accidents. Many of these accidents stem from a combination of age-related deficiencies and poor ergonomics. Although correction of ergonomic problems may not require a high-tech solution, technology might improve an older person's safety by increasing that person's control of home conditions. This is the concept underlying a smart home, an approach that relies on the use of computer-driven integration of a home's automation control system, in which the system itself makes decisions and anticipates the desires and needs of the household.

Globalization

Technology has played an important role in the development of a globalized economy and the spreading and sharing of a globalized, Internet-based culture. In the previous 100 years, the spread of technology and culture has usually been in one direction as innovations spread from the developed world to the developing world. The next 100 years might show a different side of globalization. While the regional differentiation mentioned in the introduction is a strong possibility with technology, the aspect of this trend that is most exciting for Home Economics is the possibility that technologies, including household technologies, will be developed or adapted for the specific conditions of the developing world, that then provide important solutions for the developed world. The head of international development at the Carbon Trust, Cath Bremner, has pointed out that the idea of using "technology transfer" from the developed to the developing world to solve problems related to climate change is deeply flawed because developing nations lack important infrastructure, such as electrical grids (Carbon Trust, 2009). This means that the development of technology such as solar thermal and cooling to produce clean water and refrigeration for households is much more likely to originate in the developing world than anywhere else. Home economists need to remain alert and open to the idea the problem solving by families with fewer resources may be very valuable for solving problems for all families. In addition, despite the global spread of technology, there are certain advances in household technology that have not been adopted in a widespread way. When these technologies, such as the use of machines to quickly dry clothing, are proven to be unsustainable in terms of their impact on climate change, it is important for Home Economics professionals to resist the normalization of this technology by multinational firms and instead to encourage both families and producers of household technology to retain the more sustainable household technology configurations whenever they do not dramatically reduce quality of life.

Prosperity

Purchasing of household equipment requires a large enough investment for families to make it vital to urge all consumers to purchase wisely in terms of functionality and environmental impact. Technological developments lead to a constant flow of new and/or improved equipment into the market. The improved version often comes at a higher price. Consumers in lower income groups can barely afford the equipment and would often have to purchase the cheapest item that will meet their basic needs even when they are aware of the long-term benefits, including the reduction of energy or water costs, of the improved product. Consumers in the middle-income groups have more freedom to select new equipment and they tend to consider convenience and comfort rather than cost when purchasing. The ease and speed at which the goal of completing household tasks can be reached often outweighs other aspects, including the conservation of energy or water.

The upper-income family can afford the best products on the market and equipment is often purchased to extend the sense of the self and identity rather than to fulfil a need, thus becoming a form of social signalling. Purchasing of unnecessary equipment merely to signal newly-gained wealth places an undeniable and largely avoidable burden on the environment. The wealthy consumer is very often well aware of the impact of their purchasing and use of technology on the environment but won't adopt the environmentally friendly option if it might be slightly less convenient or less prestigious to use. As global prosperity increases, home economists must make an effort to develop best practices related to the selection and use of household technology and work to increase awareness on the part of wealthy consumers of the criteria they should use to select the most efficient and environmentally friendly equipment.

Acceleration

The acceleration of change in technology is undeniable and the changes in technology serve to reshape the landscapes of industrial, public and private spheres on a continuing basis. One important consideration in terms of the impact of the trend of acceleration on household technology is the relatively large investment required for most household technology, which serves as a barrier to easy replacement as technology changes. While consumers the world over are encouraged to adopt the new and latest mobile technology, and while a more sustainable cook stove or washing machine may cost only a bit more, in the long term, than the latest iPod, consumers are not rushing to replace household appliances with the same fervour.

This resistance of the household appliance stock to rapid turnover may be caused by several factors. Technology such as water heaters, toilets and furnaces in many regions of the world are "built in" to the home in such as way as to feel part of the very fabric of the house itself. While a television, a home appliance that has been subject to this acceleration trend, can be moved around the home easily, taken out of the home to share or even left out of the home entirely without damaging the ability of the house to function as a home, other household technology is just too integrated. Just as home fashions evolve at a much slower pace than apparel fashions, the technology that is inherently tied to the home may also have a naturally slower acceleration pace. This slower rate of acceleration does mitigate the waste-related impact pointed out in the previous prosperity trend, but it also makes the home more resistant to improvements in technology designed to increase the sustainability of homes and families.

Individualization

The technology of the Internet has already changed the world. As long as there is a connection to the Internet, individuals can be "virtually" everywhere they want to be. To older consumers, it seems that younger generations, such as those who were born between 1980 and 2000, take for granted and fully use this new technology more than previous cohorts. These younger consumers are typically thought to have an innate ability to use technology, to be driven by convenience and connectivity, and to have a healthy work-life balance that helps to maintain relationships.

New ways to communicate, work and shop might change the sense of the place, including the meanings of home, in such a way that future generations might not value the traditional housing norms — owning a single family detached home with a private backyard. Younger consumers in the developed world already do more activities in "cyber space", including socializing, blogging or gaming using platforms such as Facebook. While they are always connected to the outside world, they do not need to be physically connected to make their connection to others. To them, home has become more than a shelter; it is the primary location of their interface with the virtual world. Although home economists can use their work in environmental design to change behaviors by designing spaces to promote more interactions, the reliance on Internet technology for social interaction will be exacerbated by the trend of individualization.

Commercialization

For many years, the energy efficiency of household appliances has been the driving force for the technological development of washing machines, dishwashers, refrigerators and other every day devices used in homes. However, consumers often have no way to accurately conceptualize the electricity and water consumption of specific household appliances. Like other regions of the world (e.g. the US or Canada), the point of sale labeling mandated in Europe has improved consumer understanding of the energy and water consumption and different use properties (e.g. noise emission, cleaning performance or capacity) of the appliance they are considering. Due to the technical progress, most of the appliances sold today have already achieved the best performance class, with classes ranging from dark green A (very good) to red G (very bad). The trend of commercialization however, will require companies to produce products that can be clearly differentiated from the competition. To assist in helping consumers choose the right appliance from the range of sustainable offerings, a new European energy label was introduced in December 2010 that demonstrates the ability of labeling to harness the trend of commercialization in order to improve household sustainability (Figure 11.2).

While the new energy label is currently mandatory for washing machines, refrigerators and dishwashers, it will soon cover other appliances (New Energy Label, 2011). The intention is that step by step the worst performance class will be eliminated and by 2020 all new appliances will be required to meet the new, increased standards that now range up to A^{+++}. Besides the electricity and water consumption of the appliance, the label provides consumers with additional information about performance features of appliances such as the cleaning performance, spinning performance, capacity or noise emission.

Figure 11.2

Energy label for washing machines (New Energy Label, 2011).

Health and Environment

While human health is dependent on the availability of clean water and fresh air, the need for safe and nutritious food also implies availability of energy for cooking and food storage. Finding clean energy sources for food preparation is all the more important because almost 3 billion people are currently dependent on biomass fuel such as wood for cooking and warmth. The biomass is often burned in open fires indoors, polluting the air with carbon dioxide, carbon monoxide, methane, nitrogen oxides, sulphur dioxide, volatile organic compounds and particulates causing lung diseases and eye irritation to the inhabitants. Small children and elderly are the most vulnerable to the effects of the pollutants. In 2010 the United Nations and the World Health Organization founded the "Alliance for Clean Cook stoves — a public/private partnership of different stakeholders who work together to save lives, empower women, improve livelihoods and combat climate change by creating a thriving global market for clean and efficient household cooking solutions" (GACC, 2011). The IFHE joined the alliance as a "Champion" partner and the PC HT&S supports the vision and mission of the Alliance and aims to use every opportunity to disseminate the information.

The goal of this effort is to produce cook stoves that are energy efficient, reduce the indoor pollution, reduce the resources used and emit little smoke, even when used with biomass fuels, which in many regions is still the only reliable option. A biomass clean cook stove is designed to provide sufficient ventilation, leading to improved combustion and reduced smoke emission. Improved control of the flow of hot air in these appliances leads to a much more efficient use of the biomass. In conjunction with efforts to spread the availability and use of clean cooking technology, home economists should continue to encourage the responsible harvest of biomass until such time as alternative fuels sources become globally available.

Network Organizing

Renewable energy sources such as solar and wind power will produce more energy during sunny or windy times of day. The increasing inclusion of these renewable energy sources in the future energy supply will require much closer coordination of electricity generation and demand, so that the demand for electricity by household can match the level of energy being generated, rather than the opposite, which is the case where energy is produced on demand using fossil fuels. The trend of network organizing will benefit energy plants, electricity suppliers and consumers by expanding the use of "smart grids" with bi-directional communication between the generation and the demand side in order to create a flexible load management.

To use Europe as an example, approximately 30% of all electricity is consumed by private households, specifically by home technology, making the inclusion of domestic appliances into future flexible-energy systems of obvious importance. Examination of appliances used by the typical European household identifies air conditioners, water heaters and heating circulation pumps as the devices with the highest proportion of the peak power demand in the evening. The appliances that provide the best opportunity for short interruptions in electrical supply are heating circulation pumps and water heaters. When these three thermal devices are being excluded from the load analysis, the appliances with the best potential to shift their operation in time are washing machines, tumble dryers and dishwashers; refrigerators seem to have the best potential for short-term breaks.

When considering only one average household, the potential for load-shifting by the use of smart appliances seems to be small. The maximum power demand which might be reduced at a single point in time during one day based on the assumptions made in the study ranges from 13 W per average household in the South to about 57 W in the North of Europe. But when taking all households in a region such as Europe into account, 18 GW may be shifted to flatten the load peak by using smart appliances that can respond to fluctuations in the available energy supply. This equals to the capacity of 30 conventional coal fired energy plants that would no longer be needed.

Urbanization

Urbanization puts a lot of stress on the infrastructure of a city. Service delivery in water supply and human waste removal are of the utmost importance for healthy living conditions. One flush toilet per family is generally considered as the minimum standard in the developed world and an important aim of development plans. But, the water supply in many cities falls short of the need, and with development the need will increase. Flushing toilets are the single item in the home that uses the most water. Improvements in the development of efficient, low water-consumption toilets are urgently required. The dual-flush system was a big step ahead but still not enough.

In developed countries, water is cleaned to a level safe for drinking and food preparation, but this cleaned water is used too often for flushing toilets and gardening as well. Gray water gathered from roofs after rain, from the shower and the washing machine, can be a suitable source of water to flush toilets and for watering the lawn. Using gray water for flushing requires a reserve tank, a pump and a pipe system to link the gray water with the toilet. The adaptation might seem costly to start with but would be beneficial to the family and the environment in the long run. Desalination of seawater is an expensive process used in many dry areas to provide water to all. The planning of separate water-supply systems for clean drinking water and using seawater for toilets might relieve the stress on water supply in coastal areas considerably. However, the issue remains that for the vast number of people living in the increasingly urban regions of the world, access to clean drinking water and protection from human waste remains one of the greatest challenges to sustainable household technology.

Dimensions of Practice

As an academic discipline, Home Economics is transdisciplinary and uses a wide range of methods to cover a wide range of topics all related in one way or another to the life of families and individuals within their homes. The education of future scholars who can make contributions to the area of household technology should not be neglected in the face of academic trends towards focuses on educating for currently desirable outcomes rather than planning for long-term sustainability. While only a few institutions around the world have become leaders in research and education in household technology, the development of international research teams, such as the PC HT&S of IFHE, has the potential to engage in research and development that reaches beyond previous institutional boundaries. However, these efforts must also strive for interdisciplinary projects that also reach beyond disciplinary boundaries, both within and outside of Home Economics, in order to create the synergy that will build the new knowledge needed to help our discipline help families adapt to the rapid changes in technology.

The PC HS&S has worked to develop solutions that will help bring solutions out of the laboratory and into the second dimensions of everyday life. Best Practices in dish cleaning and cooking have been developed by the committee members and will be disseminated through IFHE and other consumer education outlets. Future Best Practices will include laboratory-tested solutions for food storage and clothes laundering. These best practices can be incorporated easily into the third dimension of the curriculum. Home Economics curriculums should also be designed to incorporate changing technology concerning a wide variety of topics (i.e. nutrition and foods, interior design, textile and apparel, etc.) in order to educate all students on the role of technology, specifically household technology, in resource management for a sustainable future.

In the final dimension of practice, it is the responsibility of Home Economics professionals to influence policy to facilitate both liveable and sustainable household technologies. Because the production of household technology is the source of income for numerous, vast, multinational corporations, home economists have the responsibility to serve as advocates for families in balance to the power of these corporations whenever the health, well-being or sustainability of families is at stake. In areas where the wealth and innovation of the captains of industry are not being brought to bear, such as the provision of clean and safe water to families in rural or developing regions, it is our responsibility to work with as many stakeholders as possible to advocate for the development of technology that can solve these unprofitable problems.

Summary

- To summarize, the International Federation of Home Economics PC HT&S takes the position that the quest for alternative energy sources that can reduce or eliminate our dependence on fossil fuels will be the most important driver for the megatrend of technology in the next 100 years. The framework of the megatrends has been an excellent means to explore many issues related to household technology and to imagine how each of the megatrends will influence changes in technology for families in the future. When families do not adapt and change their methods of completing everyday tasks, even when the technology has advanced, significant

gains in sustainability are lost. For this reason, the committee encourages any professionals in a position to influence curriculum to advocate for the development and inclusion of educational objectives that relate to household technology.
- Developing a variety of affordable alternative energy sources that can be used by the wide variety of households across the globe is the most important task in the area of technological development.
- Not every important technological development in households should be "high-tech". Many families need access to clean water, waste-handling systems that do not require water and clean methods to cook their food.
- The megatrends of prosperity, acceleration and individualization may push technological developments that do not necessarily improve the quality of life for families.
- Networking by home appliances via a smart grid and the connection of appliances to the growing social networks has the potential to greatly reduce the stress of increasing energy demand on aging electrical systems.
- Among the four dimensions of practice incumbent on home economists, the curriculum area is perhaps the most vital to helping families adapt in a sustainable way to the rapid changes in technology, including household technology, that are washing over the globe.
- Teams of home economists such as the PC HS&S that actively seek members from other disciplines and regions to join their work can have a vital and revitalizing influence on any of the disciplines covered within Home Economics.

Discussion Prompts

- Why is it important for organizations that produce consumer labeling for household appliances to provide a mechanism to update the label in order to maintain differentiation for the most efficient products once the intended effect of labeling has been achieved?
- When we think of technological development, we often forget the lowly flush toilet. How will a development project such as the "peepople" (http://www.peepople.com), a portable bag system designed to collect and neutralize human waste, improve household sustainability?
- Historically, many tasks now performed by household technology were located outside the home. As home economists face the megatrend of urbanization, is it important to advocate the "sharing" of energy intensive technologies such as clothes cleaning and oven facilities by multiple households?
- It is important for education about household sustainability to be spread broadly across the Home Economics curriculum. How could Best Practices for the use of household appliances be incorporated into disciplines that focus on food, family and human development or fashion?

References

Carbon Trust, (2009). *Blueprint for global collaboration on clean energy*. Retrieved from http://www.carbontrust.co.uk/news/news/press-centre/2009/Pages/blueprint-global-collaboration-clean-energy.aspx

Copenhagen Institute for Future Studies, (2012). *Why megatrends matter*. Retrieved from http://www.cifs.dk/scripts/artikel.asp?id=1469

Hausgeräte Plus, (2012). *Washing and drying*. Retrieved from http://www.hausgeraete-plus.de/waschen_und_trocknen/index.php

New Energy Label. (2012). *Discover the new EU energy label*. Retrieved from http://www.newenergylabel.com/index.php/de/discover_the_label

National Institute on Aging. (2007). Why population aging matters: A global perspective. (Publication No. 07-613). Washington, D.C.: National Institutes of Health. Retrieved from http://www.nia.nih.gov/NR/rdonlyres/9E91407E-CFE8-4903-9875-D5AA75BD1D50/0/WPAM.pdf

Organization for Economic Co-operation and Development and International Energy Agency (2011). *World energy outlook*. Organization for Economic Co-operation and Development: Paris.

CHAPTER
12

Everyday Life of Families in the Global World

Hille Janhonen-Abruquah

This chapter discusses how the megatrend of globalization looks from the point of view of a migrant family and how it can be researched from a Home Economics science point of view. Family is here viewed through eco-cultural theory. It is seen as an active unit that is able to accommodate to each new situation. Family operates across national borders.

At the end of the chapter, the four dimensions of practice from the International Federation of Home Economics IFHE Position Statement (2008) are reviewed in light of global Home Economics.

Migration at global level

At the global level, migration has accelerated as a result of globalisation and economic integration; people may cross borders voluntarily in search of economic opportunities and social alternatives, or be forcibly displaced by conflict, natural resource degradation, disasters or human trafficking. In the century, one out of every 35 people worldwide is an international migrant, and half of them are women. Remittances, transfers of funds from migrant workers to relatives or friends in their place of origin, have become an increasingly important feature of modern economics. Funds attributable to remittances have increased the availability of household resources, and this income has the potential to improve the quality of life in the receiving areas. On the downside, migration disrupts households and family ties. Newly arrived individuals and families are often marginalised, as they have yet to integrate into the social networks that can help them meet basic requirements.

Definition of transnational family, home and everyday life

The term transnational (Basch et al. 1994) acknowledges that it is possible for people to belong to several locations at the same time, and thus have a number of identities. Grass-root level relationships — both in the new homeland and in the country of origin — are important, from both social and economic perspectives. The concept of transnational family means here that immigrants are taking actions in two or more nation states (Basch et al., 1994). They live some or most of the time separated, but are able to create a sense of 'family-hood' and form a survival unit (Bryceson & Vuorela, 2002; Schmalzbauer, 2004). Remittances play an important role in their lives (Levitt & Glick-Schiller, 2004) and the migration has produced so-called super diverse identities (Vertovec & Cohen, 1999) where referring to the passport nationality does not anymore tell much of one's identity. Carrington (2002) saw the contemporary family as a socio-space that is characterised by an imagined community, the construction and maintenance of social bonds and support networks. In the socio-space, it is possible to operate across time-space boundaries. Family members may no longer be in the same local time and place but they are able to utilise technologies such as e-mail, the Internet, and telephone to provide instant access. The transnational family operates in a space that is called home.

Home, therefore, does not necessarily refer only to a specific place of origin or homeland but may also be a place of belonging and identification that changes as individual life trajectories change (Olwig, 2003, p. 2). Personal ties give meaning to this place and it develops through time. Olwig (2003, p. 7) reminds us that home has a central role as a locus where respectability is both displayed and gained. Sending regular remittances is done as a duty but also to gain respect in the local community. For men, it is important to build a house in the place of origin. The notion of home has thus taken on a new meaning. Home is defined as the location or space where the transnational family operates. It is used in the concrete sense to describe a physical place and the surroundings of the transnational families. However, home is also used in a broader sense to describe the socio-space, in Carrington's (2002) sense, where the walls and borders are invisible.

Everyday life is the context where transnational families operate and where their homes exist. Transnational families are formed by the people and their homes are made out of the family-hood they manage to create. Everyday life is the context, the environment where they operate and act, and by doing that they change their everyday life. Everyday life is the context where the habitual and mundane daily activities of immigrant women take place. Everyday life is an active process. It belongs to everyone and is personal and uniquely experienced. Everyday life exists and also continues in transnational families' home of origin as well as in their new home country. Thus everyday life is a meaningful context to study immigrant women. Everyday life is defined as personally experienced active process and a social context where the people operate. Everyday life has dimensions like mode and space (Felski 2000/1999, 2002).

Researching and analysing transnational families

A research (Janhonen-Abruquah, 2010) was carried out amongst immigrant women who were currently living in Finland. It asked how transnational everyday life is constructed. As everyday life, due to its mundane nature, is difficult to operationalize for research purposes, mixed data collection methods were needed to capture the passing moments that easily become invisible. Thus, the data were obtained from photographic diaries (459 photographs) taken by the research participants themselves. Additionally, stimulated recall discussions, structured questionnaires and participant observation notes were used to complement the photographic data. To analyse the data content analysis was first carried out to find out the emerging themes in women`s everyday life. Then a matrix was developed based on the theoretical understanding of everyday life to reveal the modal, social and spatial dimensions of the practices.

The modal dimension of activities describes whether activities take place regularly and continuously or if they present exception to this routine. Routine is something that happens regularly e.g. daily, weekly, and is or can be planned to some extent. Exceptions take place unintentionally or require special, long-term planning.

The social dimension of daily activities describes how activities are carried out in the social context. It describes activities that are done in order to benefit us, the family, the immediate others. Sometimes things are done mainly to benefit the one who is doing them. Activities that are done 'for me', are those where one is working towards one's own goal — to improve one's future, to provide pleasure or enjoyment. In everyday life favours are done for others. Tasks carried `for immediate others` are those activities where one is caring for others, doing something for other family members' well-being. Activities are also carried out together with others, with immediate others'. There are tasks that are carried out jointly, but also events and times where people simply are together.

Spatial dimension describes the context of a practice. It highlights the location of the activity. In the simplest form it means whether activities take place in the physical home or outside; it is a category of indoors — outdoors activities. The locations are physical places where activities are taking place.

The research findings were summarized in the form of a hot air balloon flight model.

Taking a hot air balloon flight

The eco-cultural theory (Gallimore et al., 1989, 1993a, 1993b) is concerned with the relationship between humans and society, but more precisely family and its environment. Eco-cultural theory sees family as proactive, as constantly determining how the limits set by the society, global and national economy and ecology affect the family. A family changes its daily routines in order to accommodate changes to the environment. These ecological features and changes, either global or local, directly affect the daily routines of a family. For example, the hurricane in North America affected oil prices, the price of fuel went up and, as a result, a mother on the other side of the

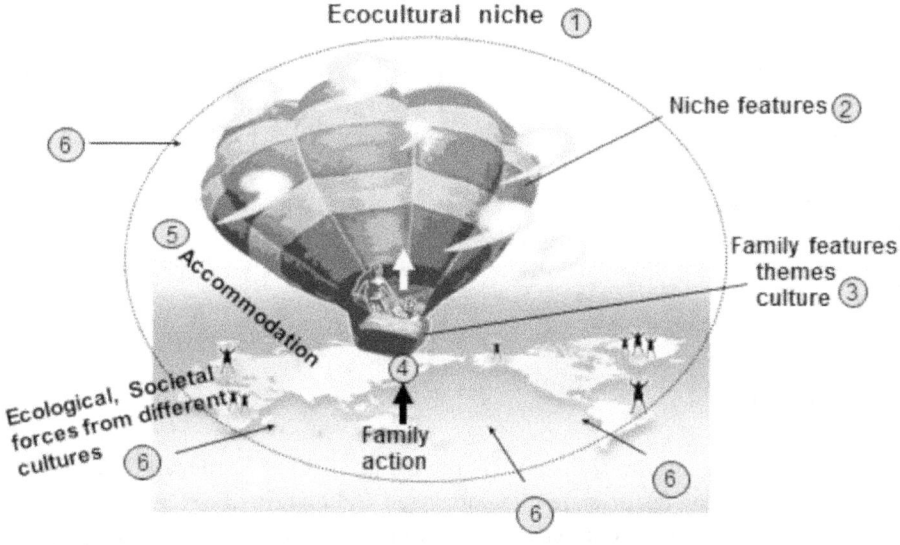

Figure 12.1

Hot Air Balloon Flight Model Describing the Everyday Life of Transnational Families.

world had to commute to work by public transportation and the picking up of the children from day care had to be reorganized. Global changes have local effects, and eco-cultural forces affect the family routines.

Below, transnational everyday life will be described through the lens of eco-cultural theory, using the model of a hot air balloon flight. This helps to see daily family life from a dynamic point of view. The hot air balloon does not fly haphazardly, nor is it under full control. There is a need to see family members as active agents who are to some extent capable of influencing their own activities. This model also helps to visualize the very essence of transnational families. There are both local and global forces which prevent as well as facilitate daily actions and accommodations.

Eco-cultural niche

Families construct their eco-cultural niches (Figure 12.1, number 1) from the mix of forces (Figure 12.1, numbers 2, 3 and 6) and actions (Figure 12.1, numbers 4 and 5). Families are strongly affected by social and economic forces but they still take individual and collective action to modify and counteract their everyday life (Gallimore et al 1989, p. 217–218). Home for the transnational families is defined as the physical place and surroundings but also a socio-space where the walls and borders are invisible. The eco-cultural niche is closely connected with concepts like proximal home environment (Bronfenbrenner, 1986) and socio-space (Carrington, 2002). Home is like an eco-cultural niche.

In the research (Janhonen-Abruquah, 2010) women defined their homes. Stina said that her home is where her heart is as she was looking forward to her boyfriend coming to her new home country. Inga commented that a person just gets richer the more homes she has and referred to the fact that she has a home in her new home country but also her childhood home in the country of origin is still important.

Tiilikainen (2003) studied multicultural families in the Finnish context. In diasporas, Somali women create their home by combining several places and locations into a place like home. Daily routines, social memories, extended family, Islam, ritual, language and collaboration with other women play an important role in building such a home in a new land (Tiilikainen, 2003, p. 282).

Niche features

The niche features (Figure 1, number 2) can be described as the statistical facts and framework for the family. They provide the fringe area where the family action can take place. The niche features are interconnected and hierarchical. These features can be either positive resources or negative constraints. A good education and high salary are not necessarily resources, and a low income is not automatically seen as a constraint. The valence of features depends on the meaning a family gives to them (Gallimore et al 1989, p. 222). Niche features set a kind of a borderline within which the families can operate.

Niche features in the research (Janhonen-Abruquah, 2010) were country of origin, language skills, education, profession, age, marital status, number of dependants and the fact that they live in a city, most likely in a block of flats. Niche features are not necessarily constraints or opportunities. It depends how they are used or how it is possible to use them.

For example, the variety of language skills might look like an opportunity, but it seemed in the study (Janhonen-Abruquah, 2010) that it was only the Finnish language that had benefited the women. They had to learn the new home country language before their other language skills could benefit them.

Family features

A group of emotionally attached people — a family — is at the centre of the eco-cultural theory. Family features (Figure 1, number 3) are like goals and future hopes of the family. They are described through the concepts family themes and family culture. Family themes are like aims or aspirations of the family. For example, providing a normal childhood for the children or keeping the family together. Family themes are put into practice through daily family activities. The specific family culture is made out of a combination of family themes. The concept of culture is not seen as national or ethnic culture but as family culture, and it is not a stereotyped view but one that sees the family as unique.

What are the aims and aspirations of these women (Janhonen-Abruquah, 2010) in the midst of their group of emotionally attached people? Family features have a future orientation. Stina says she wants to raise her children in the new home country and have family members living in her new home country as well. Lidia wants to move together with her husband to another new home country. They might move further — 'to somewhere warm'. Azra wants to live in a peaceful country, like Finland. Maria's husband likes small villages and is wondering if they should move back to the little village in North Finland. Inga is hoping to contribute to the family income now that she has graduated with a profession. Beene hopes that her daughter from Cameroon can get a permit to come to Finland. Anja hopes for the best for her daughters and if things do not go well with her daughter's fiancée, she is always welcome back home. Ida is dreaming of a nice husband. Somehow it seems that before these aims come true they require major sacrifices: moving, learning new languages, finding a job.

Family action

Families proactively construct their family ecology and routine (Figure 1, number 4). Not only are families shaped by the social world around them, they also help to shape that world. Meaningful and sustainable daily routines have a moral and cultural significance and value for family members. Daily routines are the contact point between individuals and the surrounding cultural and ecological environment. Sustainable daily routines, according to eco-cultural theory, have some stability and predictability, they are meaningful, there is congruence and balance and the available resources roughly match the activities the family engages in.

In the research (Janhonen-Abruquah, 2010) everyday activities were placed on continua which described the mode of activities, social context of activities and their spatial arrangements. Mode of activities described the distinction between routine and exceptional events. The research showed seven different spatial arrangements: place to learn, to have friends, to organize food, to provide order and cleanliness, to rest, allowing space for children and to care. The social dimension describes activities that are done in order to benefit us, the family, the immediate others. Activities are done either for the one who is doing them, for others or together with others. It was also interesting to look at activities that did not take place. Women did not talk or practice their hobbies and they did not go for holidays.

Accommodation

Daily activities reveal how the process of accommodation (Figure 1, number 5) takes place. Accommodation refers to the proactive, social construction of actions as the family is adapting, exploiting, counterbalancing and reacting to many competing and sometimes contradictory forces like income needs, health, domestic workload and the like. Such accommodation can be unconscious, and the forces that drive families may be only dimly perceived by the parents.

The accommodation process in the eco-cultural model has many similarities with Berry's (1992) acculturation model and Ong's (2003) cultural citizenship — ethnic assimilation concepts. The ability to cross boundaries, worlds and cultural borders is essential in the accommodation process; the study of cultural intelligence (Earley and Ang, 2003, p. 59) provides additional theoretical tools to understand this process better.

Earley and Ang (2003, p. 16) claimed that the challenge for an international sojourner is that most of the cues and behaviors that are familiar at home may be lacking in the new cultures, so entirely new interpretations and behaviors are required. This ability is cultural intelligence, which is an individual characteristic. Earley and Ang (2003, p. 64–65) see an 'emic construct' when cues have their basis within a given culture and are only fully appreciated and understood within this context. An emic construct gains meaning from its context and, fully absent from its contextual interpretation, cannot be appreciated. For example, witnessing a crowd of noisy people holding long sticks and gathering by the lakeside around a large bonfire at midnight in the middle of summer can have a totally different interpretation if it is not understood as part of a Finnish Midsummer celebration. An 'etic construct', on the other hand, has characteristics that exist across cultures and is universal. For example, all people have certain cognitive functions such as memory and recall, and social institutions like marriage and mourning of a lost loved one. Earley and Ang's emphasis is on etic aspects of intelligence that provides individuals with the capacity to operate across various cultural boundaries (Earley and Ang, 2003, p. 16).

Daily activities could be seen on a continuum that at one end maintains traditional practices, at some point adapts to the current situation and in the other end of the continuum new practices were created (Janhonen-Abruquah 2010). This was seen in the units of activity settings and in the transformation that took place. Information technology — and especially its easy access forms like mobile phone, cheap internet calls, and free internet services — has provided a link or bridge between family members living in different countries. Even though IT devices are more easily associated with use by men they still play an important part in immigrant women's social lives. They have provided a medium for a new kind of social interaction which resembles traditional family dining in many ways. IT devices were definitely not designed to improve the family dining moments among mass migration settlers in various countries, but this side effect has been a benefit to migrant women. Information technology is the 'mediational mean' in this study. Social interaction has dramatically changed from the times of early settlers in New World (Bryceson & Vuorela 2002). A letter across the Atlantic took months and now the relatives in America are on-line. Such technical development has opened new avenues for building virtual belongingness. Mass migration has changed from the American frontiers to the modern-day frontiers because the cultural tools have changed and cultural, historical and institutional settings are different.

In the Tan Dum (2002) concert, modern technology made it possible to join together two different musical and cultural traditions. In the live concert, Chinese village musicians and a North European symphony orchestra played simultaneously. Two remote corners of world were brought together and formed a new kind of experience. In the study (Janhonen-Abruquah 2010) 'virtual dining' has similar features. 'Virtual dining' is a concept that describes the novel-type dining emerging amongst trans-national families. Family dining is such an important part of human life that it will be recreated even when family members live apart. In 'virtual dining' family members join the table through computers and on-line applications. Some ingredients are mailed from homes of origin and combined with the local ones. Even the gender roles seem to shift. Men cook the food their mothers and sisters used to cook in their countries of origin. Information technology is playing a major role in joining and combining traditional patterns with something new and thus novel practices are created.

Accommodation is one of the key concepts. It has a major role in eco-cultural theory and is important in discussions with immigrants and their domiciling process. Accommodation has also been central to Home Economics research. Combining the demands of work life and family life, using new domestic appliances or managing with the lack of resources like time and money are key concerns that require adaptation.

Accommodation was analyzed through three phases: maintaining traditions, adapting and re-creating practices. In other words, women's narrations were analyzed in terms of how they were maintaining traditions, how they were learning to perform Finnish practices and what novel ways were invented to carry out daily activities. The units of activity settings are analyzed in the light of how traditions are maintained, how adaptation and accommodation takes place and what kind of new practices are re-created. Special attention was given to the use of tools and artefacts. For example, some kitchen tools would be needed in order to prepare some traditional dishes. Whereas some other kitchen machines, like a bread-making machine, would change the traditional way of preparing bread.

Ecological forces

Ecological forces (Figure 1, number 6) are the limiting factors and resources, constraints and opportunities set by society, national and global politics and economic factors. These are forces that a single individual has little or no power to alter.

In the research (Janhonen-Abruquah 2010) there seemed to be mainly three factors: education, refugee background and their men that operated as ecological forces to direct their route to Finland. Some of the women reached Finland with a refugee background and the hope to find peace. The men had not been very visible in the research otherwise but some of them had directly or indirectly influenced the women's route to Finland. The education system, at least programs that were in English, seemed to be attractive. It was hoped that Finnish education would open the door to the Finnish labor market and improve the quality of life.
About the Home Economics approach

Research choices were made in line with the discipline of Home Economics science. As Home Economics is an arena for everyday living (IFHE 2008, Position Statement), the research thus focused on immigrant women acting in their everyday contexts. The strength of Home Economics is that it often tries to improve everyday life from a practical point of view. Immigrant women with different ethnic backgrounds have their traditional daily practices. As they live in their new home country some of their daily practices change; they adapt and re-create new practices.

As Home Economics is also a curriculum area (Position Statement) it has potential for easing the domiciling process of immigrants. Home Economics based courses, projects and interventions would help immigrant women adapting to the Finnish socio-cultural environment. Home Economics is closely connected to learning and education as it has a straightforward connection to teaching skills needed in everyday life. Home Economics is a field of formal study including such topics as consumer education, institutional management, interior design, home furnishing, cleaning, handicrafts, sewing, clothing and textiles, cooking, nutrition, food preservation, hygiene, child development and family relationships. Combining Home Economics knowledge with domiciling practices would open new areas for course and intervention planners. As Home Economics is a societal arena (Position Statement), the research findings of this research should be implemented. Policy and decision makers would need to take into consideration the research findings whilst planning and implementing new domiciling projects.

Migration studies, and especially transnational theory, give Home Economics science as an academic discipline (Position Statement) a more dynamic starting point. The actors, the acting and the context are literally on the move all the time. Home can no longer be viewed as static, permanently fastened to specific physical location or nation. This, of course, brings new challenges to Home Economics research. As everyday life is mundane and difficult to capture for research purposes, immigrant families open a new context for research. In immigrants' everyday lives a lot of the features are easier to see, even though, actually, they take place in everyone's lives. For Home Economics research, the method used in the study (Janhonen-Abruquah 2010) is worth using and further developing. Photograph elicitations together with participant observations provided rich data. The method should be developed by involving the research participants even more closely to the analysis. Home Economics research and teaching should be based on research-backed knowledge about everyday life. What did this research technique bring to Home Economics research that is new? It provided an ethical way of entering private family lives in the sense that the researcher sees what the research participants want to show. Creative use of photographs could open new approaches not only for various immigrants' domiciling projects, interventions and family support but to Home Economics research in general.

Summary

The key concepts of this chapter are summarized below.
- The concept of *transnational* refers here to the fact that people belong to several locations at the same time. They may be taking actions in two or more nation states and have super diverse identities. *Family* as a socio-space is characterised by an imagined community, the construction and maintenance of social bonds and support networks. It is possible for the *transnational family* to operate across time-space boundaries.

- *Home* is a place of belonging and identification that changes as individual life trajectories change. It is a location and space where the transnational family operates.
- *Everyday life* is defined as personally experienced active process and a social context where the people act. Everyday life has dimensions like mode and space.
- *Ecocultural niche* is a place where a family tries to maintain a comfortable and sustainable daily life. Home.
- *Niche features* are the statistical facts and framework of the family. For example, time use of a family, organization of everyday-life domestic tasks, child-care tasks, type of work parents are doing, type of neighbourhood family is living in.
- *Family features* are family themes and family culture. Family themes are the aims and aspirations of the family. Family culture is formed by the combination of family themes.
- *Family action* is the sustainable routine of daily actions. It is characterised by A) social ecological fit B) congruence and balance C) meaningful D) stability and predictability.
- *Accommodation* refers to the adapting, exploiting, counterbalancing and reacting to many competing and/or contradictory forces.
- *Ecological forces* are the limiting factors and resources, constraints and opportunities set by society/ environment, national and global politics and economy.

Discussion Prompts

- The hot air balloon flight model can be used to describe any family. How would your own family look like if you put yourself in the hot air balloon basket?

- What other relevant definitions for family, home and everyday life can you find from literature? How do they differ from the ones presented in this chapter?

References

Basch, L., Glick Schiller, N. & Blanc, C. S. (1994). *Nations Unbound: Transnational Projects, Postcolonial Predicaments and Deterritorialized Nation States.* New York: Gordon and Breach.
Berry, J.W. (1992). Acculturation and adaptation in a new society. International Migration. *Quarterly Review, 30,* 69–85.
Bronfenbrenner, U. (1986). Ecology of the family as a context for human development: Research perspectives. *Developmental Psychology, 6,* 723–742.
Bryceson, D. & Vuorela, U. (eds) (2002). *The Transnational Family. New European Frontiers and Global Networks.* Oxford, New York: Berg.
Carrington, V. (2002). *New Times: New Families.* Boston: Kluwer Academic Publishers.
Dun, T. (2002). *The Map: Concerto for Cello, Video and Orchestra.* [electronic source] Available at http://www.tandunonline.com/biography.php, http://www.tandunonline.com/ composition.php?cmd=view&id=59&part=intro
Earley, C. P. & Ang, S. (2003). *Cultural Intelligence. Individual Interaction Across Cultures.* Stanford. California: Stanford University Press.
Felski, R. (2002). Introduction. *New Literary History, 4,* 607–622.
Felski, R. (1999/2000). The invention of everyday life. *New Formations, 39,* 13–31.

Gallimore, R., Weisner, T.S., Bernheimer, L.P., Guthrie, D. & Nihira, K. (1993a). Family responses to young children with developmental delays: Accommodation activity in ecological and cultural context. *American Journal on Mental Retardation, 2,* 185–206.

Gallimore, R., Goldenberg, C.N., & Weisner, T.S. (1993b). The social construction and subjective reality of activity settings: implications for community psychology. *American Journal of Community Psychology, 4,* 537–560.

Gallimore, R., Weisner, T.S., Kaufman, S. Z. & Bernheimer, L.P. (1989). The social construction of eco-cultural niches: Family accommodation of developmentally delayed children. *American Journal on Mental Retardation, 3,* 216–230.

IFHE International Federation for Home Economics (2008). Position Statement. *Home Economics in the Century.*

Janhonen-Abruquah, H. 2010 *Gone with the Wind? Immigrant Women and Transnational Everyday Life in Finland. Home Economics and Craft Studies Research Reports* 24. University of Helsinki. Faculty of Behavioural Sciences. Department of Teacher Education.

Levitt, P. & Glick-Schiller, N. (2004). Transnational perspectives on migration: conceptualizing simultaneity. *International Migration Review, 145,* 595–629.

Olwig Fog, K. (2003). Migrant's visions and practices of home: perspectives from a Caribbean family network. *Journal of the Finnish Anthropological Society, 2,* 2–14.

Ong, A. (2003). *Buddha is Hiding: Refugees, Citizenship,* the New America. Berkeley, California: University of California Press.

Schmalzbauer, L. (2004) Searching for wages and mothering from afar: the case of Honduran transnational families. *Journal of Marriage and Family, 5,* 1317–1331.

Tiilikainen, M. (2003). *Arjen islam: Somalinaisten elämää Suomessa.* [Everyday life Islam: life of Somali women in Finland]. Tampere: Vastapaino.

Vertovec, S, & Cohen, R. (1999). Introduction. In S. Vertovec & R. Cohen (eds) Migration, Diasporas and Transnationalism. *The International Library of Studies on Migration, Vol. 9* (pp. xiii–xxviii). Cheltenham, UK & Northampton, Mass.: Edward Elgar.

CHAPTER
13

Home Economics, Mega-Crises and Continuity

Vuokko Jarva

> "The rise and fall of images of the future precedes or accompanies the rise and fall of cultures. As long as a society's image is positive and flourishing, the flower of culture is in full bloom. Once the image begins to decay and lose its vitality, however, the culture does not long survive." (Polak 1973, p. 19)

Home Economics encounters new challenges in the 21th century because of the ever-increasing entangling of households with the world system. There are at present two dominant views of this development: the continuity view presented through Megatrends and the discontinuity view presented by the Mega Crisis approach. In this article, I study the different requirements the continuity and crisis phases pose to Home Economics, and propose suggestions towards reaching future consciousness and versatility.

Household is a care economy institution

The IFHE Position Statement (2008) characterizes Home Economics as following:

> "Home Economics is a field of study and a profession, situated in the human sciences that draws from a range of disciplines to achieve optimal and sustainable living for individuals, families and communities. Its historical origins place Home Economics in the context of the home and household, and this is extended in the century to include the wider living environments as we better understand that the capacities, choices and priorities of individuals and families impact at all levels, ranging from the household, to the local and also the global (glocal) community. Home economists are concerned with the empowerment and well being of individuals, families and communities, and of facilitating the development of attributes for lifelong learning for paid, unpaid and voluntary work and living situations. Home Economics professionals are advocates for individuals, families and communities."

This statement explicitly expresses that Home Economics is a moral economy science, serving people who strive for their survival and welfare, as well as their empowerment. It also has contextual references to all levels of the world system, from the individual to the global, and even at the planetary level.

The relationships between economy, social issues and ethics in the household have been previously studied by Brown and Paolucci (1979, pp. 40–47; Turkki 1999, pp. 12–18). They state that production of such services, which have an explicit social goal, is typical of the activity of the household. Activities serving material goals have connections with psychological, socio-cultural and even political factors. In households, these connections interweave tight bonds between social, ethical and economical.

The production, consumption and distribution of utilities form the core process of a man's livelihood. Sociologist Max Weber considers maintenance the basic function of the household. Maintenance implies stability and continuity. While other economic institutions specialize in other functions, the household is the basic economic institution, which is specialized to this function (see Figure 13.1). (Weber 1968, pp. 356–360).

The American Association of Family and Consumer Sciences have defined the family functions as following:

- emotional care and physical maintenance of group members and relatives.
- addition of new members.
- socialization and education of children into adult roles and responsibilities.
- social control of members (e.g., setting boundaries, disciplining, mentoring) and protection of family members against all forms of violence.
- production, consumption, exchange and distribution of goods and services.
- maintenance of family morale and motivation to ensure task performance both within the family and in other groups. (McGregor 2009, p. 4)

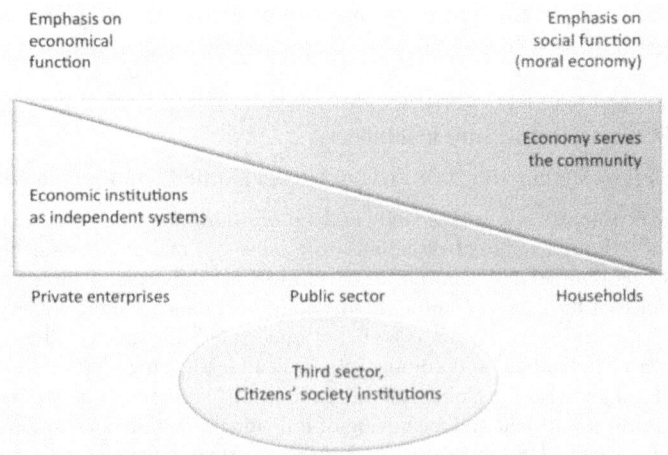

Figure 13.1

Economic institutions. Illustration©Vuokko Jarva 2011

According to anthropologist Karl Polanyi (1968), economy is the utilization of natural resources for livelihood. In present societies the relationship between economy and livelihood is more complicated. The basic economic tasks of the household, however, remain unchanged:
- To offer maintenance and shelter for its members;
- To create safety and continuity and;
- To strive towards welfare of the members.

Home Economics and future consciousness

The question of understanding futures has become paramount to Home Economics, as globalization binds each single household more and more tightly to the world system as a whole. To answer this challenge, home economists are required to study futures and existing futures images. One of the classic icons of futures research, Fred Polak (1973, p. 19), was convinced that as long as a culture is able to offer positive futures images, it flourishes. When futures images lose their strength and become pessimistic, the culture begins to decompose. He believed that Western culture is no longer able to offer positive and flourishing futures images.

Economist Kenneth Boulding (1973, p. V) stated that the same principle concerns an individual as well. When one's futures images are positive, they are empowering:

> "The image of the future, therefore, is the key to all choice-oriented behavior. The general character and quality of the images of the future which prevail in a society is therefore the most important due to its overall dynamics. The individual's image of the future is likewise the most significant determinant of his Personal behavior."

The motivationally attractive positive futures images express the quest of both individuals and institutions towards a better future and create hope to be able to influence in one's own, as well as the world's, future. The basis of stimulating and realistic futures images are found in our emotion-based motivation and the cognitive consciousness oriented towards the future. Thomas Lombardo defines future consciousness as following:

> "…future consciousness is the human capacity to have thoughts, feelings, and goals about the future. It includes the normal human capacities to anticipate, imagine, and think about the future, to have hopes and fears about the future, and to have desires, set goals and make plans for the future. Future consciousness includes evaluating different possibilities and preferable futures, solving problems about the future, and making choices and decisions concerning the future … Connected with hope and fear, people can learn mindsets and modes of behavior ranging from helpless and depressed to hopeful and proactive …" (Lombardo 2006, pp. 4–5)

For any action our future consciousness is the best planning tool. Not only a tool for planning, future consciousness is also useful in understanding the present and the past, since they are entangled with the future in our minds. Many philosophers and psychologists agree that human beings are basically futures oriented, and that the *possible*, *probable* and *preferred* futures are present even in our everyday decisions. The possible refers to futures which can possibly be realized in some limited time perspective (futures research works mainly with time intervals from 5–50 years). The *probable* refers to futures which are probable, if the events follow continuity. The preferred refers to futures which people actively strive towards. The *wildcards* describe some possible but unexpected events of major influence.

Mega Crisis and Megatrends

Futures research already has a history of decades. Ossip K. Flechtheim was the first to define futures studies. He launched the term 'futurology' in the 1940s. Futures research was molded into more scientific modes in the 1960s, mainly in the USA, and several of its methods were constructed: delphi, scenario, trend extrapolation etc. In Europe, a more critical approach was formed, the symbol of which is Bertrand de Jouvenel's (1967) book 'The Art of Conjecture'. New directions were also formed in Europe, often symbolized by *Limits to Growth* (Meadows—Meadows—Randers—Behrens 1972), world modeling, and Robert Jungk's (1987) *Futures Workshops* for grassroots futures work. Those interested in futures research can get a good holistic picture in Eleonora Masini's book: '*Why Futures Studies*' (1993) or Thomas Lombardo's '*Contemporary Futurist Thought*' (2008), and a more in depth view in Wendell Bells extensive, two volume opus: '*The Foundations of Futures Studies*' (1996). The relationships between past, present and futures are studied in Figure 13.2.

Trends represent the probable future approach. Trends do have their origin in the statistical construction of time series, which can be extrapolated into the future.

Mega Crisis and scenarios of possible developments.

Two advanced futures researchers, Willian Halal and Michael Marien (2011, p. 65–84) have recently created a Mega Crisis Scenario and four scenarios of its possible developments.

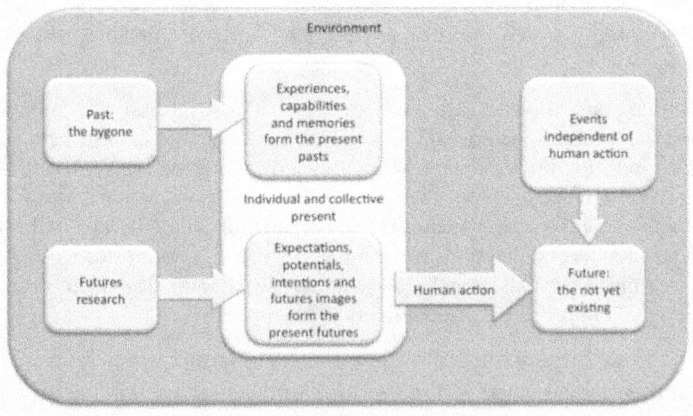

Figure 13.2

Futures research and future consciousness. Illustration©Vuokko Jarva 2011

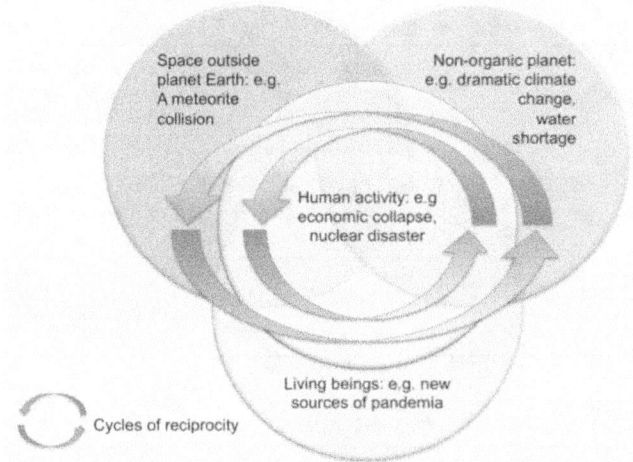

Figure 13.3

Mega Crises Sources. Illustration©Vuokko Jarva 2011

"The unfolding Mega crisis cuts across all sectors in an era of multiple transformations. The Iraq war demonstrated the limits of military power, and the Great Recession highlighted the limits of poorly regulated free markets. With the foundations of the old global order shaken badly, the threat of growing climate change, looming food and energy price escalation, huge government deficits, terrorism and a host of wild cards now form a complex interplay of destructive forces that are straining old systems to the breaking point. These multiple threats now appear as interlocking elements of a failing global order that looks like a train wreck in slow motion. If it had not been bad mortgages and arcane derivatives, some other flaw in these complex systems could have caused roughly the same type of global failure. And more failures seem all too likely in our Anthropocene age of 'wicked complexity' that we don't understand. (Allenby & Sarewitz, 2011)". (Halal-Marien 2011, p. 66)

Their definition of Mega Crisis covers events from the personal level to the global level. However, they do not consider it as a catastrophe, but more of a turning point. The sources of a Mega Crisis are studied in Figure 13.3.

Their four survival scenarios are constructed on an axis of the most pessimistic to the most optimistic. They are:

- *Decline to Disaster:* World fails to react. More global warming, widespread energy and water shortages, economic depression, conflict, etc. Loss of civilization in many parts of the globe.
- *Muddling Down:* World reacts partially, but problems continue to outdistance policies and technologies, ecological damage continues, increased poverty and conflict.
- *Muddling Up:* World reacts out of need and the help of IT/AI (Information technology/Artificial intelligence). Policies and technologies gain on problems. Disaster avoided but some disorder and disappointment.

Table 13.1
MegaTrends and suggestions to responses by Home Economics.

MegaTrends (– or +) by Halal and Marien	MegaTrends (statistical) by Copenhagen	Suggestions to Home Economics' responses
World system	Globalization Acceleration Urbanization	Undercurrents: planetization, localization and glocalization
Population	Ageing Individualization	The problem of useless people

Economy
  Recession likely for years (–)
  Industrialization growing rapidly (–)
	Prosperity
	Commercialization
		The Sampo principle

Technology
  Cyber insecurity (–)
  Weapons of mass destruction (–)
  The technology revolution
    introduces new powers (+)
  The world is accelerating use
    of alternative energy (+)
	Technological development	The Papanek principle

Health	Health and environment	Itinerari saludable and planetary everyday

Environment
  Scientific forecasts for climate
    change are grim (–)
  Dangerous environmental
    impacts are likely (–)
  Methane a growing new threat (–)
  Reducing CO_2 is costly (–)
  Increasing water scarcity (–)
  Countries and urban areas
    going green (+)
		Planetary consiousness

Political and social structures
  Organized crime continues
    to grow worldwide (–)
  Institutional failures could
    grow severe (–)
  Little political will (–)
  Forces of Social Change:
  The rise of women
    into positions of power, citizen
    revolts in the Middle East, the
    Millennial generation modeling
    the first "global citizens, and other
    movements are introducing fresh
    perspectives and energy (+).
	Network organizing	Occupy your life

- Rise to Maturity: Ideal transition to a humane and responsible global order. (Halal-Marien 2011, pp. 73–74).

They list trends, which either are driving the Mega Crisis (−) or influence its resolution (+). The trends are listed in Table 1 below (Halal-Marien 2011, pp. 69–72). Halal and Marien (2011, p. 72) also draft some wildcards, such as: global pandemic kills tens of millions, internet crippled for months by cyber war or cyber terror, huge volcanic explosion cuts food production by half, clear discovery of extraterrestrial intelligence, cheap and widely available life extension techniques, nuclear power plant failure puts industry on hold, synthetic biology creates many new life forms and stadium-size asteroid hits earth. These wildcards include any extraterrestrial, planetary or human sphere threats.

Mega Crisis and Megatrends challenge Home Economics

The challenges to Home Economics by the trends of Halal-Marien (2011, pp. 69–72) and the *Copenhagen Institute for Futures Study* (Why Megatrends Matter? 2006) are presented in Table 13.1. In the documents the trends are not presented in a systematic order, but in the table they are organized into 7 groups to improve visualization.

Suggestions to responses by Home Economics

In Table 13.1 are proposed suggestions to relevant responses by Home Economics. I have chosen suggestions which appear in current discussions, but are less well known.

World system undercurrents: planetization, localization and glocalization

Changes in values, attitudes, policies, enterprises and lifestyles towards caretaking of our planet, both locally and globally, spread as separate small rivulets in our communities. The question then, is when do they reach the critical mass of influencing decisively?

Localization. This undercurrent has its most visible expression in the formation of new states. Inside societies it appears as more or less revolutionary movements, like the Arab Spring and Occupy movement in 2011. One case of economic democracy is the microfinance pioneer Grameen Bank in Bangladesh, as well as local co-ops. Local democracy has its expressions as the activities of the citizens' society (e.g. Non Governmental Organizations) and its direct democracy.

Planetization. Planetary consciousness has been developed mainly in ecological questions, and has lately culminated with the Global Warming discourse. Though the dominant politics have not yet been ready to accept radical activities to save the living planet, planetization has still advanced: recycling, utilization of renewable energy, green industry, animal and nature protection and greening of lifestyles has accumulated quickly.

Glocalization. A combination of the former two, movements like green consumption, permaculture, slow life, slow cities and downshifting are spreading. One prominent case is the Green Belt movement in Africa, created and organized by Nobelist Wangari Maathai. On the intellectual and scientific level, good practices mesh with the recognition of the necessity to sustain the living planet.

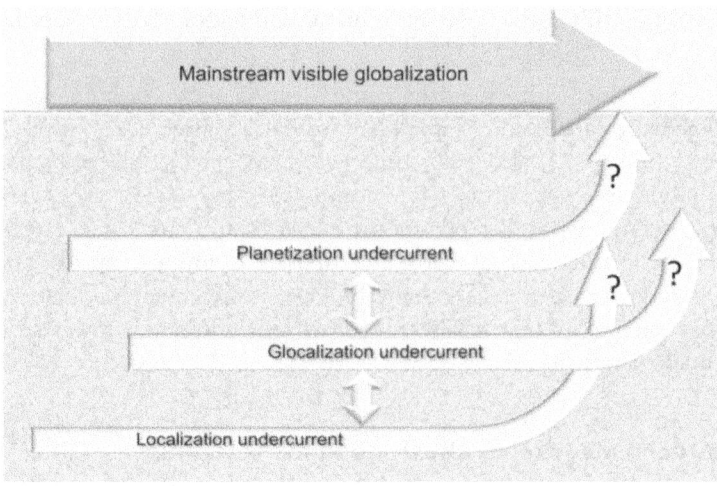

Figure 13.4

The undercurrents are described in Figure 13.4. Illustration©Vuokko Jarva 2011

What can then be the role of Home Economics in relation to these currents?

To be versatile, Home Economics needs to be aware of these three undercurrents of human action. The capability to tackle both problems caused by a Mega Crisis, as well as the continuous development phases, depends on one's ability to understand one's respective position in time and place. It is not only cultures which have different experiences of time and place, but even individuals in everyday situations shuttle between different times and places. Unfortunately, there is an additional complication. The Home Economics researchers or teachers have to understand, as well as act, in all the different time-spaces they encounter in their life and work.

Population — The problem of useless people

There is one special blind spot in the analyses of the present problems that needs to be pointed out: the catastrophic waste of human resources. In the sphere of labor, incredible amounts of work-force are wasted on production of vanities and non-necessities. The accumulating unemployment results in a remarkable percentage of waste. Poverty, war and malnutrition prevent vast amounts of people from developing and utilizing their resources. All of this, combined with an inner loss of purpose, is a huge resource, which is being squandered.

Aging. One of the central forms of segregation is to divide people into age groups. The elderly are considered useless. Especially in well-educated and welfare societies, the elderly form an ever-widening resource reserve, which governments attempt to utilize by increasing the retirement age. On the contrary, the elderly should be viewed as an active self-steered resource. This has already been seen in many citizens' society institutions.

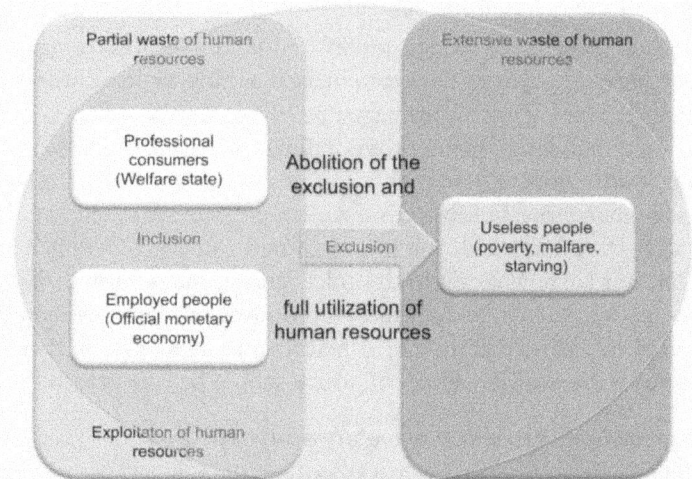

Figure 13.5

Undercurrents of human action. Illustration©Vuokko Jarva 2011

Paideia for all. The Norwegian criminologist Nils Christie (1977) wrote in *Hvis skolan ikke fantes*, that *paideia* originally referred to leisure time. Only later was it taken to mean education and schooling. Takis Fotopoulos (2005) defines two modes of *paideia*. *Paideia as civic schooling* is to educate people to be responsible citizens. The newest European proposals for consumer education emphasize the education of consumer-citizens (Consumer Citizenship Education Guidelines 2008; Teaching Consumer Competences 2009). To them, the ideal citizen is a consumer who takes responsibility on all levels whether it is locally, nationally or globally. In a sense, they are both the chicken and the egg. This is a lofty goal for Home Economics, but this direction is necessary for planetary every day. *Paideia as personal training* educates individuals into becoming autonomous and capable of self-reflection and deliberation.

Economy — The Sampo principle

In the Finnish National Epic Kalevala, the blacksmith Ilmarinen forged Sampo, the horn of plenty. Sampo is a good example of downshifting and moderating consumption. The Sampo ground only one barrel of wealth a day. The division into three; for consumption, for the market and for the store-house, is as up-to-date today as before. If those in the wealthy countries would follow this principle, then the future of the living planet would be less threatened and there would be a solid basis for the redistribution of the wealth.

> "Well the Sampo grinds when finished, To and fro the lid in rocking, Grinds one measure at the day-break, Grinds a measure fit for eating, Grinds a second for the market, Grinds a third one for the store-house." (Kalevala 10th rune).

Technology — The Papanek principle

The principle of the famous design professor Viktor Papanek is very useful. He claims: "Any attempt to separate design, to make it a thing-by-itself, works counter to the inherent value of design as the primary, underlying matrix of life." (Papanek 1985, p. 322). He insists that design has to produce things which are useful for the user and not only things with monetary or aesthetic value.

The basic human struggle for survival and management of their lives leads them to observe, to try to understand, and to give certain patterns to all phenomena they encounter. The human tendency is to control, to create, and to formulate phenomena into wholes, creating patterns and organizing the interplay of wholes and parts. While the mainstream of technological development crafts the high-tech, there are many efforts to improve the everyday low-tech, which should be encouraged.

Health — Itinerari saludable and planetary everyday

Here in Catalonya, one can often see at a crossroads the sign '*Itinerari saludable*' — 'A healthy hiking route'. Home Economics can in many ways promote healthy hiking routes to people, not only in the terrain, but in their whole life. One can count their own Happy Planet index at: http://survey.happyplanetindex.org/

Planetary everyday. The shrinkage of our planet in our minds, as well as the ongoing globalization, has caused the everyday to be even more tightly tied into the whole world system. The new dimension, brought by these processes, is the responsibility of how our everyday activities influence the global system. A moderate consciousness of our influence is a necessary part of our decision-making and action. In the field of Home Economics this concerns especially consumption: what we buy, what kind of supra-local effects e.g. our energy consumption has and what we throw away as waste.

Planetary consciousness

Connected with the planetary every day, the educational focus needs to be the development of planetary consciousness. However, this is not enough, for we need motivation and ethics on the planetary level.

Dalai-Lama and Erwin Laszlo published in 2001 the 'Manifesto on planetary consciousness' document. They defined planetary consciousness:

> "An individual endowed with planetary consciousness recognizes his or her role in the evolutionary process and acts responsibly in light of this perception. Each of us must start with himself or herself to evolve his or her consciousness to this planetary dimension; only then can we become responsible and effective agents of our societies' change and transformation. Planetary consciousness is the knowing as well as the feeling of the vital interdependence and essential oneness of humankind, and the conscious adoption of the ethics and the ethos that this entails." (Laszlo 2003)

Political and social structures — Occupy your life!

The well known Indian activist Vandana Shiva was asked: "What would you say to the people of the occupy movement?" She answered: "Occupy your own life." Joanne

Poyourow (2011) interprets it as "taking back your life". She presents five points on how it can be done:

1. Take back your food. Every dollar you spend to Big Agribusiness — every dollar you spend at Big Box stores or conventional grocery stores — reinforces, supports, and endorses the horribly broken system Vandana Shiva campaigns against.
2. Take back your money ... Urge your community bank or credit union to invest in our future — to invest in, support and promote local projects which better prepare your neighborhood for post-petroleum lifestyles...
3. Take back your health care. Learn the skills of basic wellness, yourself ... Learn the skills of traditional healing modalities and practice them with your family...
4. Take back your livelihood. The hours of your working day, your time, are the very fabric of your life ... In your times of unemployment or underemployment — or in your leisure time — what new skills can you pick up which better prepare you, your family, and your neighborhood for a power down future? As we localize our economies with the end of cheap oil and easy credit, what basic goods or services can you provide for your local community? What need can you fill?"

El son de la eternidad — The sound of eternity

In our turbulent world, there are counter-movements, which are more and more acute, and get their expression for example in the slow-life movement. These kind of things are discussed under the term spirituality, which does not refer only to traditional religious spirituality. Sprituality does not emphasize dogmas or rituals but the emotional — sometimes even ecstatic — spiritual experience. In the core of this experience is unitedness, either with other people or communities or with nature. Recently I found a strong example in music: Ensueño (Dreaming) by Freddie Mercury and Montserrat Caballe, with lyrics in English and Spanish, http://www.youtube.com/watch?v=vrqsjEUrvKM.

Day to day survival, anticipation and crisis survival

The study of futures can only give us contingent knowledge and we must keep our minds open for alternative futures. This concerns all types of futures, from the local to the global.

These stories, which we construct for ourselves on possible, probable and preferred futures, have an immense influence in our actions. In this article, the stories on futures are reduced into two basic modes: the continuity story (Megatrends) and the Mega Crisis story. Each challenges Home Economics in a different way. In crisis, the focus has to be on everyday survival; in more continuous phases, the focus can be moved over into long-range planning and anticipation. There cannot be only one Home Economics strategy for different societies, communities and situations. The greatest transformation needed is the cultivation of planetary consciousness, because the layers of the world are deeply entangled from the level of the world system to the level of households and individuals.

Because our emotions and feelings are the dynamic source of action, the crucial capability in the planetized everyday is to learn to love future living beings as well as having a commitment to a better future. Humans create themselves stories about everything that happens and might happen. Why shouldn't Home Economics create positive and motivating images of futures?

One crucial task is to define work in a radical new way. In Finland, researchers Johanna Varjonen and Kristiina Aalto (2005) evaluated the monetary value of household work in the year 2002. Their results show that, even in a highly industrialized country, the value of household work was 40–45 % of the GDP. It was about the same as the whole industrial production. The unpaid household work, as well as the voluntary social and other work in one's society has to be valued as important as the paid work now.

Literature professor Hamid Dabashi considers the phenomenon which has the name Arab Spring to be a mental creation. Dabashi uses **as a case** a scene from the film *Divine intervention* by Palestinian film director Elia Suleiman. (The man in a car eating an apricot, http://www.youtube.com/watch?v=jYsZhF5ciGQ)

> "What we see happening in *Divine Intervention* is nothing other than cinematic *montage* playing tricks on our minds. The individual shots are independent, but like Sergei Eisenstein, Elia Suleiman slices them together and leaves the rest to the viewer …we do the *montage* — creatively, critically and hopefully — with Elia Suleiman and Sergei Eisenstein implanted inside our mind's eye. What we call the Arab Spring is the mental editing of a succession of shots that demand and exact a reading and a recreation to render things meaningful. The individual shots produce a sequence with significance, and the sequence gives a teleological meaning to otherwise disparate shots..."
>
> There is a scene in John G Avildsen's *The Karate Kid* (1984) in which Mr Miagi (Pat Morita) is teaching his young protégé Daniel LaRusso (Ralph Macchio) how to prune a bonsai. As soon as he is given the gardening shears, the rash young man starts cutting the delicate branches away. "Stop," says Mr Miagi. "First close your eyes and imagine the bonsai you want to create. Now, open your eyes and start pruning." (Dabashi 2011)

The Dabashian way of thinking suggests a startling way to see the world: even the household or Home Economics is created in our minds from various real world institutions and events. The whole everyday is a story we tell ourselves. Futures consciousness helps us to imagine which kind of bonsai tree we want. To quote the ex director of UNESCO, Federico Mayor, at a futures methodology seminar in the year 2000: "We cannot let the others create our futures".

Summary

The classic icon of futures studies, Fred Polak, believed that positive futures images are essential for the flourishing of a culture. Economist Kenneth Boulding considered this to apply to individuals as well. The core question is, if Home Economics is able to create motivating, positive futures images for the 21th century?

William Halal and Michael Marien have written an article on Mega Crisis and four scenarios on how it could turn out. The great challenge for Home Economics as a study of a care economy institution in the 21th century is: can it tackle the problems both in state of a Mega Crisis and in the long-term continuity of different trends. The challenges to Home Economics are studied in relation to Halal-Marien Mega Crisis and the Copenhagen Institute for Futures Study Megatrends. Suggestions are given for some possible solutions for the discipline. In a crisis situation the challenges are directed towards basic survival strategies of the families, in continuity phases the planetary level gets a heavy weight in this century — this division also concerns societies on the border of survival versus more wealthy societies. Commitment and love of the future (generations, living planet) are focal motivational goals in the framework of a planetary every day.

Discussion Prompts

- How is the household entangled in the whole world system?
- How can home economists influence in the three phases of obtaining, production and consumption?
- How can recycling be strengthened in everyday life?
- How can people be educated to become responsible consumer citizens?

References:

Bell, W. (1996). *Foundation of Futures Studies: Human Science for a New Era*. Vol.1–2. New Brunswick: Transaction Pubs.

Boulding, K. (1973). Foreword. In: Polak, Fred (1973). *The Image of the Future*. Translated and abridged by Elise Boulding. Amsterdam: Elsevier.

Brown, M. & Paolucci, B. (1979). *Home Economics: A Definition*. Washington DC: American Home Economics Association.

Christie, N. (1977). *Hvis skolen ikke fantes*. Oslo: Universitetsforlaget.

Consumer Citizenship Education Guidelines Vol 1: Higher Education (2008). Victoria Thoresen (ed.). Retrieved 10.3.2009 from http://www.hihm.no/Prosjektsider/CCN/About-CCN/CCE.

Dabashi H. (2011). *Imagining the Arab Spring: A year later*. Retrieved 7.12.2011 from http://www.aljazeera.com/indepth/opinion/2011/12/2011125132335754716.html.

de Jouvenel, B. (1967). The Art of Conjecture, New York: Basic Books.

Fotopoulos T. (2005). From (mis)education to *Paideia*. *The International Journal of Inclusive Democracy*, Vol. 2, No.1 (September 2005). Retrieved 10.1.2012 from http://www.inclusivedemocracy.org/journal/vol2/vol2_no1_miseducation_paideia_takis.htm.

Halal W. and Marien M. (2011). Global megacrisis, *Journal of Futures Studies*, December 2011, 16(2).

Happy Planet Index. Retrieved 15.12.2011 from http://survey.happyplanetindex.org/.

IFHE Position Statement (2008). *Home Economics in the 21th Century*. Retrieved 10.1.2012 from http://www.ifhe.org/136.html?&0=.

Jarva, V. (2008). Foresight — the hidden dimension in The Art of Everyday. In *Reinventing art of everyday making*. T. Tuomi-Gröhn (ed.). Bern: Peter Lang.

Jarva, V. (2011). Towards planetary consciousness. *Journal of Futures Studies*, December 2011, 16(2): 115–120.

Jungk, R. & Müllert, N. (1987): *Future workshops: How to Create Desirable Futures*. London, England, Institute for Social Inventions ISBN 0948826398.

Kalevala, The Finnish National Epos, Rune 10. http://www.sacred-texts.com/neu/kveng/kvrune10.htm

Laszlo E. (2003). *Manifesto on Planetary Consciousness*. Revised version: February 2003. Retrieved 15.1.2012 from http://www.newciv.org/nl/newslog.php/_v76/__show_article/_a000076-000108.htm.

Lombardo T. (2006). Developing Constructive and Creative Attitudes and Behaviors about the Future: Part One — Deep Learning, Emotion, and Motivation. *WFSF Futures Bulletin*, Vol. 31, No. 6, November, 2006. Retrieved 10.1.2012 from http://www.centerforfutureconsciousness.com/FC_Readings.htm (Reprinted PDF version).

Lombardo T. (2008). *Contemporary Futurist Thought*. Bloomington — London: Author House.

Masini, E. (1993). *Why futures studies?* London: Grey Seal Books.

McGregor, S.L.T. (2009). Becoming family literate: A new construct and platform for practice. *Journal of Family and Consumer Sciences,* 101(1), 60–66. (Reprinted PDF version).

Meadows, D. H., Meadows D. I., Randers. J. & Behrens. W.W. (1972). *The Limits to Growth*. New York: Universe Books.

Papanek, V. (1985). *Design for the Real World, Human Ecology and Social Change*. Second Edition Completely Revised, Thames and Hudson, London.

Polak, Fred (1973). *The Image of the Future*. Translated and abridged by Elise Boulding. Amsterdam: Elsevier.

Polanyi, K. (1968) *Primitive, Archaic and Modern Economies*. G. Dalton (Ed.). New York: Anchor Books.

Poyourow J. (2011). *Occupy your life*. Retrieved 1.1.2012 from http://www.vandanashiva.org/?p=772 .

Teaching Consumer Competences — a Strategy for Consumer Education. Proposals of objectives and content of consumer education (2009). TemaNord 2009:588. Copenhagen: Nordic Council of Ministers. Downloadable 29.1.2012 as PDF on http://www.norden.org/en/publications/publikationer/2009-588

Turkki, K. (1999). Kotitalousopetus tienhaarassa. Teknisistä taidoista kohti arjen hallintaa. Helsingin yliopiston Kotitalous-ja käsityötieteiden laitos.

Varjonen, J. & Aalto, K. (2005). *Kotitaloustuotannon satelliittitilinpito Suomessa 2001*. Helsinki: Tilastokeskus ja Kuluttajatutkimuskeskus.

Weber, M. (1968). *Economy and Society,* G. Roth & C. Wittich (eds.). New York: Bedminster Press.

Why Megatrends Matter? (2006). Copenhagen Institute for Futures Research. Retrieved 30.12.2011 from http://www.cifs.dk/scripts/artikel.asp?id=1469 .

CHAPTER
14

A Systems Approach to Food Future Proofs the Home Economics Profession

Jane Kolodinsky

Issues surrounding food span across all ten megatrends outlined in Chapter 1, from technology to prosperity, and individuality to networking. And, food serves as both a great equalizer and un-equalizer with regard to the environment, prosperity and health. The food system from production to disposal can enable or inhibit the prosperity and health of individuals and households (see Figure 14.1). This chapter explores the food system as it relates to future proofing the Home Economics profession.

While some people around the world have an abundance of "cheap food" at their disposal, others face severe food shortages and high food prices. Diet-related diseases, especially obesity, are a global problem, regardless of food availability. Food safety issues span harvest, storage, processing, preparation and preservation of food. Newer technological advancements have yet to be proven safe, including genetically-modified versions of seeds, plants and even animals. We are losing the earth's agricultural land base as commercial development replaces farmland. Combined with an aging population and migration away from rural areas there are limits on the number of farmers who will produce food in the future.

Consumer demand for animal protein (e.g., substitution of meat for rice) in quickly developing nations is growing as the prosperity of these economies increases. This, combined with pressures to use tillable land to produce biofuels places increasing pressure on existing resources for food production.

"Cooking" has been seen as an expendable activity as women have continued to add labor market hours to their milieus of daily activities, leaving a perception of less time available for food preparation. As a result, knowledge of food preparation skills has been lost over the past 50 years.

During the same time period, we have seen growth in convenience foods, an increasing share of the household dollar spent on food away from home, and a consolidation of the food industry to a few multinational corporations. Marketing, advertising, consumer information and propaganda about all of the items presented above are shared immediately and widely through the internet and social media. Looking at it holistically, it is clear that food, our relationship with it, and its effect on well-being, make it part of a large and complex system. These mega-trends are aligned with the food system. This chapter explores these alignments and discusses how a food systems approach future proofs the Home Economics profession.

Embedding the Home Economics Profession into a Food System Model

Figure 14.2 places the food system in the context of the Home Economics profession. Three ways of "knowing" are included in every component of the system. Two of these ways of knowing, everyday and historical, have long been the basis for our food knowledge. Our ancestors learned through trial and error (and error often meant death) which foods were safe to eat. This knowledge was passed on through generations. They developed food preservation techniques: drying, salting, and freezing. "Eat your vegetables," and "No dessert before you finish your dinner," were phrases of guidance about eating passed from generation to generation through historical and everyday knowledge. These two types of knowledge are at the heart of everyday living concepts and the well-being of households. The third way of knowing, scientific knowledge, includes the generation of theory, and the empirical testing of hypotheses. This is how science gives meaning to everyday knowledge. Information helps households make better food decisions, and home economists must be able to translate scientific knowledge into the practices that fit within the economic, environmental, and social character of a household in a particular setting.

Home economists have also long recognized the importance of several areas of scientific research including basic, applied and action (Touliatos & Compton, 1988).

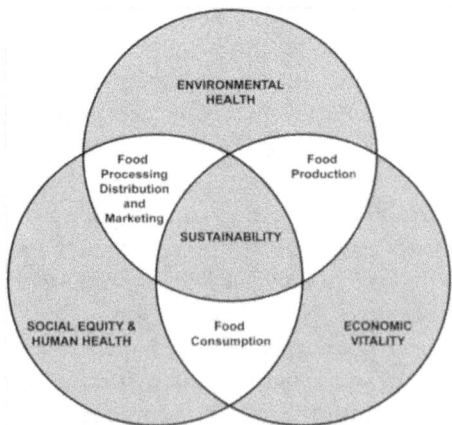

Figure 14.1

The Food System

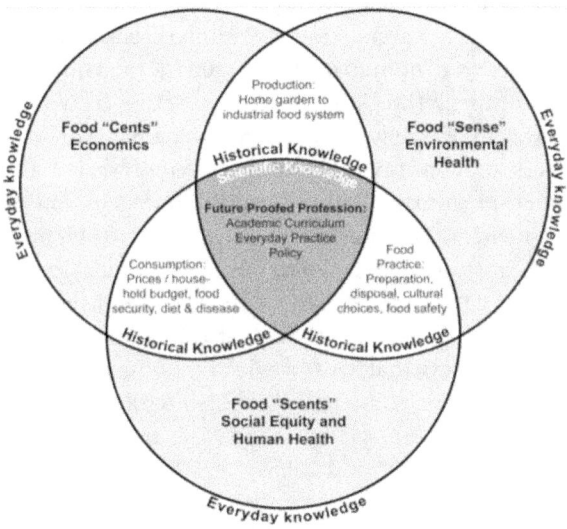

Figure 14.2

Home Economics Profession

We understand how science works in the everyday context of the household. Yet, reductionist approaches to scientific inquiry about food have been stressed over the past 100 years. Household and personal meanings of a balanced meal, enjoyed slowly, have been lost in a scientific world of individual vitamins, minerals, protein, carbohydrates and fats. We must transcend such a reductionist approach (Hoffman, 2003). The Home Economics profession faced an increasingly reductionist approach until the movement toward a Human Ecology or systems approach began to emerge in the 1980s (see McGregor, 2010, 2011a). The next 100 years provides the opportunity to embrace an approach that pays attention to the complexity of the *food system* using a holistic lens. This approach reveals the relevancy of Home Economics for academics, curriculum development, everyday living, organizations representing both business and the non-profit sectors and policy recommendations (the four dimensions of Home Economics set out in the 2008 IFHE position statement). The following narrative discusses each of these and introduces a conceptual framework pertaining to the three senses of the food system.

Complexity and Transdisciplinarity in the Home Economics Profession
Academics
Scientific knowledge, broadly defined to include a variety of research approaches and methods, is at the center of the model in Figure 2. To translate research findings to curriculum, everyday living guidelines and policy, we must have our finger on the pulse of the entire food system. Our historic embrace of multidisciplinary

approaches to research and problem solving helps us to understand the next generation of transdisciplinary research. Transdisciplinary acknowledges multidimensionality and complexity (Thompson Klein, 2004). In complex systems, actors adapt to their environment (McGregor, 2012), reacting to what others do in an interrelated food system. Complex systems are dynamic. For example, when the health consequences of consuming trans-fats were revealed through scientific evidence, the popular press translated the science into steps consumers could take to avoid the consequences. But consumers needed way to identify products containing these fats. A consumer campaign to boycott a popular cookie with trans-fat ingredients began in the U. S. media. The U.S. government then promulgated laws requiring nutrition labels to list the amount of trans-fat in foods, and businesses reformulated many products that had previously contained trans-fat (American Heart Association, 2010). The complex food system and actors within it acted and reacted until a new equilibrium was reached. The trans-fat example spanned a period of ten years, between 1993 and 2006.

There are few, if any, disciplines as ready as ours to integrate the study of the complexities of the food environment, the links between scientific and everyday knowledge, the importance of the family and household on food decisions and intake of this generation and the next. The roots of our profession indicate that we have been multifaceted generalists who have the well-being of the household as our goal. Because well-being encompasses a variety of constructs, we have never been beholden to striving for economic, environmental, health, *or* social equity (McGregor, 2011b). Instead, our paradigm is holistic. We substitute *and* for *or* in the previous sentence.

Most of us are familiar with the trend of disbanding of Schools, Colleges, and Departments of Home Economics and their scattered placements around Universities including Economics Departments, Colleges of Agriculture, Departments of Nutrition, Schools of Education, and Departments of Human Development. This trend may have done the profession a short term disservice, but it has the potential to offer longer term gain as transdisciplinary approaches to research gain acceptance by academics.Thompson Klein (2003) provides a useful list of concepts to consider as we embrace transdisciplinary in the Home Economics Profession. We must go from:

- segmentation to boundary crossing and blurring;
- fragmentation to relationality;
- unity to integrative process;
- homogeneity to heterogeneity and hybridity;
- isolation to collaboration and cooperation;
- simplicity to complexity;
- linearity to non-linearity and
- universality to situated practices.

In summary, a transdisciplinary approach to Home Economics requires boundary crossing and blurring relations among things, integrative processes, hybridity, collaboration, complexity, non-linearity and situated practice.

The academic home economist who embraces transdisciplinarity has an opportunity to lead teams of nutritionists, behavioralists, sociologists, statisticians, psychologists, and physicians as they study the complexities of food as it contributes to disease, culture, the environment, the economy, well-being, and the contexts in which we live in the food environment.

Curriculum and Everyday Living

Higher education Home Economics curriculum (related to the food system) must be transdisciplinary. Business courses such as consumer behavior and financial management, natural science classes in nutrition and foods, educational philosophy and human development courses, journalism and media literacy courses, global, consumption, micro, and time use economics courses, ethics courses and courses in management and public administration and policy remain relevant. An envelope that places these within Home Economics theory (McGregor, 2011a) and research methods provides cohort "glue." Our ability to reach and work with audiences of all ages, disciplines and sectors will remain relevant. Examples are illustrative.

The growth in convenience foods, fast food chains, and the substitution of purchased meals for home prepared meals has led to the loss of everyday knowledge of what is in our food and how to prepare it. Time scarcity, perceived or actual, is a constraint faced by households spanning the spectrum of rural to urban, impoverished to wealthy — each contributes to the substitution of home cooked foods for away-from-home prepared foods using minimally processed (whole) ingredients (Jabs and Devine, 2006). Yet, evidence shows that using cooking skills contributes to better food choices in terms of health outcomes (Kolodinsky & Goldstein, 2011). Everyday knowledge of how to combine three to five simple unprocessed ingredients into a meal in under 30 minutes, therefore, is a skill that can have a large impact on the well-being of the population. Home Economist James McIntosh shows this with his Gourmand Award winning series of cookbooks (Whisk, n.d.).

Home Economics curriculum must also include teaching about computer and smart phone technology to enable students to search for and obtain *legitimate*, important information and to share it within their networks, and how to tell the difference between information and advertising. Media literacy about how to navigate an increasingly unhealthful global food environment is also necessary.

There are other examples of why a transdisciplinary education is necessary for future Home Economics professionals. With regard to economics and marketing: the two major soft drink companies, Pepsi-Co and Coca-Cola (11 and 25 percent of the world market, respectively), have chosen a global approach to expansion over the last decade, increasing sales of soft-drinks and snack foods worldwide, and especially to developing countries. The largest growth in global sales has been of "high value" increasingly processed foods to "low-income" countries (Bolling, 2002; Gehlhar & Regmi, 2002). With regard to nutrition knowledge: Packaged and processed foods are more expensive and are higher in sodium, fats, and calories. Soft drinks are one of the three foods that contribute most to excess calorie consumption and obesity (Ready & Krebs-Smith, 2010; Malik et al., 2006) and intake of sweeteners has been increasing over the past two decades worldwide (Popkin & Neilson, 2003). With regard to the ability to translate research into practice, implications for everyday living guidelines have been translated to messages around the word, as illustrated by this slogans: *Limit the intake of sugar, particularly from soft drinks, confectionery and cakes* (Denmark); *Sugars, sweets, sweet drinks — just the right amount* (Italy), and *Limit intake of free sugars* (WHO, 2004).

Policy

There is increasing evidence that home economists can play a role in policy formation, thus having impact beyond the scope of individual households. Our next tasks must include advocating for policy changes that provide consumers with the information they need to make healthy food choices and to understand the diet-disease link. Food labeling legislation in restaurant venues is needed; as are food labels that list ingredients from most-to-least used in the package. Policies that strengthen food delivery programs will remain important, as are those related to competitive foods in schools (vending machines and fast food).Given that we are faced with the possibility of a global food security disaster in the coming decades, policies that span the food system are paramount to success.

Food insecurity is not simply a "food issue" (FAO, 2011a), an idea analogous to "poverty is not a money issue." Poverty is accompanied by many related social issues, including lack of education, poor health, crime and substance abuse. Similarly, food security is an issue that has a social and political side. Food policy must include components that improve educational opportunities, provide safety nets, improve agricultural productivity while preserving the environment, and open trade doors to increase food availability. And, as with all complex issues, consultation with those who are experiencing food insecurity is necessary in order to develop the most appropriate policy recommendations. Home economists have access to and understand the household unit that is affected by the food insecurity dilemma. Working at the individual household level can have sweeping policy effects if enough households are able to self-organize, develop patterns and networks, and create order out of what may appear to be a chaotic situation. These are all aspects of addressing complexity (McGregor, 2012).

Buycotts and boycotts are examples ofindividual actions having an impact on a wider system. Theseactions have been effective at both the national and international level for decades (Allan & Albala, 2007; Friedman, 1999). With the advent of technology, including Facebook, boycotts become easier to organize, as was the case with a boycott of Whole Foods Markets in 2009 ("Boycott Nestle", 2012; Friedman, 2009). Even with lower technology, one of the most famous international consumer boycotts was that of the 1979 Nestle Corporation's selling of infant formula. The boycott, which highlighted problems associated with feeding infants formula in developing countries, contributed to the 1981 joint WHO/UNICEF code on breastfeeding recommendations, including labeling of infant formula to indicate that breastfeeding is the best approach to infant feeding.

The context of the household and the current economic, social, educational and political situation must be understood and woven into our study and action. These situations are dynamic and can be influenced quickly by structural changes including natural disasters and war, or more slowly, as is the case with cultural changes in gender roles and social mores. Regardless, when the current state of societal issues and the complexity of the food system are understood at the professional level, and applied at the household level and beyond, the relevance of Home Economics is future proofed.

The final section of this chapter presents a three-pronged approach to understanding food systems, using a sense metaphor. Senses provide humans with inputs for their perceptions of the world around them. This chapter shares an approach to Home Economics practice that involves three food-system inputs: economic, environmental and social/cultural.

Three "Senses" of the Food System and Relevance for the Home Economics Profession

Figure 14.2 presents food systems in terms of three "senses" that encompass economic, environmental and social/cultural concepts. Each sense overlaps another, as shown inthe Venn diagram. Each "sense" is described below, in the context of megatrends and future proofing the profession. Home economists can use these receptors to perceive the food-world and augment their practice, accordingly.

Food "Cents"

Household financial management is a permanent component of Home Economics research, curriculum, and everyday living. Rising global prosperity is a double-edged sword. This prosperity fosters an industrial food system that has replaced many local and regional food systems and has had both positive and negative effects on the wellbeing of households and their communities, around the globe. Financial issues related to the food system require more than household financial management knowledge. Home Economics professionals must understand household financial management within a global economy. For example, national and international monetary and trade policy affect prices that households face. In addition, economic policy must include household safety nets when food prices, scarcity or crop failure impact household food security. The effects of a multinational, concentrated food industry, and its ability to control the amount and types of food made available,must also be considered.

Issues closer to a household level include the tradeoffs faced in the production, preparation, consumption and disposal of food. From a management perspective, home economists have historically considered the cost of food purchased and the time spent in preparation and eating. In the future, we must also consider the *full cost approach* of food. Full costing includes concepts such as food miles, a measure of the impact on the environment (see Food 'Sense," below). We must also consider the full cost of substituting convenience and fast foods that require less preparation, but often contain more sugar, sodium and fat — all known to have adverse health effects on the consumer (Variyam, 2005). The impact of these choices reaches beyond a household's pocketbook to the physical environment and health.

For academic home economists, there are many food "cents" research questions to which we can contribute expertise. For example:
- How do tradeoffs in where and how food is purchased and prepared impact people's weight, well-being and health?
- What are the most economical choices for households in terms of local and regional purchasing versus purchasing national/international brands?
- How do household food consumption choices affect global warming and vice-versa?
- What is the optimal allocation of home prepared, convenience and food away from home that maximizes household well-being, and minimizes cost in both dollar and health?

The list of questions that require research in order to obtain the answers will grow over the next decades. Academic home economists who have a broad, transdisciplinary understanding of the food system, and of how households make choices with regard to food "cents," will be of central importance on research teams. These academics will need a broad based curriculum, as described earlier in this chapter.

These research questions might prove to be "too scientific," but there are implications for everyday living. No longer is it enough for a household to have skills to allocate a budget to food and other items. There are many food "bowls" that must be considered. Home economists must develop new toolkits that can be adapted to various levels of household prosperity. Answers to the research questions above, translated into everyday language, will, for example, help households determine the optimal allocation of home-produced versus market-purchased ingredients and the optimal split between food prepared at home and that purchased away from home.

This said we cannot assume that households automatically have both the tools and skills to prepare meals. The "art" of cooking in many developed nations has been lost. Clearly, the obesity epidemic and other adverse impacts on physical health of poor diets imply that the everyday skill of cooking is once again needed in Home Economics curricula at the primary and secondary grade levels and in lifelong learning initiatives. There have been cases made for such curriculum to return (Kolodinsky & Goldstein, 2011; Lichtenstein & Ludwig, 2010).

Food "Sense"

Choices about the production, distribution, marketing, consumption and disposal of food impact the environment. The same trends that affect our food "cents" also impact food "sense" in terms of environmental health. Other megatrends, including globalization, increasing technology, commercialization, urbanization, acceleration and prosperity, all lead to an increased supply and demand for mass produced foods that leave a negative environmental footprint from production through disposal.

There are environmental impacts of large scale production methods, designed to meet food security needs across the globe, but requiring increasing amounts of fertilizer, insecticide, herbicides, and water resources. All have potentially negative environmental implications, including global warming, poisoned land, water shortages, and decreased land fertility. The Green Revolution approach of the 1960s is appearing again. A campaign that began in 2011 is engaging leaders from African, Asian, and South American countries, led by the U.S., on a "new" large scale food production approach (Feed the Future, 2011). The Food and Agriculture Organization of the United Nations (FAO) has critiqued these approaches and notes the positive and negative effects of large scale efforts at the expense of smaller scale approaches (FAO, 2011b). As society struggles with the approaches that are best suited to "feed the world," the place for home economists in the discussion is strengthened.

Internationally, academic home economists might consider research about how households and families in a particular region have been affected by food policy decisions of their country. In the U.S. and Canada for example, home economists have researched the use of and consumer demand for food labels indicating genetic engineered ingredients or production methods (Kolodinsky et al., 2003). Research on this issue will remain salient as more and more countries around the globe debate issues surrounding food production using genetically altered seeds and, now, animals.

Home Economics curriculum must include coursework on global economies and environmental impacts. We must inform ourselves about the causes and consequences of climate change and how the way food is produced impacts the environment. Only with a systems approach will we then be able to translate research-based findings on sustainable concepts of everyday living. Through a human ecosystem lens, we understand the impact that choices made at the household level can have on the larger environment.

Household demand ultimately drives the variety of foods available in the market and the packaging in which they are sold. Food manufacturers do respond to consumer (non)spending. Everyday living concepts of purchasing in season, regionally, and of reading ingredient labels all have larger implications for food production and its environmental effects. Household choices have an impact on the waste stream as well. The teaching of everyday living concepts by home economists must include information about reducing, reusing, and recycling of food packaging and waste in addition to our historical roots in food choice and preparation.

At the policy level, home economists advocating for a "place at the policy table" can include several legitimate policy options. For example, home economists can lobby for regionally-based and smaller scale food production approaches and food labeling initiatives. The latter should include process attributes (how foods are produced) related to the ways in which animals are raised/fish is caught, the use or not of insecticides and pesticides, whether producers are paying fair wages to farm workers, and any climate change impacts of the food production process. Individual consumers often do not understand how food policy is made, regardless of whether they reside in developed or lesser developed countries. Home economists can inform policy at the government level and translate policy initiatives in understandable ways to households in order for them to "vote with their food dollar."

Home economists of the future must be in touch with the history, and future trends, of food production, and the implications beyond individual household choice on the environment in order to make sustained and informed contributions to academics, curriculum, everyday living, and policy. Issues of environmental degradation and sustainability of the planet as megatrends will remain important and using a food systems approach helps future proof the profession

Food "Scents"

The manner in which food is produced and prepared, "food ways" and cultural heritage, diet-health links, and changes in all of these provide a framework for considering how "modernization" of the food system both enhances and threatens equity and human health. And, because culture is dynamic over time, using food in the framework for academics, curriculum, everyday living and policy helps future proof the Home Economics profession.

The megatrends of globalization, prosperity, individualism, and technology all play into changing cultural influences on food choice. A global movement away from traditional vegetable/rice-based diets to one more inclusive of meat protein was mentionedin this Chapter's introduction. Academic home economists can help answer research questions related to influences that have changed traditional food ways. A brief review of the literature shows that sociologists and anthropologists have been most active in this area of inquiry (see Hoogland et al., 2005). Yet, the question of what changes occur due to the megatrends and the implications on food security and health is transdisciplinary. Academic home economists can be leaders in these investigations as we understand the value of examining well-being as a system. Publishing these transdisciplinary approaches to important research questions in a diversity of journals not limited to traditional Home Economics outlets can increase the reach of our expertise.

In a globalized society, there is danger of losing cultural heritage in terms of food ways. An increasingly industrialized food system takes away from the preservation of specialized food preparation techniques, including the loss of specific types of foods consumed on a smaller scale. The simple loss of access to a food product can change a family food tradition. On the other hand, home economists must question cultural heritage impacts on human health. The traditional recipe used to make plum pudding, for example, uses an animal-based fat, clearly not on the list of healthy fats.

Cultural food considerations are important in the area of food "scents" and are a good segue into how "modernization" of the food system leads to a possibly distorted view of foods. To continue the plum pudding example, it has been enjoyed at special occasions since the 15th century (Davidson, 2000). Contemporary advertising and marketing have led to over consumption of foods that just twenty years ago were reserved for "special" occasions. Serving sizes have also become increasingly distorted. Fast food and soft drink consumption are two such examples (Young & Nestle, 2002). Changes in serving sizes are not only found in food away from home. Wansink and Payne (2009) note that even the famous *Joy of Cooking* cookbook has increased portion sizes in its recipes over the years.

Food and culture are not limited to traditional foods attributed to specific areas around the globe or ethnic group. Culture can be more broadly defined and home economists must consider concepts such as "food for families," "food for gender," and "food for class" as well as "food for ethnicity or religion" (Bonnekessen, 2010). This approach further contributes to future-proofing the profession.

Modernization of the food system has also led to food safety issues including increased incidence of food borne illness. Attention to food preparation techniques that guard against food borne illness is a concept that home economists have historically translated to everyday living. In addition, some older problems we may have believed to be solved resurrect again. For example, the importance of milk pasteurization was an early 20th century issue. It has resurfaced in the 21st century as segments of consumers are interested in purchasing raw milk directly from farmers (Jay-Russell, 2010).And, many people living in developing economies routinely use unpasteurized milk.

Home economists can make a difference through everyday education stressing consumer knowledge of distorted portions and continued emphasis on nutrition education and food safety. Such issues will not disappear even when we have an "educated" public. New products, new marketing pitches, and continued advertising designed to sell more product using engaging and persuasive messages suggest that impartial information without a marketing spin will continue to be needed in the future. There are several areas of policy relevant in the arena of food "scents." On a local level, home economists can influence school menus to include a variety of cross-cultural menu items. Providing information to organizations that advocate for standardized portion sizes or information about portion sizes is another. Lobbying for corporate responsibility for, and increased government regulation of, food safety are other areas to which we can contribute.

Home economists of the future face many of the same issues we have in the past decades, just in different contexts (e.g., the megatrends). Yet, the dynamics of the food system have led us to consider these both in traditional and new ways. Although in the early 20th century, everyday teaching may have included ways to acculturate new immigrants to the U.S. food system, we are now faced with preserving and encouraging the preservation of culture in our diets. And, food safety issues include both old and new problems associated with food "scents." Understanding the food system and its complexity will allow home economists to continue to find relevance in research, curriculum planning, everyday living and make contributions to policy discussions, effectively future proofing the profession.

Summary

A food system approach is a powerful way to future proof the Home Economics profession. It embeds the notions of transdisciplinarity, complexity, dynamism and megatrends. It also generates a host of examples where home economists can play a major role in the next 100 years with regard to academics, curriculum, everyday living and policy. There are a few major points to highlight:

- Home Economics professionals have a holistic view of the world; therefore, we are well suited to be leaders in the transdisciplinary, complex future where a systems approach implies continual change, adaptation and reorganization;
- The holistic approach to well-being indicates that academic Home Economics professionals are well suited to lead teams of transdisciplinary researchers who address increasingly complex food systems problems;

- Home Economics curriculum must be transdisciplinary and include integrated coursework from numerous disciplines ranging from business and nutrition to media literacy and public policy, and held together by a core of Home Economics theory, philosophy and content;
- As problems facing households become more complex, Home Economics professionals will continue to be useful translators of scientific knowledge into everyday knowledge, which is useful "on the ground" and
- Home Economics professionals can add to policy discussions as they understand how the individual and household level of influence impacts the global and visa-versa.

Discussion Prompts

- Explain why Home Economics professionals are in an ideal situation to lead teams of academic researchers in transdisciplinary research endeavors;
- What is the value of embedding the Home Economics profession into a food systems model? What was your impression of the food sense approach in Figure 14.2?
- To address the messages contained in this chapter, what academic courses would you include in a University-level Home Economics curriculum, and why?
- Discuss the idea that "old" Home Economics topics related to the food system are new again and that "old" topics become relevant again in new ways. How will this view of the food system future proof the Home Economics profession?
- Discuss why Home Economics professionals should have a place at the "food policy table." What are some of the ideas they can contribute?

References

American Heart Association. (2010). *A history of trans-fat*. Dallas, TX: Author. Retrieved from http://www.heart.org/HEARTORG/GettingHealthy/FatsAndOils/Fats101/A-History-of-Trans-Fat_UCM_301463_Article.jsp.

Allen, G., & Albala, K. (2007). *The business of food: Encyclopedia of the food and drink industries*. Westport, CT: Greenwood.

Bolling, C. (2002, December). Globalization of the soft drink industry. *Agricultural Outlook*, pp. 25–27. Retrieved from www.ers.usda.gov/publications/agoutlook/Dec2002/ao297h.pdf.

Bonneskessen, B. (2010). Food is good to teach. *Food, Culture & Society,13*(2), 279–296.

Boycott Nestle: Facebook. (2012). Retrieved from http://www.facebook.com/group.php?gid=2299841105.

Davidson, A. (2000). *Oxford companion to food*. Oxford: Oxford University Press.

Food and Agricultural Organization of the United Nations. (2011a). *The state of food insecurity in the world 2011*. Rome, Italy: Author. Retrieved from http://www.fao.org/publications/sofi/en/

Food and Agricultural Organization of the United Nations. (2011b). *What does FAO do? Food forever! The Green Revolution*. Rome, Italy: Author.

Feed the Future. (2011). *About*. Washington, DC: Author. Retrieved from http://www.feedthefuture.gov/.

Friedman, E.(2009). Health care stirs up whole foods CEO John Mackey, customers boycott organic grocery Store. *ABC News*. Retrieved from http://abcnews.go.com/Business/story?id=8322658&page=1.

Friedman, M. (1999). *Consumer boycotts*. New York: Routledge.

Gehlhar, M. & Regmi, A. (2002, December).Shaping the global market for high-value foods. *Agricultural Outlook*, pp. 38–42. Retrieved from http://www.ers.usda.gov/publications/agoutlook/Dec2002/ao297k.pdf.

Hoffman, I. (2003). Transcending reductionism in nutrition research. *American Journal of Clinical Nutrition, 78* (Supplement), 514S–516S.

Hoogland, C.T., de Boer J., & Boersema, J.J. (2005). Transparency of the meat chain in the light of food culture and history. *Appetite, 45*(1), 15–23.

Jabs, J., & Devine, C. (2006). Time scarcity and food choices: An overview. *Appetite, 47*(2),196–204.

Jay-Russell, M. (2010). Raw (unpasteurized) milk: Are health-conscious consumers making an unhealthy choice? *Clinical Infectious Diseases, 51*(12),1418–1419.

Kolodinsky, J.,DeSisto, T., & Labrecque, J. (2003).Understanding the factors related to concerns over genetically engineered food products: Are national differences real? *International Journal of Consumer Studies, 27*(4), 266–276.

Kolodinsky, J. & Goldstein, A. (2011).Time use and food pattern influences on obesity. *Obesity,19*(12), 2327–2335.

Lichtenstein A.H., & Ludwig, D.S. (2010). Bring back home economics education. *Journal of the American Dietetic Association, 303*(18),1857–1858.

McGregor, S. L. T. (2010). Integral leadership and practice: Beyond holistic integration in FCS. *Journal of Family and Consumer Sciences, 102*(1), 49–57.

McGregor, S. L. T. (2011a). Home economics as an integrated, holistic system: RevisitingBubolzand Sontag's 1988 humanecology approach.*International Journal of ConsumerStudies, 35(1),* 26–34.

McGregor, S. L. T. (2011b). *Well-being, wellness and basic human needs in home economics.McGregor Monograph Series No. 201003.*Seabright, NS: McGregor Consulting Group. Retrieved fromhttp://www.consultmcgregor.com/documents/publications/well-being_wellness_and_basic_human_needs_in_home_economics.pdf

McGregor, S. L. T. (2012). Complexity economics, wicked problems and consumer education,*International Journal of Consumer Studies, 36*(1), 61–69.

Popkin, B., & Nielsen, S. (2003). The sweetening of the world's diet. *ObesityResearch, 11*(11), 1325–1332.

Reedy, J. & Krebs-Smith, S. (2010). Dietary sources of energy, solid fats, and added sugars among children and adolescents in the United States, *Journal of the American Dietetic Association, 110*(10), 1477–1484.

Thompson Klein, J. (2003). History of transdisciplinary research: Contexts of definition, theory, and the new discourse of problem solving. In *Encyclopedia of Life Support Systems.* Ramsey, England: Eolss Publishers. Retrieved from http://www.eolss.net/Sample-Chapters/C04/E6-49-01.pdf.

Thompson Klein, J. (2004). Prospects for transdisciplinarity. *Futures, 36*(4), 515–526.

Touliatos, J., & Compton, N. (1988). *Research methods in human ecology/home economics.* Ames, IO: Iowa State University Press.

Variyam, J. (2005). *Nutrition labeling in the food-away-from-home sector: Aneconomic assessment [Economic Research Report Number 4].* Washington, DC: United States Department of Agriculture.Retrieved from http://ageconsearch.umn.edu/bitstream/7235/2/er050004.pdf

Wansink, B., & Payne, C. (2009).The joy of cooking too much: 70 years of calorie increases in classic recipes. *Annals of Internal Medicine,150*(4), 291–292.

Whisk.(n.d.).*A fresh approach to home economics.*London, England: Author. Retrieved from http://www.whisk.biz/james_mcintosh.htm.

WHO/UNICEF. (1981). *International code of marketing of breast-milk substitutes.* Geneva, Switzerland: Office of Publications. Retrieved from http://www.who.int/nutrition/publications/code_english.pdf.

World Health Organization. (2004). *Global strategy on diet, physical activity and health.*Geneva, Switzerland: Office of Publications. Retrieved from http://www.who.int/dietphysicalactivity/strategy/eb11344/en/index.html

Young, L. R., & Nestle, M. (2002). The contribution of expanding portion sizes to the U.S. obesity epidemic. *American Journal of Public Health, 92*(2), 246–249.

CHAPTER
15

Sustainable Consumption Through an Environmental Lens: Challenges and Opportunities for Home Economics

Sylvia Lorek and Stefan Wahlen

We bring an environmental lens to our discussion of how to future-proof Home Economics in light of the 10 megatrends toward 2020 discussed in the stimulus chapter for this book. Environmental problems, upcoming resource scarcity and attendant global social inequity indicate that our contemporary, global structures will not be reliable in the future. Both academic research and civil-society bottom up initiatives for sustainable consumption expect an increasing need to ensure that products and services (e.g., food and energy) are supplied from local or regional sources. With its focus on the well-being of consumers, families and communities, Home Economics has much to contribute to the issue of sustainable consumption.

As home economists with expertise in environmental issues, we wish to paint a different picture of selected megatrends and go further than suggested by the Copenhagen Institute for Future Studies (Anderson, Kruse, Persson, Mogensen & Eriksen, 2006). Examining some of these megatrends with the assumptions dominating the debates within the sustainable consumption research community, which is international and quite transdisciplinary (Jackson, 2006; Lorek, 2010; Princen, Maniates & Conca, 2002; Røpke & Reisch, 2004; Tukker, 2008), we arrive at different estimations about the future — less optimistic than the predictions of the authors of the Copenhagen Institute's analysis. The consumer sustainability research community at large is not as optimistic about the future as is the Copenhagen Institute for Future Studies (Anderson et al., 2006), especially regarding the issues of climate change, which has the potential to alter the entire world, and technology (two megatrends).

Many environmental and social factors are jeopardizing our future and making it very unlikely that business can go on as usual. In the following section, we provide some arguments from an environmental point of view, partly combined with societal ones, for moving beyond the megatrends identified by Anderson et al. (2006), in the first chapter. We especially address the issues of climate change and the overuse of resources and of peak oil as examples of the seriousness of our present situation (Lorek, 2010; Lorek & Fuchs, 2011). Similar cases can be made for each of the other megatrends identified in this book's stimulus chapter. We chose climate change and technology because both of these are our areas of expertise which truly have the potential to change the future of the world and because Home Economics has much to contribute regarding the potential to change.

Reframing Climate Change

The environmental threat most discussed these days is climate change or, more precisely, the possibility of a climate disaster. Accepted wisdom is that humans must prevent the earth from warming more than two degrees Celsius if we are to prevent apocalyptic climate outcomes. To stay within the limit of a two-degree warming, the International Energy Agency (2008) clearly points out that even if the 34 OECD countries were to reduce their emissions to zero, it would not be sufficient to reach the goal of not heating earth above two degrees. Thus, strong measures have to be taken and they have to be taken right now. The Intergovernmental Panel on Climate Change (IPCC) (2007) calculates that governments only have until 2015 to manage the turnaround to decreasing greenhouse gas (GHG) emissions. If this reduction/turn around does not happen, weather extremes, desertification, a rise of the sea level, etcetera will affect many countries and their peoples — causing suffering and migrations replete with attendant tensions and conflict.

In addition to the threats of climate change, the production capacities of planet earth are also over-stressed. The Global Footprint Network (2012) regularly calculates the availability of renewable resources, measured in the amount of biologically productive lands and their overuse. The resources available for a year (for all humans on the planet) are consumed earlier year by year. The day when human beings start living beyond the annual reproduction capacity of the globe is annually calculated as the Earth Overshoot Day. In recent years, this date now falls in September. This date means that humanity uses about 30% more resources in one year than nature can regenerate within this year.

And, this figure is only an average. A closer examination of the figures of resource consumption offers clear insights into inequity on Earth. In Europe (excluding Russia), around 36 kg of resources are extracted per person per day, while every European consumes 43 kg per day in average (a 19% shortfall). This shortfall indicates that Europeans need resources from the other regions of the world to maintain their current level of unsustainable consumption. This unbalance is even higher in other world regions. An average North American consumes around 90 kg per day; inhabitants in Oceania about 100 kg per day. In Asia, resource consumption is about equal to resource extraction at around 14 kg per person per day. The average resource consumption of an African is only 10 kg per day, lower than the extraction of 15 kg per day. These figures mean Europeans consume three times as many resources as an inhabitant of Asia and more than four times as much as an average African. Inhabitants of other rich countries consume up to 10 times more than people in developing countries (SERI, Global 2000 & Friends of the Earth Europe, 2009).

At the centre of the global industrialized economy is a specific non-renewable resource, crude oil. It is not only that transport depends upon it, but so do petrochemical industries, which produce pesticides, fertilizer and fibres. For some time now, it has been predicted that oil production will peak in the near future, and then decline. This shrinking supply of oil faces an increasing demand from growing developing and developed economies (Campbell & Laherrère, 1998; Hirsch, Bezdel & Wendling, 2005; International Energy Agency, 2008). The effects are predictable: rising prices and potential conflicts about access to available oil reserves. The same thing applies to other resources, such as phosphor. These alarming figures demand that we manage austerity in time, as the precautionary principle demands (Diederen, 2009). This principle implies that there is a social responsibility to protect the public from exposure to harm, when scientific investigation has found a plausible risk (Kriebel et al., 2001).

Reframing Technology

Those who accept that the problems presented by the earth's limited capacity are indeed serious tend to offer, as solutions, new technological developments that bring efficiency and build on renewable resources. Doubling wealth with a halving of resource use is a popular concept in this context, promoted as 'Factor 4' (Weizsäcker, Lovins & Lovins, 1998). Those advocating for this approach envision that resource use can be decoupled from economic growth. Although relative decoupling can indeed be observed (the pressure is growing, but slower than economic growth), an absolute decoupling, where ecological pressures are stabilised independently from the monetary growth of economies, is not in sight. The rebound effect regularly undermines technological efficiency gains through behavioural or other systemic responses to the introduction of new technologies that offset the intended beneficial effects. For example, in cars, despite more efficient engines, the km driven per litre of fuel is nearly at the same level as in the 1980s, due to heavier cars, air conditioning in cars, etcetera. What would be necessary in the long run is a progressive decoupling where the pressure is significantly reduced (Watson, Carlsen & Szlezak, 2008). And, this reduction is not insight so far — at least not economy wide. Relying on efficiency will quite likely not work, and is even less likely to work in the context of growing economies.

There are high hopes for the further use of renewable energy sources and quite a few initiatives have already been set in motion. Optimistic estimates expect that, for example, 35% to 50% of German energy provision could come from renewable sources by 2050. But what about the rest (if we remember that even a reduction of GHG emissions to zero in the developed countries is not enough)? The title of

Trainer's (2007) book reflects this concern: Renewable Energy Cannot Sustain Consumer Society. Critical minerals needed for photovoltaic energy production, for example, are scarce and their calculated demand is up to 6 times higher than current extraction rates (Institut für Zukunftsstudien und Technologiebewertung, 2009). Also, bio-fuel will be not able to satisfy current and growing world energy demands. There is simply not enough land from which to get bio-fuel and, anyway, bio-fuel is already competing with the land needed for food production (Heinberg, 2003; Kunstler, 2006), another disconcerting aspect of inequity (Martinez-Alier, 2002).

All these examples show that the technologies that the Anderson et al. (2006) praised for potentially overcoming the limits on growth are themselves subjects to limits. With foreseeable limits of (cheap) oil and the lack of alternatives, our energy-based, highly industrialized and globalized lifestyle is obviously under strain. It is not just a matter of how to produce goods and services with less energy or how to transport them around the globe. Resource scarcity also challenges our suburban lifestyle wherein we live, work, care, recreate and shop in different places, and thus have to travel constantly between them.

Home Economics' Contributions toward More Sustainable Consumption

As home economists, we share this more pessimistic view on the future so we can make suggestions for how Home Economics can future-proof itself relative to helping individuals and families deal with the fallout and the opportunities pertinent to these and other megatrends. From our point of view:

(a) Environmental limits will have a much stronger influence on future developments than suggested by the Copenhagen projections (Anderson et al (2006);

(b) This pressure on the environment will strongly influence future processes of globalization in the direction of more regionalization and localization;

(c) Resource scarcity will also affect prosperity or, said another way, worsen the inequity between those who can afford higher resource prices and those who will suffer from disturbing mining, production and distribution conditions;

(d) Also, the *solving potential* of new technologies is seriously in question, from our standpoint and

(e) Social networks are rising on countless bottom-up initiatives, beyond the digital reality, which can overcome people's search for individualization. Elinor Ostrom's research on 'the commons' serves as an indication of how seriously people are taking the development of bottom-up globalization (Ostrom, 1990) (she received the Nobel Memorial Prize in Economic Sciences in 2009).

From this more critical perspective of two of the most pressing megatrends (environment and technology), we now highlight how the rich knowledge of Home Economics can contribute towards more sustainability for society's future, doing so in ways that ensure we future-proof the profession at the same time.

> "Home Economics is a field of study and a profession …to achieve optimal and sustainable living for individuals, families and communities"(IFHE, 2008, p. 6).

The above quote clearly indicates that 'sustainability,' as well as 'the well-being of individuals, families and communities,' are located at the core of Home Economics. With its focus on individuals, families and communities, our profession will have truly relevant answers when food and energy supplies no longer derive from globalized markets, but have to be provided through local structures. While technological developments have driven the last century, social innovations are needed most in the century ahead. The re-cultivation of old and partly forgotten cultural knowledge seems a possible opportunity. The increasing incapability to grow food, and even too cook it, opens opportunities for Home Economics. The same could be said for other areas dealt with by Home Economics (clothing, housing, child rearing, caring, resource management) and opportunities abound by which we can tender social and family-oriented innovations as well as technological innovations.

The following text discusses how Home Economics can contribute to the challenges outlined above, and to various aspects of the 10 megatrends toward 2020 (Anderson et al. 2006). The four dimensions of Home Economics mentioned in the introduction of this book (see also IFHE, 2008; Pendergast, 2008) will serve as an orientation for this discussion. Wahlen, Posti-Ahokas and Collins (2009) provide a vision of Home Economics. Using empirical examples, they discuss how the understanding of Home Economics differs across regions as well as over different generations. This divergent cultural knowledge about how to cope with the everyday (see argumentation above) might serve as a starting point across generations as well as for future developments and the next century of Home Economics. We do not *do* Home Economics the same way around the world, and this diversity should be respected and used to our advantage as we future proof the profession.

Dimension 1: Everyday Living

Everyday life is the fundamental focus of Home Economics and can be understood as what seems to be the most familiar to us. Everyday life is the fulfilment of everyday tasks, in routine settings, in households and families (Felski, 1999). The everyday is specific for each of us and might be experienced in settings like a family or a household, in the context of care-taking institutions such as elderly homes, or in other settings. All other dimensions of Home Economics then gather around everyday life. Rationalizing and modernizing forces have affected the organization of everyday life in households and families since the second half of the last century, promoting more 'efficient resource management in households.' However, the resources that were to be used efficiently were often time and men/women's power. These human resources were often optimized at the cost of the overuse of natural resources, from biomass to energy. Although home economists are aware of cultural differences in the everyday, the increasing use of industrial food can be found amongst all consumers, around the globe, more than half in developing countries already (Worldwatch Institute, 2010). Nevertheless, Home Economics also taught people, for example, how to sustain healthy diets despite the flood of pre-prepared meals and drinks containing unnecessary amounts of fat, sugar and huge varieties of additives.

The most interesting questions then are, "how does everyday life relate to the discussion of consumption patterns outlined above, especially as we struggle to reframe towards less climate change or to sensitize people to rely less on blind confidence in the solving potential of new technologies?" "How can everyday life contribute towards more sustainable consumption patterns?" As Lorek and Spangenberg (2001) and Spangenberg and Lorek (2002) point out, housing, food and mobility (transportation) matter most in our efforts to ensure strong, sustainable consumption. Their findings are confirmed by other studies (Gatersleben, Steg & Vlek, 2002; Lähteenoja et al., 2007; Nissinen et al., 2007; Noorman, Biesiot & Moll, 1999; Vitterso, Strandbakken & Stø, 1999). To be more precise, it is the following products, services or activities that matter the most in our efforts to consume responsibly:

- Housing: the square meters used; the way of heating/cooling, isolation, the type of house;
- Food: the share of animal products in the diet, the type of production, the distance between production and consumption, reduction of food waste and
- Mobility: the mode of traveling (ranging from plane, car, other motorized vehicles to bicycle and foot.

In these three areas, households can make a difference. Home Economics can increase efforts to support developments towards more sustainable consumption patterns in order to address climate change, not only relying on more efficient technology, but also considering social innovations. This support would involve closer investigations into how consumption in these areas can be fulfilled in more sustainable ways. For example, how do we enable living in urban communities, which allows for lower use of living area for the individual? How do we narrow the distance between farmer and consumer? How do we create public or other ways of non-individual mobility, which is attractive? How do we encourage the development of social networks which, from our point of view, will form a vital part of the changes needed?

Dimension 2: Academic discipline

The academic discipline of Home Economics is concerned with the training and socialization of emerging scholars and practitioners and manifests in the arena of research with new knowledge by applying certain methodologies, including scientific, interpretive and critical (McGregor & Murnane, 2010); however, being epistemologically and ontologically diverse, and calling, for example, for transdisciplinary research (McGregor, 2007), home economists can focus on everyday life in common. Accordingly, there is no single and unified approach to Home Economics research, although a call for a more coherent approach has been made (Pendergast, 2008). Home Economics as an academic discipline should strive to provide knowledge on the everyday life and on sustainable consumption in order to assist (a) in the development of curricula as well as (b) in influencing policies and (c) advocating for sustainable consumption patterns that ensure the wellbeing of individuals and communities and that ensure the latter can contribute to sustainability.

Even though Home Economics has been addressing sustainable development in general, further exploration is needed. Especially, these further explorations could be taken up by home economists in the academic and research arenas, collaborating with practitioners engaged with the other three dimensions of Home Economics (everyday life, community and societal). Together, they can grasp the whole picture of sustainable consumption and how Home Economics, in particular, can contribute. Working in isolation and in specialized areas of Home Economics expertise is not enough anymore. These specializations have to be integrated into holistic practice.

Home Economics is in a qualified position to theoretically develop sustainable consumption approaches and to implement these in good practice examples. For example, they can suggest new theoretical approaches to overcome consumption theories that perceive households as fulfilling the main function as players in economic markets. home economists can turn this on its head by emphasizing that the wellbeing of people is what matters most (not the market), especially as this concerns sustainable consumption. Peoples' needs can be fulfilled via market and non-market activities — as they have done for centuries. This idea is not to be misunderstood as a nostalgic wish to recreate the past; however, being aware of the cultural past helps people cope with the present and with getting ready for the future. With the dominant focus on market activities — reflected in the paralysing effect of a focus on Gross Domestic Product (GDP) development — non-market activities are ignored. Engaged Home Economics research could help to bring these aspects of everyday life to the public's attention again.

Joint efforts among home economists working in diverse career paths, from the practical perspective, should also be taken into account in research for sustainable consumption. There are home economists who are active in schools, teaching pupils. There are opportunities to influence stakeholders in policy, for example, from home economists working in research institutes or as politicians. In the end, all home economists are specialists in everyday life practices of families and they should be able to articulate how these mundane practices have profound impacts on future sustainability.

To generate further research-based knowledge about sustainable consumption and production, home economists, especially in the academic arena, should use the principle of interconnectedness that is associated with our discipline. Not only can they examine what can be understood as sustainable consumption, they can address, maybe most importantly, how to answer the question of how far sustainable consumption can be enacted in practice? The knowledge of how to enable sustainable consumption, for instance, by educating or by influencing policies, has to be reflected theoretically in order to highlight the changes and challenges that occur in society, in everyday life and in enacted sustainable practices.

Dimension 3: Curriculum area

As outlined above, there are three decisive consumption clusters in which consumers can make a change: food, housing and mobility (transportation). For example, food has been, and continues to be, a key focus of Home Economics. Capabilities for how to cope with, adapt to and affect the everyday have been addressed since the establishment of Home Economics. Accordingly, Benn (2009) calls for practical wisdom and an understanding of coherence and competencies for everyday life. She provides objectives for education in the area of Home Economics. Her concept of competence development can be applied to realizing sustainable lifestyles in order to reduce GHG-emissions, as well as to live life in more sufficient ways. The empowerment of consumers, for example, can be facilitated by Home Economics education. The IFHE programme committee on consumer issues has established an online e-book on education for sustainable development (O'Donoghue, 2008). This knowledge database on the promotion of sustainable consumption is continuously growing and includes a variety of approaches to the challenges outlined above, approaches developed solely by home economists. Other home economists are encouraged to avail themselves of these rich intellectual and practical contributions.

Education serves as a stimulus to enable sustainable consumption and to empower consumers and families to live a more sustainable and responsible way of life. Once there is agreement amongst home economists on how to practice sustainable consumption in the areas of food, housing and mobility, consumers and families need to be educated accordingly. It is important to not just point the finger at families' bad habits, but rather to promote some kind of critical approach so that new, future challenges can be addressed as well. It must be clear that society will change. Accordingly, education in the domain of Home Economics must draw upon its and others' ever-changing knowledge base to educate individuals and families to be critical towards the present situation in everyday life and how to encourage them to always sustainably and responsibly address the ever present challenges they face in their everyday context.

Dimension 4: Societal arena to influence and develop policy

Home economists should be aware of the potential uses for their knowledge about everyday practices. This knowledge can be useful when formulating policy measures that, for instance, might not follow classic economic theory and principles, such as a consideration of the consumer as sovereign. With the everyday as a locus of practice, the perspective shifts and allows for different theories of the economy (feminist, ecological, behaviourist) and of sustainable development in order to address the challenges inherent in reframing climate change and technology.

One such approach could be to strengthen home economists' and others' recognition of the satellite system of accounting for households in the context of alternative measures for well-being. Satellite systems of accounting for GDP re-value the contributions of non-market based activities, like traditional family work, care giving, charity or neighbourhood help (Egerton & Mullan, 2006; Schäfer, 2004; Schiess & Schön-Bühlmann, 2004). This approach would be a valuable contribution to the ongoing debate on alternative measures of well-being (Stiglitz, Sen & Fitoussi, 2009), the raison d'être of Home Economics.

Political contexts set the conditions for consumption (Lorek, Spangenberg & Oman, 2008; Wolff & Schönherr, 2011). In order to help families change their lifestyles towards a more sustainable way, the political conditions and systems of provision (consumption and production) should make it easier to enable lifestyle changes (Thøgersen, 2005). In the domain of mobility, for example, consumers will not use more public transport if there is no public transport; they will not use the bicycle unless it is not dangerous to drive (e.g. cycling lanes). Sustainable food has to be available or being made available.

Also of relevance to this discussion is Wahlen, Heiskanen and Aalto's (2011)discovery that practitioners bring different interpretations of what can be understood as sustainable food consumption. Policy makers and catering professionals (e.g., in school canteens), as well as consumers, describe and interpret sustainable consumption differently. Thus, it is important to be aware of the multiple interpretations that can be evoked by introducing sustainability measures in curricula as well as in policy initiatives. These should be aligned with the various understandings prevailing in everyday life of individuals as well as communities. Home economists can serve as mediators or facilitators between these different professionals and between the professionals and families, even among families. Wider, more informed dialogue is needed if Home Economics is to future-proof itself around the issue of sustainability.

Summary

Home Economics, with its vital history over the past century, has played important roles for individuals and families in their everyday lives. In order to gain further relevance, it would prove important to actively engage in debates and activities promoting sustainable consumption from a Home Economics perspective. The quaternary character of Home Economics, with its foundations in everyday life and a knowledge base in the academic arena, serves as a pivotal connection that can develop curricula as well as influence policy. This interconnectedness might serve as an imperative aspect in overcoming the knowledge-practice gap for establishing sustainable consumption patterns (Lebel et al., 2006; Lebel & Lorek, 2008). There is a vast amount of knowledge on sustainable consumption; yet, in practice, little change has been achieved, as we have demonstrated above. Change would requirecorresponding curricula innovations in conjunction withmeasures ranging from policy to the everyday lives of consumers. The challenges outlined in this chapter can and should be addressed by Home Economics. The next century will show how it might be possible that Home Economics becomes more involved in the discussion on sustainable consumption, better yet, leading the discussion and proposed changes:

- Environmental problems, resource scarcity and global inequity will challenge our lifestyles more than expected;
- How home economists address thesechallenges will strongly influence further processes of globalization, ideally in the direction of more regionalization and localization;
- Resource scarcity will affect prosperity and worsen the inequity of society because ttechnological optimism has not proven to be justified;

- Social attempts towards more sustainable lifestyles, in turn — however blooming — are underestimated and insufficiently supported;
- In order to address these challenges with sustainable consumption patterns, the everyday has to be acknowledged as an arena that enables sustainable consumption;
- Further research on everyday sustainable consumption and its enactment in practices is needed, for example overcoming the theory-practice gap;
- Education for sustainable development has to be supported in order to empower consumers to strive to live more sustainably and responsibly and
- Policy should recognize everyday life as a network of practices associated with sustainable consumption.

Discussion Prompts

- How can Home Economics contribute to the further development of social and service innovation to complement the previous emphasis on technological development?
- How can Home Economics enhance the contributions of non-market based activities, like traditional family work or neighbourhood help?
- How can Home Economics support individuals and communities to live a sustainable, everyday life?
- What kinds of concepts, theories and research methodologies are needed in order to promote more sustainable consumption in the context of everyday living?

References

Anderson, K., Kruse, M., Persson, H., Mogensen, K., & Eriksen, T. (2006). *10 megatrends toward 2020*. Copenhagen, Denmark: Copenhagen Institute of Future Studies.

Benn, J. (2009). Practical wisdom, understanding of coherence and competencies for everyday life. *International Journal of Home Economics, 2*(1), 2-14.

Campbell, C. J., & Laherrère, J. H. (1998).The end of cheap oil.*Scientific American, 278*(3), 60-65.

Diederen, A. M. (2009). Metal minerals scarcity: A call for managed austerity and the elements of hope. Rijswijk, The Netherlands: TNODefence, Security and Safety.

Egerton, M., & Mullan, K. (2006). *An analysis and monetary valuation of formal and informal voluntary work by gender and educational attainment*. Colchester: University of Essex: ISER Working Paper.

Felski, R. (1999). The invention of everyday life. *New Formations, 39*, 15–31.

Gatersleben, B., Steg, L., & Vlek, C. (2002). Measurement and determinants of environmentally significant consumer behavior. *Environment and Behavior, 34*(3), 335-362.

Global Footprint Network. (2012). *Earth overshootsday*. Retrieved from http://www.footprintnetwork.org/en/index.php/GFN/page/earth_overshoot_day/

Heinberg, R. (2003). *The party's over*. Gabriola Island, BC: New Society Publishers.

Hirsch, R. L., Bezdel, R., & Wendling, R. (2005). *Peaking of world oil production. Impacts, mitigation, & risk managements*. Pittsburgh, PA: National Energy Technolgy Labratory.

IFHE. (2008). Position statement "HE21C". *International Journal of Home Economics, 1*(1), 6-7.

Institut für Zukunftsstudien und Technologiebewertung. (2009). *Rohstoffe für Zukunftstechnologien [Raw materials for future technologies]*. Karlsruhe, Germany: Author.

International Energy Agency. (2008). *World energy outlook 2008*. Paris, France: Author.

IPCC Intergovernmental Panel on Climate Change. (2007). *Synthesis report of the IPCC Fourth assessment report.* Gland, Switzerland: Author.

Jackson, T. (2006).*The Earthscanreader on sustainable consumption.* London: Earthscan.

Kriebel, D., Tickner, J., Epstein, P., Lemons, J., Levins, R., Loechler, E. L., et al. (2001). The precautionary principle in environmental science. *Environmental Health Perspectives, 109*(9), 871–876.

Kunstler, J. H. (2006). *The long emergency: Surviving the end of oil, climate change, and other converging catastrophes of the twenty-first century.* New York: Grove Press.

Lähteenoja, S., Lettenmeier, M., Kauppinen, T., Luoto, K., Moisio, T., Salo, M., et al. (2007). Natural resource consumption caused by Finnish households. *Paper presented at the Proceedings of the Nordic Consumer Policy Research Conference.* Helsinki, Finland. Retrieved from http://www.kuluttajatutkimuskeskus.fi/files/5359/proceedings_consumer2007.pdf

Lebel, L., Fuchs, D., Garden, P., Giap, D., Hobson, K., Lorek, S., et al. (2006). *Linking knowledge and action for sustainable production and consumption systems.* Chiang Mai, Thailand: Sustainable Production Consumption System Project.

Lebel, L., & Lorek, S. (2008). Enabling sustainable production-consumption systems.*Annual Review of Environment and Resources, 33*, 241-275.

Lorek, S. (2010). *Towards strong sustainable consumption governance.* Saarbrücken, Germany: LAP Publishing.

Lorek, S. & Fuchs, D. (2011). Strong sustainable consumption governance: Precondition for a growth path? *Journal of Cleaner Production.* Advance online publication. *http://dx.doi.org/10.1016/j.jclepro.2011.08.008.*

Lorek, S. & Spangenberg, J. H. (2001).Indicators for environmentally sustainable household consumption. *International Journal of Sustainable Development, 4*(1), 101-120.

Lorek, S., Spangenberg, J., & Oman, I. (2008).*Sustainable consumption policies effectiveness evaluation (SCOPE2) — Conclusion.*Vienna, Austria: Sustainable Europe Research Institute.

Martinez-Alier, J. (2002). *The environmentalism of the poor: A study of ecological conflicts and valuation.* Surrey, England: Edward Elgar.

McGregor, S. L. T. (2007). Consumer scholarship and transdisciplinarity. *International Journal of Consumer Studies, 31*(5), 487-495.

McGregor, S. L. T., & Murnane, J. A. (2010). Paradigm, methodology and method: Intellectual integrity in consumer scholarship. *International Journal of Consumer Studies, 34*(4), 419-427.

Nissinen, A., Grönroos, J., Heiskanen, E., Honkanen, A., Katajajuuri, J. M., Kurppa, S., et al. (2007). Developing benchmarks for consumer-oriented life cycle assessment-based environmental information on products, services and consumption patterns. *Journal of Cleaner Production, 15*(6), 538–549.

Noorman, K. J., Biesiot, W., & Moll, H. C. (1999).Changing lifestyles in transition routes towards sustainable household consumption patterns.*International Journal of Sustainable Development, 2*(2), 231–244.

O'Donoghue, M. (Ed.). (2008). *Global sustainable development: A challenge for consumer citizens*[e-Book]. Bonn, Germany: IFHE. Retrieved fromhttp://www.educationforsustainabledevelopment.org/index.html.

Ostrom, E. (1990). *Governing the commons: The evolution of institutions for collective action.* Cambridge, England: Cambridge University Press.

Pendergast, D. (2008). Introducing the IFHE position statement.*International Journal of Home Economics, 1*(1), 3–7.

Princen, T., Maniates, M., &Conca, K. (Eds.). (2002). *Confronting consumption.* Cambridge, England: MIT Press.

Røpke, I., & Reisch, L. (2004).*The ecological economics of consumption.* Cheltenham, England: Edward Elgar.

Schäfer, D. (2004). *Unbezahlte arbeit und bruttoinlandsprodukt 1992 und 2001 — Neuberechnung des haushalts-satellitensystems.* Wiesbaden, Germany: Federal Statistic Office, Germany.

Schiess, U. & Schön-Bühlmann, J. (2004). *Satellitenkonto saushaltsproduktion — Pilotversuch für die schweiz.* Neuchatel, Switzerland: Swiss Federal StatisticOffice.

SERI, Global 2000, & Friends of the Earth Europe.(2009). *Overconsumption? Our use of the world's natural resources.* Vienna, Brussels: Authors.

Spangenberg, J. H., & Lorek, S. (2002). Environmentally sustainable household consumption: From aggregate environmental pressures to priority fields of action. *Ecological Economics, 43*(2/3), 127-140.

Stiglitz, J., Sen, A., & Fitoussi, J. P. (2009).*Report by the Commission on the Measurement of Economic Performance and Social Progress*. Paris, France: Commission on the Measurement of Economic Performance and Social Progress.

Thøgersen, J. (2005). How may consumer policy empower consumers for sustainable lifestyles? *Journal of Consumer Policy, 28*(2), 143-178.

Trainer, T. (2007). *Renewable energy cannot sustain a consumer society*. Dordrecht, Germany: Springer.

Tukker, A. (Ed.). (2008). *System innovation for sustainability 1*. Sheffield, England: Greenleaf.

Vitterso, G., Strandbakken, P., & Stø, E. (1999). Sustainable consumption and the consumer: Introducing the green household budget. *Paper presented at the Second International Symposium on Sustainable Household Consumption*.Groningen, The Netherlands: Center for Energy and Environmental Studies.

Wahlen, S., Heiskanen, E., & Aalto K. (2012). Endorsing sustainable food consumption: Prospects from public catering. *Journal of Consumer Policy 35* (1): 7–21. doi: 10.1007/s10603-011-9183-4

Wahlen, S., Posti-Ahokas, H., & Collins, E. (2009). Linking the loop: Voicing dimensions of home economics. *International Journal of Home Economics, 2*(2), 32-47.

Watson, D., Carlsen, R., & Szlezak, J. (2008).*An SCP indicator set for EEA reporting — Draft working paper*. Copenhagen: European Topic Centre on Resource and Waste Management.

Weizsäcker, E. U., Lovins, A. B., & Lovins, L. H. (1998).*Factor four: Doubling wealth, halving resource use — Areport to the Club of Rome*. London: Earthscan.

Wolff, F., & Schönherr, N. (2011). The impact evaluation of sustainable consumption policy instruments. *Journal of Consumer Policy, 34*(1), 43–66.

Worldwatch Institute. (2010). *State of the world 2010: Transforming cultures*. New York: W.W. Norton.

CHAPTER
16

Anchoring Skills for Sustainable Development in Vocational Training: Curricula for Home Economics and Hospitality Professions

Nancy Mattausch, Carola Strassner and Irmhild Kettschau

Humanity is the main driver of environmental changes on earth. The boundaries in systems such as biodiversity, climate change and human interference with the nitrogen cycle have already been exceeded. For global freshwater use, change in land use, ocean acidification and interference with the global phosphorous cycle humanity may soon be approaching the boundaries. Such changes might lead to an eroding resilience of major components of the earth-systems (Rockström et al. 2009, p. 472f). In due consideration of an increasing world population and its orientation to adopt the consumption patterns of the western world, the change towards sustainable lifestyles is inevitable.

In conjunction with sustainable development, the production and processing of food plays an important role, as it requires huge amounts of limited resources, e.g. energy, drinking water and arable land. Multiple and diverse products and services, and with them corresponding professions, are necessary to secure and design the food supply and feeding of our populations. The food economy has to take over responsibility for creating sustainable products and services, for which well trained staff are required. Despite the high relevance of our food systems for sustainable development, there is insufficient systematic consideration of it in subject-specific vocational training.

In order to address this we need to be clear about sustainable development. A sustainable food system, and central points of sustainable food service, is a necessity for today's society and future societies. Together with a detailed understanding of working processes in this industry we then have to apply a competence model which puts forward the essential competencies required of professionals to meet the challenges within our food system.

The concept of sustainable development

Sustainable development is a global movement and is by now applied to almost all parts of our lives. In Germany it is closely associated with historical developments in silviculture. In 1713 Hannß Carl von Carlowitz from Saxony (Germany) reported on the basic concept of a sustainable silviculture in his thesis called *"Sylvicultura Oeconomica"*. At that time Europe was undergoing dramatic losses in forests, due to coal mining and wood being the most important fuel for the industry and households. Carlowitz postulated that this kind of silviculture would lead to severe ecological and thus economic problems. He therefore demanded that only as many trees as could grow again be cut down. This is also known as the resource-economic principle, as it balances economic and environmental interests. For a long time this principle was limited to silviculture and fishery. Until the 20th century people did not carry over this principle to other industries, because technological and scientific progress seemed to allow unlimited growth. Around 1970 it became obvious that technological progress and the lifestyle of the industrialized nations threatened what the economy relies on — the environment. *"The limits to growth"*, a report for the Club of Rome (Meadows et al, 1972) and the first oil crisis in 1973 contributed to a public debate about limited resources and environmental problems. These are linked to social aspects such as allocation and access to limited resources, e.g. drinking water (Grunwald & Kopfmueller 2006, p. 17ff). The 1st Environmental Conference in 1972 discussed these relations with the keyword Ecodevelopment, which later became characteristic for the understanding of sustainable development.

Today's understanding of sustainable development dates back to the report of the World Commission on Environment and Development in 1987 in which it is explained as the "development that meets the needs of the present without compromising the ability of future generations to meet their own needs" (WCED 1987). Also known as the Brundtland-Commission, after its chairwoman Gro Harlem Brundtland, it paved the way for the United Nations Conference on Environment and Development (Earth Summit) in Rio de Janeiro in 1992, where the Agenda 21, a comprehensive action plan adopted by 178 governments attending, was passed.

Since the 1990s sustainable development is linked with the three dimensions 'ecology', 'economy' and 'social equity' (see Figure 16.1). Social equity relates to today's societies on our planet, signifying equity between industrialized and developing countries, and also between today's generation and future generations. That means we are asked to reduce our consumption of natural resources in a way that provides good living conditions for future generations as well. The dimensions are in mutual dependence on each other and their attainment is to be well balanced.

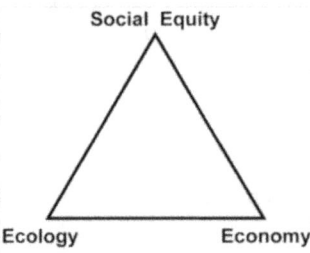

Figure 16.1

The sustainability triangle.

Education for sustainable development

The world population faces several challenges as mentioned in the introduction. It is clear that education must play a central role in the transition towards a sustainable future, which is the central challenge in the 21st century. It can neither be achieved by single groups nor nations nor by a centrally managed "top-down strategy". The process of change — and this is what sustainable development is about — rather has to be created by all individuals. Sustainable development is indeed a complex model, encompassing economic development, social equity and environmental protection. This is where education comes into play. Agenda 21 includes a whole chapter on education, and its key role for sustainable development is stated as follows: "Education is critical for promoting sustainable development and improving the capacity of the people to address environment and development issues" (Agenda 21, chap. 36.3).

Education for sustainable development (ESD) is an educational process, meaning education that:

- enables people to foresee, face up to and solve problems that threaten life on our planet;
- spreads values and principles that form the basis of sustainable development, such as intergenerational equity, gender parity, social tolerance, poverty reduction, environmental protection and restoration, natural resource conservation, just and peaceful societies and
- points out the complexity and mutual dependence of the three dimensions ecology, social equity and economy (UNESCO 2006, p. 5).

ESD helps individuals to fully develop the attitudes, values, skills, perspectives and knowledge necessary to make informed decisions, so that the quality of life on a local and global scale is improved. ESD encompasses both formal and non-formal education for everyone, at all stages of life and in different learning contexts. Koichiro Matsuura, Director-General of the United Nations Educational, Scientific and Cultural Organization (UNESCO), calls for ESD to become a concrete reality for all of us, on an individual, organisational and governmental level and in all of our daily decisions and actions (UNESCO 2006, p. 3).

United Nations World Decade "Education for Sustainable Development 2005–2014"

At the World Summit on Sustainable Development 2002 in Johannesburg, South Africa, the United Nations Organisation decided to declare the years 2005–2014 as the "United Nations World Decade of Education for Sustainable Development". The overall mission of the movement is to implement the principles, values and practices of sustainable development in all areas of education and learning worldwide. The Decade functions on a broad basis. Governments, civil society, NGOs and the industry are invited to join and all stakeholders take part in achieving these aims through (UNESCO 2006, p. 5):

- promoting and improving the quality of education;
- reorienting curricula from pre-school to university;
- raising public awareness of the concept of sustainable development and
- educating the employed (especially directors and workers in trade and industry).

Translated to a country level, take the example of Germany. The Decade was implemented by the German Commission for UNESCO under the patronage of the Federal President and with support from the Federal Ministry of Education and Research. The German Commission for UNESCO presents all ESD-related activities on a web portal, enabling cooperation and networks on a national level (www.bne-portal.de). The platform also provides learning and teaching materials for different target groups. Within the Decade every single year focuses on a special theme ('cities' in 2011, 'food' in 2012). The German Commission for UNESCO also awards recognition biennially to Official German Projects of the UN-Decade for ESD. By the end of 2011 more than 1400 awards were given. Amongst these is the project "Vocational training for sustainable development in the food industry and Home Economics" presented later in this chapter.

Sustainable development in vocational education and training

"Training is one of the most important tools to develop human resources and facilitate the transition to a more sustainable world" (Agenda 21, chap. 36.12). In the Agenda 21 several activities to achieve this goal are listed, such as "Countries and educational institutions should integrate environmental and developmental issues into existing training curricula and promote the exchange of their methodologies and evaluations" (Agenda 21, chap. 36.16). Irrespective of ESD, vocational schools and training centres (in Germany) have to fulfil an educational mission, to address the main challenges and problems of our time — problems that students of vocational schools must be able to face in vocational settings and their everyday life. Each era has its typical key problems. Ours are, for example, the conservation of natural resources and the protection of our own health, the handling of new media, creation and protection of our own identity in a society characterized by pluralism, living together in a globalized world with many different cultures and being prepared for a discontinuous working life.

Sustainable development as part of German training curricula has — up to 2011 — been realised for very few professions such as tourism management clerks or industrial clerks. Education for sustainable development still depends on the motivation of vocational teachers and trainers. However, at least 'environmental protection' is an integral part of all training curricula in Germany. No matter if someone becomes a home economist, hairdresser, bricklayer or sales person, environmental issues related to the profession have to be addressed. In the next step now necessary, curricula must be expanded for the aspects of social equity and economic development or the three dimensions, and reorganized in a way that the focus is more on the interdependencies between these dimensions.

Sustainable feeding

Food is one of the most fundamental needs of humans everywhere. Its consumption is a practical concern of individuals, families and communities (groups) in life every day. This brings it into the essential dimension of Home Economics as the IFHE Position Statement (2008) so clearly explains. Our food systems today are a mix of local, national and global structures and interdependencies, in some cases highly sophisticated while in others not even meeting the most basic needs of the chronically hungry.

Challenges of sustainable feeding on a global scale

Taking such a central part in the daily lives of humans, food and feeding will be particularly impacted upon by the global megatrends described in Chapter 1. They will bring challenges and opportunities alike to our food systems which we now recognize as having to be met in a sustainable way.

Ageing will increase the need for food-related services in the health and aged care sectors — commercialisation and technical development will support this development. The continued decoupling of our diets from our neighbourhoods and seasons will require further energy and technical resources for production and transport, with potentially damaging consequences for our environment. Globalization of our food ways will bring questions about the balance of power and the rights of marginalized groups (via the food sovereignty movement). Prosperity and urbanization bring a higher demand for meat, for dairy and for processed foods while commercialization will raise the demand for convenient food services for a more western diet. These foods and this lifestyle (eating style) need more resources than currently used, such as arable land (to grow crops to feed intensive animal husbandry), water (for the crops too) as well as operating materials (such as fossil fuel based fertilizers and pesticides). This process will result in more greenhouse gas emissions unless we change our production systems and our consumption habits. Meat, or more precisely its high use, is being discussed as one of the central problems in the climate debate. We consume about twice the recommended servings of meat per week in the western diet. So voices calling for restraint are doing not just our health a favour but the overall balance on our planet as well. Adopting a more vegetarian-oriented diet needs experts to steer us clear of simply exchanging meat for non-endemic fruits, vegetables and cereals whose production may put further pressure on already overburdened regions of the world.

All these will require home economists and hospitality professionals that are sensitized to interdependencies, knowledgeable about options in the food system and able to see consequences of their decisions in all spheres. Especially they will need to know the central points about sustainable production and consumption.

The central points of sustainable feeding

The central points of sustainable production and consumption in the food system can be approached from a number of perspectives. We can place Home Economics and hospitality professionals in the context of the food and agriculture systems worldwide by looking at the global issues according to the Food and Agriculture Organisation (FAO), a specialized agency of the United Nations. In the past five years these have continually included biodiversity, bioenergy, water, climate change, hunger, food safety and the worldwide food situation. The past decades have brought us evidence of the negative impact of our current resources management. This evidence requires of us to learn to think and act as part of an ecosystem.

Taking food service as a particular example of production and consumption in the food system, we can focus on the resources commonly used to provide the service (see Figure 16.2). Decisions professionals need to make about the resources in the food service sector can be divided into short-term and long-term decisions. Short-term decisions include those about foods bought, use of preparation methods and skills and to a certain degree use of energy, water and finances. Long-term decisions

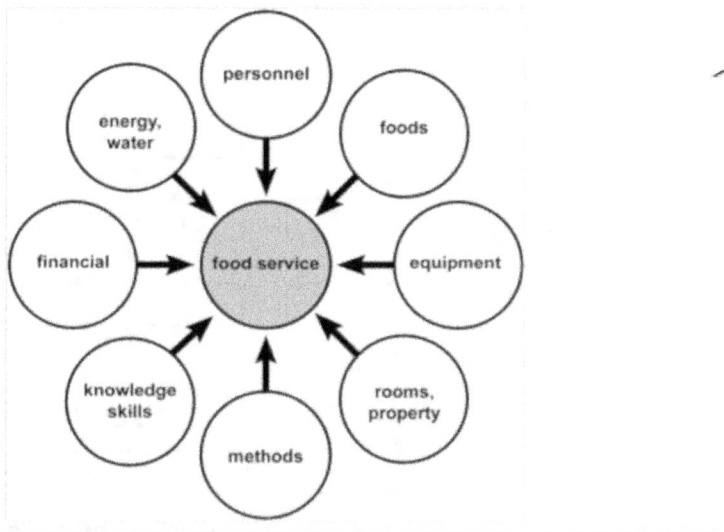

Figure 16.2

Diagram of resources commonly used in providing food service.

include maintenance or procurement of machines, technology, rooms and property. As the two most important areas in terms of their potential impact we can identify staff (people) and foodstuffs. The former is a central point because it essentially impacts on every other resource employed in food service, on their utilisation and care, drawing on the knowledge present and skills mastered. The latter is a central point because decisions made about which foods and which food qualities (e.g. organic) will be procured, have an impact on the production within the food system. Technology (and machines), in turn linked to energy and water use, would be a third central point, though not so quick to change per unit of operation.

A third approach to identifying central points of sustainable feeding focuses on the value chain underlying food services (see Figure 16.3). The values of a food service provider are conveyed to the consumer by the menu, whether these are explicit or implicit. The menu tells a story about which foods are important, in what volumes, frequencies and forms they are included in the service provision, and what self-concept the provider has. The act of drawing up the menu is preceded by decisions about, for example, the amount of meat versus the vegetarian options or whether fruits and vegetables included are in season. This menu planning is a central point in sustainable feeding. It is closely connected to the next link in the chain, the act of procurement. Again, the potential impact of procurement decisions up the line on food production and on foodways is greatest at this juncture. This has been recognized in the European Union in the field of public procurement, especially for public institutions such as hospitals, homes for the aged and schools. Toolkits to assist professionals are already available for green (GPP) and/or sustainable public procurement (SPP). Preparing the food means using available equipment and technology. Appropriate training in the use of the hardware can impact strongly on other resource use such as water and energy.

Thus Home Economics and hospitality professionals need especial knowledge

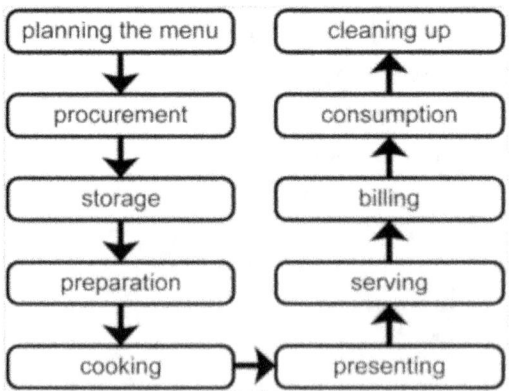

Figure 16.3

Schematic representation of the value chain for a food service provider.

about the various food production and processing systems, and about the differing impacts of these systems on the ecosystem, including the human element (e.g. fair trade). This means that the more limited system boundaries accepted by professionals up to now will need to change to ones including elements both upstream and downstream. It is this increased ability for home economists to make informed choices in a professional setting, that we seek to be able to convey to consumers at home, too. (IFHE Position Statement 2008). As such these competencies need to be embedded in Home Economics and hospitality curricula.

Sustainability-oriented core curriculum for vocational training of home economists and hospitality Professionals

How can a complex concept such as sustainable development be integrated into training curricula? Which are the core competencies to enable professionals to manage the multi-dimensional challenges they are confronted with? In the previous sections we have learned that staff and foodstuffs are the resources having a main impact on the quality and sustainability of food services. Their impact is greatest during menu planning and procurement.

We now have to combine these facts with a competence model, which in turn fulfils two requirements:

- appropriateness for the promotion of competencies with relevance to sustainable development and
- connection to the leading pedagogical and didactical ideas of vocational training (country specific).

A European project about sustainability management in the food industry (EuKoNa, 2007–2009) distinguishes between competencies specific to a profession and core competencies relevant for acting in a sustainable way, which are both essential for apprentices. The latter are:

- systemic and cross-linked thinking;
- availability of inter-professional knowledge and its application in concrete situations;
- the ability to deal with complexity;
- understanding closed-loop structures and life-cycles and
- social sensitivity, intercultural competence and willingness of the individual for a global perspective (Tiemeyer 2009, p. 43).

If we now look at the vocational requirements of Home Economics (according to IFHE 2008) we will find that it is surprisingly close to the competencies mentioned above. As explained in the IFHE Position Statement (2008) Home Economics combine several disciplines in an interdisciplinary approach. Everyday life is a complex challenge necessitating professionals to bridge one-dimensional thinking, which enables home economists to make an optimal living for individuals, families and communities. This is in some aspects similar to the concept of sustainable development. Being multi-dimensional, too, it aims to maintain and promote good living conditions for us, our children and grandchildren, here with a stronger focus on maintaining our natural resources at the same time. From these similarities we can conclude that Home Economics offers excellent preconditions for integrating the concept of sustainable development into curricula. Home Economics indeed seems to be predestined for implementing sustainable development for another reason: the ethics of the profession is based on values such as caring, sharing, justice, responsibility, communicating, reflection and visionary foresight (IFHE 2008). Comparing these values with the concept of ESD, we again find similarities, e.g. to foresee problems, display social tolerance and justice. And finally, sustainable development itself is a future-proofing strategy that will only succeed if every one of us takes over responsibility in occupational, societal and individual settings. These values and competencies form a robust basis for making informed choices. Nevertheless, the ability of thinking in (biological) cycles has to be strengthened within Home Economics (and the hospitality industry). Professionals must be aware of themselves being part of the cycle. They must recognize interdependencies and gain a deeper understanding of how they can change parameters in different working processes along the value chain so that their decisions contribute to the collective good.

With regard to the competencies specific to a profession, it is essential to check existing training curricula for elements which are already adequately included and connected to sustainable development. Insufficient contents must undergo a systematic development. The following excursus will exemplify this analysis for the German vocational training system.

The German vocational training system is a dual-system (duration of training is usually three years), divided into practical training in businesses and education in vocational schools (one or two days a week). Hence, there are two curricula for each profession:

- general training schedule for the practical training in businesses and
- core curriculum for vocational schools according to the Standing Conference[1].

The content of both curricula is matched, so that the more theoretical training in vocational schools complements the more practical work in businesses and vice versa. Therefore both curricula must be analysed and renewed.

Excursus on the project "Vocational training for sustainable development in the hospitality industry and Home Economics"

The project is operated by the Institute of Teacher Training for Vocational Education at the University of Applied Sciences in Muenster/Germany (runtime 2010–2012). The aim is to anchor skills for sustainable development in vocational training curricula for Hospitality-professionals and home economists.

The methodology used to develop the core curriculum mainly is a mixture of analysing existing curricula and examining typical working processes of the mentioned professions. These tools are necessary to identify significant action situations that are highly relevant for sustainable development. Curricular analysis has been carried out exemplarily for four skilled professions:

- Chefs;
- Home economists;
- Restaurant specialists and
- Professional caterers.

All curricula did not contain the term 'sustainable development'. They were then examined for terms with reference to sustainable development such as *'ecology'*, *'environment'*, *'social equity'*, *'economy'* and *'health aspects'*. An extract from the core curriculum of the Standing Conference for home economists shows some results:
- considering qualitative, economic and environmental aspects at procurement (learning field 2);
- knowing about the hygienic, economic and environmental importance of appropriate storage (learning field 3) and
- during the preparation process: keeping in mind the relevance of high-quality food and beverages for a healthy diet (learning field 4).

The existing curricula contain several important aspects of sustainable development, but predominantly fragmented. Connecting these to a comprehensive curriculum is the basis for recognizing interdependencies within the food system and finding solutions. To become successful, the new curriculum must also link more strongly to the central points of sustainable feeding.

Raising attractiveness of Home Economics and Hospitality professions

May a sustainability-oriented curriculum have the potential to future-proof a profession and raise its attractiveness? In Germany, professions in the hospitality industry and Home Economics are not highly regarded by many young people. Hospitality professions such as chefs are to some extent less regarded because of strenuous working conditions (e.g. heat, humidity, working hours and overtime). Salaries are often low compared to other service professions. Commercial and clerical professions are — among others — more popular. Figure 16.4 exemplifies the decline of apprenticeships for chefs, home economists and restaurant specialists in Germany. For professional caterers the number is on a more stable level possibly because chain restaurants are becoming more important. A further decline of apprenticeships finally might result in a skills shortage. Even though the data in Figure 16.4 represent the situation in Germany, it can be assumed that the tendency is similar in other industrialised countries, as one reason for the decline is the demographic change.

Providing professionals with skills and competencies for developing and realising strategies of sustainable food services is both essential and reasonable. It is essential to contribute to the reduction of environmental and to some extent the economic burden connected with food production and procession and to establish equitable feeding on a global scale. It is reasonable to provide young professionals with a modern, future-oriented occupational profile, especially in less regarded professions. Society is constantly and rapidly changing. We therefore require pro-

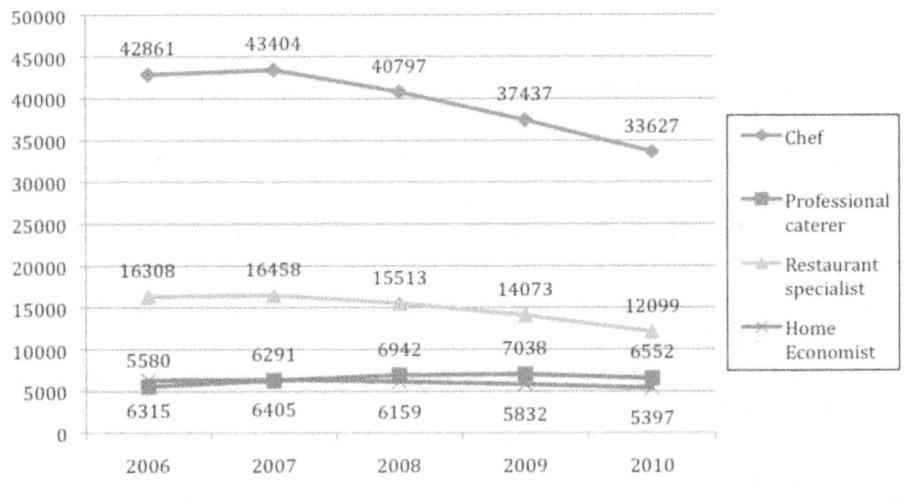

Figure 16.4

Decreasing number of apprenticeships in Germany (Source: BIBB database)

fessionals that are 'expert novices', good at learning new things and able to find solutions for emergent issues and challenges (IFHE Position Paper 2008). Being flexible and thinking multi-dimensionally are characteristics which might increase their options for good jobs with higher salaries. The change towards a sustainability-oriented curriculum may contribute to move away from the image of old-fashioned housekeeping and make the brand 'Home Economics' recognisable, attractive and future-proofed.

We are facing the challenges of sustainable development in the vocational context but also from a societal and individual perspective. The combination of these three levels applies to Home Economics in general, as it deals with the basic needs of humanity. However, with all the challenges arising from the global depletion of natural resources, we need new daily living skills. The competencies gained during vocational training can be transferred into daily life. That is one of the great potentials of Home Economics. With a deeper understanding of life cycles and our impact on them, professionals have the opportunity to go further than simply mastering daily life. This serves to raise awareness that our professionals can make contributions to sustainable development at all different levels in life.

Sustainable development is a future-oriented, "21st century thinking concept". It should be mandatory for all curricula. Those industries that implement ESD into their curricula will set the standards for further debates about vocational training. Consequently there will be an increasing pressure on other industries to follow the concept.

Summary

Education and training are the keys for the transition towards a sustainable world. The UN-Decade of Education for Sustainable Development strengthens global activities to implement the principles, values and practices of sustainable development in all areas of education and learning worldwide. The chapter discusses how to design new curricula for professions such as Home Economics, enabling professionals to create food services that contribute to sustainable development. This future-proofing strategy in turn contributes to make Home Economics a recognizable brand.

- Training is one of the most important tools to develop human resources and facilitate the transition to a more sustainable world (Agenda 21, ch. 36);
- Against the background of a growing world population we have to change our food patterns by consuming less meat and dairy and focusing more on what is in season;
- Menu planning and procurement of foodstuffs are the most important processes along the value chain of food services in terms of sustainable development. Considering resources, foodstuffs and personnel having the greatest potential for impact;
- Home Economics is predestined for integrating the concept of sustainable development as both require inter-disciplinary knowledge and takeover of responsibility and
- The integration of modern concepts such as sustainable development into curricula may increase the attractiveness of Home Economics to young people, which is in turn important to avoid skills shortages in the future.

Discussion Prompts

- Why is it essential, mainly for western societies, to change our consumption patterns and with them our foodways and diets?
- What are processes and resources with the greatest potential impact regarding sustainable food services?
- Which role are education and training playing for the transition to a more sustainable world? And which skills and values should therefore be promoted?
- To what extent do Home Economics and the hospitality industry have to make a contribution to sustainable development?
- What are the core competencies for home economists and other food-related professions for making informed choices in vocational settings?
- How can the attractiveness of professions in Home Economics and the hospitality industry be raised?

Endnotes

1 The Standing Conference of the Ministers of Education and Cultural Affairs of the Laender in the Federal Republic of Germany

References

Agenda 21. [Online] http://www.un.org/esa/dsd/agenda21/ (Retrieved December 28, 2011)

BIBB, Bundesinstitut für Berufsbildung [German Federal Institute for Vocational Education and Training]: number of apprenticeships — time series. Database apprentices.http://www.bibb.de/de/1108.htm (Retrieved January 30, 2012)

Grunwald, A. & Kopfmueller, J. (2006). *Nachhaltigkeit.* [Sustainability]. Frankfurt a.M.: Campus.

Rockström, J.; Steffen, W.; Noone, K.; Persson, Å; Chapin, F. S.; Lambin, E. F.; Lenton, T.M.; Scheffer, M.; Folke, C.; Schellnhuber, H.J.; Nykvist, B.; de Wit, C.A.; Hughes, T.; van der Leeuw, S.; Rodhe, H.; Sörlin, S.; Snyder, P.K.; Costanza, R.; Svedin, U.; Falkenmark, M.; Karlberg, L.; Corell, R.W.; Fabry, V.J.; Hansen, J.; Walker, B.; Liverman, D.;Richardson, K.; Crutzen, P. Foley, J.A.: A safe operating space for humanity. *Nature 461,* 472-475(24 September 2009)

Tiemeyer, E. (Ed.) (2009). *Europäische Kompetenzentwicklung zum nachhaltigen Wirtschaften in der Ernährungsbranche. Herausforderungen, Projektergebnisse und Transferkonzept.* [European competency development for sustainable management in the food industry. Challenges, project results and transfer concept.] Ministerium für Schule und Weiterbildung des Landes Nordrhein-Westfalen.

UNESCO, United Nations Educational, Scientific and Cultural Organization (2006*): Promotion of a Global Partnership for the UN Decade of Education for Sustainable Development (2005-2014). The International Implementation Scheme for the Decade in brief.*http://www.bne-portal.de/coremedia/generator/unesco/de/Downloads/ Hintergrundmaterial__international/IIS_20englisch.pdf (Retrieved December 28, 2011)

WCED, World Commission on Environment and Development (1987). *Our common future.* [Online] http://www.un-documents.net/wced-ocf.htm (Retrieved December 29, 2011).

CHAPTER

17

Envisioning an African-Centric Higher Education Home Economics Curriculum for the 21st Century

Lois R. Mberengwa and Fungai M. Mthombeni

Home Economics as a discipline of study was introduced into Africa mainly through missionary activity in the first half of the 20th century. However, training educators to teach in higher education institutions on African soil did not begin until the last half of the 20th century. To fill this gap, teachers were trained abroad, mostly in England, Canada and the United States. They then returned to teach in African institutions. As a result, the content of most Home Economics higher education and public school programmes in Africa reflects a strong Western influence. The relevancy of these programmes has oftentimes been criticized, warranting programme evaluation and review. Africa is a unique continent (54 countries) with particular challenges for its individuals and families. While embracing similarities and the leadership provided by Western paradigms, African home economists need to be sensitive to these unique challenges and to their own culture in order to create an appropriate curriculum that is relevant to their context. This chapter first explores the current challenges that are faced by Black African families in the Southern African Development Community (SADC) region. This overview is followed by a discussion of the challenges that emanate from professional Home Economics practice. It concludes by envisioning an ideal Africentric Home Economics higher education curriculum for socializing future generations of African home economists.

Historical background

As noted, Home Economics, as a discipline of study in African schools, was introduced during the first half of the 20th century, mainly through missionary activity (Atkinson,

1972; Kiamba, 2005). Teachers were often missionaries' wives who wanted to train women and girls so they could become better maids and housewives. The women were therefore taught basic housekeeping skills, including hygiene, in order to improve the living conditions in homes (SIAPAC-Africa, 1990).

Today, Home Economics professionals, including those in Africa, agree that the scope of Home Economics is much broader. It is no longer just limited to the home, but expands into the larger community, including the world of work. By focusing on the "trilogy of prevention, education and development" (McGregor, 2010, p. 28), home economists work to improve the quality of life of individuals and families by paying attention to the practical perennial problems encountered on a daily basis from generation to generation. To ensure continuity of this important work into the 21st century, Africa needs Home Economics educators with the right attributes, skills and knowledge.

Provision of such educators has always been a challenge in Africa, as previously noted in the Introduction to this chapter. Because the content of most African Home Economics programmes reflects a strong Western influence,critics have described the programmes and curricula as irrelevant for African professional practice, highly foreign, and not taking into account African developmental needs and problems. As well, curricula are criticised for lacking any focus on critical thinking, and for lacking qualified personnel, at all levels (Waudo, 1993).Such criticisms, and related ones, have provided the basis for programme reviews in most African countries.

To focus the discussion offered in this chapter, we will set out the challenges faced by Black African families in the 15 countries (Angola, Botswana, Democratic Republic of Congo (DRC), Lesotho, Madagascar, Malawi, Mauritius, Mozambique, Namibia, Seychelles, South Africa, Swaziland, United Republic of Tanzania, Zambia and Zimbabwe) making up the SADC. These countries constitute a common trading region. The economic, political and social development levels of these countries are highly diverse, with some countries being far more developed than others. The populations are also diverse in terms of ethnicity, race and gender. Despite this diversity, the majority of the SADC countries have similar developmental challenges. Because all of the 15 countries have subscribed to the United Nations Millennium Development Goals (Economic Commission for Africa, 2005), they also have common social development agendas for the first quarter of the 21st century. The major challenges faced by families in the SADC are issues related to poverty, health and disease, food security and nutrition, migration and urbanization, conflict, and technological changes (similar to the megatrends identified in the Chapter 1 for this book, but lived out differently in Africa). Home Economics has the potential to contribute towards these national development goals. We discuss the aforementioned challenges in the following section.

Challenges confronting Black African families in the SADC

Poverty

Poverty can be defined in different ways according to the context in which the concept is being applied. We use Wodon and Zamani's (2010) definition of economic poverty, defined as a state of one's income being inadequate to maintain quality of life. Every family wishes to meet its basic needs for shelter, food and clothing, but this reality remains a dream for most African families. Political instability and harsh economic factors have forced governments to resort to budgets cuts — eliminating access to even the most basic services such as health and education. Jobless youth are a common sight in the SADC. Poor harvests caused by natural disasters result in hunger and starvation in rural households, and food prices in urban areas increase. Conflict and war have also worsened famine in some countries, thus exacerbating poverty.

Conflict (including domestic violence)
Southern Africa is not a stranger to wars and conflict. Wars, regardless of what causes them, expose the family and its members to many risks including: death, injury, orphan-hood, sexual abuse, and rape, which may culminate in illegitimate children. Children are left without the needed care, protection and support from families. Some become 'street children' and are at risk of abuse. Women, like children, are also exposed to vulnerability through widowhood. Female-headed households are also vulnerable because men are engaged in combat. Education and socialization are disrupted because schools are destroyed. Other basic survival needs tend to dominate the time and energy of the adults, leaving little time for education.

Education
Educating a child is generally expensive in the SADC. Primary school education is free in most of these countries, or only a minimum fee is charged, but families are expected to pay for both secondary and tertiary (college or university) education. Most families strive to send their children to school in the hope that their children will live a better life and help take care of their parents and siblings. However, the high tuition fees are beyond the reach of most families. This situation, compounded by the negative effects of HIV/AIDS, forces most children to drop out of school in order to look after their younger siblings.

Health and Disease
The face of the African family has been affected by wars and diseases, more so than any other factor. Millions of African children have been orphaned by HIV/AIDS. The pandemic is concentrated disproportionately among younger, economically active and, often the best educated, family members — impacting the economic performance of the family. Malaria is another big killer among African children. About 20% of Africa's children die before they reach the age of five. Orphaned children are usually left with no older blood family members to care for them. The extended family system, which traditionally cushioned such children, is severely challenged as it fails to cope with the ever-increasing number of orphaned children (Washi, 2002).

Aside from disease, other health-related issues such as sanitation, clean drinking water and fuel supply remain chronic challenges for most African families. Without a permanent supply of clean water, it is impossible to achieve good sanitation. Food security and nutrition are also pressing health issues faced by families living in the SADC.

Food Security and Nutrition

Basic food security is achieved when all people have access at all times to the food required to maintain a healthy life. At the household level, food security refers to the ability of a household to secure adequate food that will meet dietary intake requirements for all members of the family. In the SADC, malnutrition, due to inadequate food intake and poor nutritional quality of diets, causes death among children and women of child-bearing age. For example, it is estimated that 20% of African women have a low Body Mass Index (BMI) due to chronic hunger (Lartey, 2008).

Several reasons have been attributed to Africa's insecure food resource base. These include: erratic rainfall patterns which cause droughts, dependence on rain (not complemented with irrigation during the growing season), inadequate agricultural inputs for subsistence farmers and poor harvests and food wastage resulting from inadequate and inappropriate storage mechanisms which prevent families from having access to food during the dry months. These challenges have formed, and should continue to form, an integral part of the work of Home Economics extension officers so that, together with other development partners in the field, they can assist families to be food secure. With Botswana, South Africa and Lesotho rated as the only three SADC countries likely to meet the MDG target of eradicating extreme poverty and hunger by 2015, the work for home economists in this area is immense.

Migration and urbanization

Migration, identified as one of the megatrends, is the largest source of urban expansion in Africa and has placed extra burdens on families. Whether voluntarily or involuntary, men and women are leaving their homes in search of better economic opportunities in cities, neighboring countries, and internationally. Working women have now joined the workforce and are forced to combine their traditional roles of childrearing and household chores with earning money to supplement household income. Some children try to escape from hunger or bereavement and quickly become street kids. Living environments in cities become congested, thus creating environmental disasters and health risks that threaten people's lives. Urbanization has also caused people to increasingly depend upon purchasing food commodities rather than producing their own. As a result, people's diets and eating patterns change as they adopt new values and lifestyles. International migration has caused disruption in family set-up and marriages. The effects of urbanization and migration are likely to continue well into the 21st century, as the world moves more and more towards becoming a global village.

Globalization, technological changes and industrialization

Technology drives development and is a major determinant for classifying the status of countries as developed or underdeveloped. Most SADC countries are regarded as underdeveloped mostly because they lag behind in technological advancement in most economic and social sectors. Although rich in natural resources, sectors such as mining and agriculture are underexploited due to a lack of appropriate technologies that facilitate value added to most products (SADC, 2008). Although the role of small and medium enterprises (SMEs) in Africa's development has always been recognized, the challenge in the 21st century is to make sure that they are viable and sustainable. This success depends partly upon the acquisition and use of appropriate technologies, supported by the creation of a conducive environment and relevant and effective implementation of policies that support growth and trade, and empower SMEs. home economists need to be aware of the challenges in the employment/industry sector so that they can strategize towards minimizing the negative effects of globalization on families, and the proliferation of cheap quality products on African markets.

Information technology has both positive and negative impacts on the manner in which family members interact, and on the structure of African families. With increased access to television, computers and the internet, traditional ways of interaction are challenged. The structure of African families is also changing, with the trend towards nuclear families. Single parenting and cohabitation are becoming more acceptable (Washi, 2002). To be able to work with families, home economists need to be aware of all these developments and how they influence family life.

Challenges emanating from professional practice

The first section of this chapter profiled the profound challenges SADC families are facing in the new millennium, ranging from life threatening conflict and diseases, through life-altering urbanization and changing family structures, to the ubiquitous challenges of globalization and technological innovations. The magnitude of these problems is perennial, never going away, and experienced differently by each generation. These problems will likely dominate the social development agendas of most African nations throughout the 21st century. Home Economics has a role to play in contributing to Africa's future as it is affected by strong families.

But, home economists in Africa are truly challenged as they strive to embrace this professional challenge. It is necessary to acknowledge and give voice to their challenges before suggesting a new vision for a higher education curriculum for socializing future generations of African home economists. Lessons learned from struggling with the current situations can inform plans on how to future-proof the African Home Economics profession. Home economists are grappling with the absence/ineffectiveness of professional Home Economics associations, the hyper-specialization of the discipline, and the declining popularity of Home Economics as a school subject.

Absence/ineffectiveness of professional associations

McGregor (2008) argues that home economists need to build professional communities of practice where professionals can engage each other and deliberate on concerns affecting their field of study so that the body of knowledge does not become stagnant and so that the profession is future-proofed. One major player in this process is professional associations, which serve several key functions in the role of future-proofing the profession. They seek to further the interests of the profession, its members, and those of the public. Many professional associations are involved with the development and monitoring of professional educational programs, the certification of practitioners and/or the upgrading and professional development of members (Harvey, 2009).

The Home Economics Association for Africa (HEAA) was active during the 1990s. Its mission was to "facilitate the process for individuals, families and communities to become responsible for improving their well being in relation to their economic, social, cultural, political and [the] physical environment" (the 1993 HEAA Constitution as cited in Kiamba, 2005, p. 22). HEAA slowly slipped away in the early 2000s as it tried to stand on its own after sustained funding from the Canadian Home Economics Association (CHEA). Since then (2003), the IFHE-Africa Region, which is affiliated to the International Federation of Home Economics (IFHE), has been formed. It is headed by two Vice Presidents and members come from approximately 10-15 countries out of a possible 54 African nations. Each Vice-President of IFHE-Africa is keen to build synergy amongst home economists from the African nations, but this task is challenging due to the geographical logistics of meeting, a lack of contact information, and inadequate responses for calls to contribute to the association's efforts. In addition, many African home economists do not have reliable access to social networking technology, such as email, Facebook, Twitter, Linkedin, Nings or Wikis (SidigaWashi, personal communication, January 23, 2012). Lack of access to each other makes the dissemination of information and the process of networking and acting in solidarity, very challenging.

Indeed, there is little continent-wide networking and solidarity amongst practicing home economists in Africa, which could be promoted through a viable continent-wide professional association. There is no centralized website, common conferences nor professional journal or newsletter(s). Despite the fact that some African nations have their own professional Home Economics associations and journals, sometimes their roles are undermined due to the lack of effective leadership, committed and adequate membership and funds. All these inadequacies indicate a strong need for a vibrant professional community for African home economists, without which it is difficult to lobby for or effect, curricula changes required in higher education to help address the challenges faced by African families.

Hyper-specialization in the discipline

The hyper-specialization of Home Economics is evident in African nations. Most Home Economics programmes in universities and colleges in Southern Africa have been reviewed during the last five years in order to address the needs of the changing market and of the programmes. The general trend has been to do away with the 'family focus' in preference for specialization (Kiamba, 2005). For example, in 2010, the University of Swaziland revamped its programmes and is currently emphasizing consumer science/education issues. Similarly, in South Africa, consumer issues now dominate what were traditional Home Economics programmes (van Wyk, 2005). The niche for Home Economics programmes, the family, has been de-emphasized in these programmes, thus making the concept of family well-being vulnerable.

Hyper-specialization has the tendency to divert Home Economics from its traditionally holistic mission of facilitating family-well-being and quality of life. Ogwu

(2010) observes that Home Economics in Africa seems to be threatened and is losing its visibility and its position in the curriculum. This decline reflects dwindling enrolments of students opting to study the subject in schools. Such trends raise concerns about the future of Home Economics in Africa.

As well, with increased hyper-specialization, those who graduate from related training programmes are no longer labelled as 'home economists,' but carry other specific job titles. Eventually, by the end of the 21st century, professional Home economists will be eradicated if something is not urgently done. Unfortunately, this loss is happening at a time when Home Economics is needed to help steer community development in Africa and to reach the MDGs agreed to by the SADC.

Declining popularity of Home Economics as a subject of study
The educational level at which Home Economics is taught in public schools in Southern Africa varies from country to country, with some countries offering a strong component of Home Economics in primary schools, while others place it as part of other subjects, such as Creative and Performing Arts (e.g., Botswana), and still others teach it in non-formal sectors, or it is not taught at all. Regardless of when it is introduced into the public school curriculum, most Home Economics programmes in African schools, including colleges and universities are characterized by a shortage of human resources and equipment, by irrelevant textbooks, and by irrelevant content, among others (Mberengwa, 1997; Ogwu, 2010).

Most African governments also fail to consistently provide a safe, rich and progressive environment where children can pursue their educational dreams. In those locales were war prevails, education and socialization are disrupted because schools are destroyed. Other basic survival needs, therefore, tend to take precedence, leaving little time and energy for education.

It is a fact that some African children as young as 12 years of age are already heads of families due to loss of parent(s) or their abandonment. It is important to expose children to the basic skills and knowledge they need in order to make decisions in their everyday life, even when they are still in primary school. Home Economics is one vehicle that can be used to transmit this knowledge. Inadequate provision of a stable and resource-rich educational environment is, therefore, a threat to the sustainability of African Home Economics programmes in the 21st century.

The proposed Africentric higher education Home Economics curriculum

Tertiary or higher education is a critical component in the shaping of empowered Home Economics professionals who will take charge of development efforts in their communities. We should emphasize that the role of the home economist in contributing towards Africa's future is even more crucial in the 21st century than it was a century ago. The magnitude and nature of the problems in Africa is perennial, never going away, experienced differently by each generation. As noted, these problems will likely continue to dominate the social development agendas of most African countries throughout the 21st century.

In the light of IFHE's (2008) four dimensions of professional practice in Home Economics, we make the following suggestions for an Africentric Home Economics curriculum for the 21st century. Figure 17.1 summarises our ideal curriculum for Home Economics in Africa. It is organized using the four dimensions of Home Economics proffered by the IFHE Position Statement (2008). The dimensions should not be seen as separate entities, but as an integrated whole. The cross-cutting themes influence the orientation of Home Economics in all the arenas.

Home Economics as a societal arena

The curriculum should uphold African core values and strengths. Values of respect, tolerance, togetherness, sharing, caring, honesty, morality, discipline, dignity, solidarity, communication and others characterize many traditional African societies

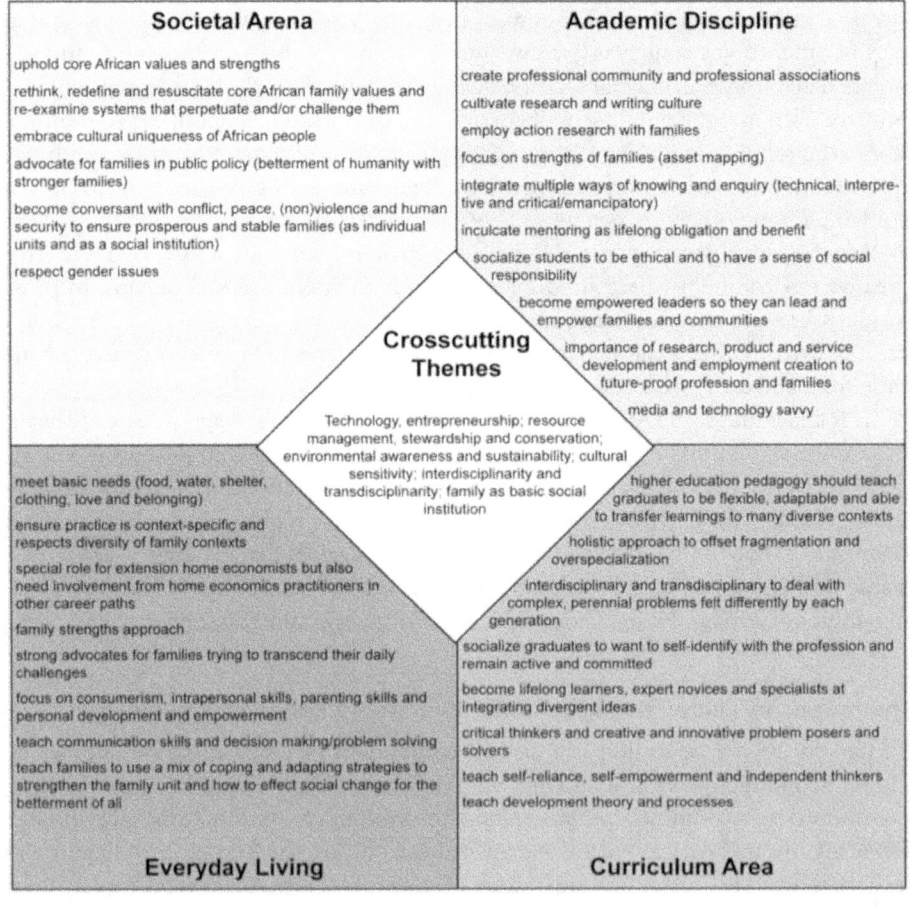

Figure 17.1

Home Economics in Africa: The four dimensions.

(Mberengwa, 2003). The setup in traditional African families, including ways of communication, where the elders were the 'teachers,' facilitated the nurturing of these values and made them achievable. Today, these values are threatened with modernization and with the issue of human rights (where even children can challenge their parents). These threats tend to undermine the desired aspirations expressed in the African traditional values. Home economists need to rethink, redefine and, if possible, resuscitate some of these values, and re-examine the systems in which they function in an attempt to redress the social challenges confronting African families. The curriculum should also embrace the cultural uniqueness of African people. For example, African hospitality, diets, shelter, parenting, child-rearing practices and artifacts should be woven into the higher education curriculum. As well, Home Economics university students should be trained in, and socialized into, the processes needed to be advocates for effective public policy for the betterment of humanity through strong families. As well, in order for families to prosper, peace and stability are needed in African homes. Home Economics university students should be conversant with these issues (conflict, (non)violence, peace and justice and human security).

Home Economics as an academic discipline

Training programmes should strive to socialize and generate Home Economics graduates who have the required core competencies needed to sustain the profession beyond the 21st century. Professionals are needed who will work tirelessly as advocates for families and their communities. Home Economics professionals who are themselves empowered can in turn empower those they work with also. University students need to be socialized to be ethical, to have a sense of social responsibility and to value their role as leaders of their communities (and be able to lead communities forward). These professional attributes can be nurtured through a sustained socialization and training programme. It must value research and product and service development as ways of creating new knowledge. It must teach leadership skills and foster in university students the belief that mentoring is an important socializing function of Home Economics professionals. The university degree program must integrate various modes of enquiry and knowing, including the technical, interpretative and emancipatory approaches.

We have also observed that there is poor documentation of research activities and of information about the existence and focus of higher education programmes by African scholars in general. African Home economists need to cultivate a research and writing culture among themselves and infuse relevant research practices into their practice. Research opportunities with African families are abundant and action research strategies should be encouraged. All research efforts should be carefully documented so that they can inform future generations about their past in order to plan for their own future. The future of Home Economics in Africa deeply depends upon the creation of a professional community supported by sustainable professional associations (which, in cooperation with the academy, can contribute to the development of conferences, networking opportunities, professional development, and publishing avenues like journals, edited books, working papers and monographs).

Home Economics as a curriculum area

The teaching/learning methods (pedagogy) that are used to teach Home Economics in higher education play an important role in influencing university students' outcomes and socialization processes. Home Economics skills university students learn should be flexible, adaptable and transferable to many different situations. This flexibility can be achieved if interdisciplinary and transdisciplinary approaches, philosophies and subject matter are used to address the multipronged nature of complex problems faced by families. A holistic approach will discourage the fragmentation that is created by overspecialization in the various Home Economics content domains. It will also help transcend the negative stereotypes and other challenges that have characterized the Home Economics profession since its inception. We have observed that some home economists have a negative attitude towards their own profession. Negative attitudes are a symptom of disempowerment. So, addressing the issue of attitudes and stereotypes during training and the socialization process will better ensure that future home economists can confidently make decisions about their life, take an active role in their work and in the profession and self-identify with being a member of the profession.

Above all, Home Economics professionals should be lifelong learners, people who are willing to continuously learn about new things in view of the vast technological changes and other mega changes taking place on a daily basis. They need to be socialized to be expert novices and to be specialists at integrating divergent, complex ideas. They need to be taught to be critical of what is happening in their world and of how these events impact family well-being and quality of life. More importantly, they need to be taught to be creative and innovative in their problem posing and solving. This approach to practice should be possible if the teaching environments for Home Economics (both the physical and psychosocial environment) promote the communal and professional traits discussed earlier.

Home Economics as an arena for everyday living

Home Economics is a comprehensive discipline that teaches everyday life skills, which are applied on a daily basis in people's lives — in their homes and communities, including the workplace. Most African families grapple daily with how to meet basic survival needs: food, shelter, love and belonging, clothing and others. Conceptualizing Home Economics as an arena for everyday living should therefore focus on meeting the basic needs of individuals, families and communities, in ways that recognize and respect their dynamic contexts. Issues such as sanitation and hygiene, water, what to eat, child health and care, and fuel for cooking preoccupy the African woman's time and energy. Families need help to enable them to transcend these challenges, and they need resources and personnel who are actively engaged at the grassroots as their advocates — and that would be us as home economists. Qualified Home Economics extension workers in Africa should have both the theoretical knowledge and the practical skills needed to help tackle such problems. We believe they should embrace the family strengths approach and use asset mapping, as well as needs assessments, all drawing on the strengths of families instead of their weaknesses. Home economists in media, politics, development, private enterprise, as well as in civil society, all have roles to play as African home economists work together to future-proof the profession for the next century, all from an Africentric perspective. Home Economics higher education curriculum should reinforce all of these ideas.

Summary

The purpose of this chapter was to explore and envisage an ideal Africentric Home Economics higher education curriculum for socializing future generations of African home economists. It first discussed the current challenges that are faced by Black African families in the SADC region. This overview was followed by a discussion of the challenges that emanate from Home Economics practice in Africa. On the basis of all these theoretical and contextual underpinnings, an ideal Africentric Home Economics higher education curriculum, which is modeled along the four IFHE dimensions of Home Economics, was then suggested.

- The major challenges faced by families in the SADC region are issues related to poverty, health and disease, food security and nutrition, migration and urbanization, conflict, and technological changes;
- Major criticisms for existing African Home Economics educational programmes and curricula include (a) irrelevant content that is operationalized through Western paradigms of the what, how and why of Home Economics, and (b) a lack of qualified and committed Home Economics professionals at all levels;
- African home economists are encouraged to be sensitive to the unique challenges besetting African families and to their cultural context. Practitioners need to infuse this knowledge into their programmes of study in higher education and
- The IFHE (2008) four dimensions of Home Economics can effectively be used to define the parameters of Home Economics in higher education.

Discussion Prompts

- How can Home Economics higher education programmes socialize and empower home economists who can play a strategic and effective role in helping families improve their quality of life (that is, strengthen the home for the good of humanity)?
- What strengths do African families have that can be respected and fostered in efforts to overcome and transcend the challenges they face in everyday living?
- Rethink the role of professional associations in future-proofing Home Economics. (a) How can African home economists be motivated to join and take an increasingly active part in the activities of a continent-wide Home Economics association? (b) How can the association be self-sustaining?

- Given the megatrends identified in the Chapter 1, and the powerful context within which African families are living, how can Home Economics as a discipline of study in Africa be future proofed, especially in view of its declining popularity, coupled with its profound need in the 21st century?

References

Atkinson, N. D. (1972). *Teaching Rhodesians: A history of educational policy in Rhodesia.* London: Longman Group Ltd.

Economic Commission for Africa. (2005). *MDGs in Africa: A challenge for change.* Addis Ababa, Ethiopia: Author. Retrieved from http://www.uneca.org/mdgs/MDGS_page.asp

Harvey, L. (Ed.). (2009). Professional body. In Analytic Quality Glossary.Birmingham, England: *Quality Research International.* Retrieved from http://www.qualityresearchinternational.com/glossary/

International Federation for Home Economics (2008). *IFHE Position statement. Home economics in the 21st century.* Bonn, Germany: Author. Retrieved from http://www.ifhe.org/31.html

Kiamba, J. M. (2005). Home economics in contemporary society. Plenary paper presented at the *10th Anniversary Regional Home Economics Conference,* University of Botswana, Gaborone.

Lartey, A. (2008). Maternal and child nutrition in Sub-Saharan Africa: Challenges and interventions. *Proceedings of the Nutrition Society, 67*(1), 105–108.

Mberengwa, L. R. (1997). Reflecting on future actions and issues teaching family and consumer sciences in Zimbabwe and the United States: A comparative examination. *Journal of Family and Consumer Sciences Education, 15*(2), 61–70.

Mberengwa, L. R. (2003). Strengths of Southern African families and their cultural context. *Journal of Family and Consumer sciences, 95*(1), 20–25.

McGregor, S. L. T. (2008). Keynote: Individual empowerment as a home economist. In D.Pendergast (Ed.), *Proceedings of the International Federation of Home Economics Centennial Congress* (pp. 131–142). Bonn, Germany: IFHE.

McGregor, S. L. T. (2010). Name changes and future-proofing the profession: Human sciences as a name? *International Journal of Home Economics, 3*(1), 20–37.

Ogwu, E. N. (2010). *Home economics in basic education curriculum and implications for the realization of Vision 2016 and beyond in Botswana.* (Unpublished doctoral dissertation). University of Botswana, Botswana, Gaborone.

Social Impact Assessment and Policy Analysis Corporation (Pty) Ltd. (1990). *Evaluation of home economics programmes in Botswana.* Gaborone, Botswana: SIAPAC-Africa.

Southern African Development Community. (2008*). Executive summary: Towards a common future.* Gaborone, Botswana: Author. Retrieved from http://www.sadc.int/index/browse/page/106

vanWyk, R. (2005). Global perspective of home economics: An entrepreneurial emphasis. Plenary paper presented at the *10th Anniversary Regional Home Economics Conference.* University of Botswana, Gaborone.

Washi, S. (2002). Family issues and concerns in Africa: A home economics perspective. *AhfadJournal, 19*(1), 30–43.

Waudo, J. (1993). Home economics education in Africa: Reflections and prospects. *Canadian Home Economics Journal, 43*(4) 150–152.

Wodon, Q., & Zaman, H. (2010). Higher food prices in Sub-Saharan Africa: Poverty impact and policy responses. *The World Bank Research Observer, 25*(1), 157–176.

CHAPTER
18

Food Security, Street Food and Family Insecurity in Nigeria: Repositioning Home Economics in the 21st Century

Nwakego Molokwu and Elizabeth M. Kembe

Home Economics as a field of study needs to connect and key into the political, economic and technological conditions of the 21st century. It is a profession that impacts on family and community well being and will continue to show concern over issues in the society that directly affect individuals and families. Home Economics is a versatile field of study that draws knowledge and training from disciplines in the sciences, social sciences and the humanities and is in a very unique position of strength to meet the challenges of improving the quality of life and well being of individuals, families and communities. Nigeria is the most populous country in Africa and referred to as the "Giant of Africa", but as a developing country it continues to grapple with inadequate resources in the area of food, shelter, health, education, environment, sanitation and other needs of the community that are necessary for the quality of life and well being of the people. Since independence in 1960, Nigeria has remained a developing country for the past 51 years despite its numerous human and material resources. Unfortunately, these resources are poorly managed due to corruption and lack of good governance. For these reasons, Nigeria is incapable of sustaining its teaming population of over 160 million people (World Bank 2012). In a country where population is constantly on the increase and where food production is lower than the population growth rate, food security is a problem. This chapter will discuss food security, increase of street-food vendors, family insecurity and the role of Home Economics vis-à-vis the well being of the people.

Food Security and Family Insecurity

The most critical issues that confront Nigeria are the problem of food security and family insecurity. Food security exists when people have physical and economic access to sufficient, safe and nutritious food to meet the dietary needs and food preferences of family members. The food security problem is multifaceted since it relates to poverty, in terms of the family's purchasing power and food practices (preparation and service) that may enhance the nutritive value of food in the correct quality and quantity. Food security for a household means access to nutritious meals by all members at all times. Inadequate food supply affects family security. According to FAO (2011), food security includes, at a minimum, the availability of nutritionally adequate and safe foods and the ability to acquire acceptable foods in socially acceptable ways without resorting to emergency food supplies, scavenging, stealing and other coping strategies. In the absence of a secured source of food supply, there are bound to be hunger problems, and its manifestation in malnourishment — especially of children and women. The three main causes of malnutrition are: lack of food, health and care. Food security, health and family security have an important link to nutrition.

Food insecurity occurs when majority of people do not have access to food that is adequate in quantity and quality consistent with decent existence at all times. Food insecurity has adverse effects on individuals and the nation as it slows down a nation's developmental plans and affects family security. In Nigeria, the quantity and quality of food produced is low. In general, traditional diets in Nigeria are based on cereals and root crops, with significant amount of legumes, fruits and vegetables. Often, fish, poultry, meat and dairy products provide only a small proportion of the total energy. Malnutrition is common where there is inadequate supply of the right type of food nutrients in the correct proportion, which has been known to be the cause of high morbidity and mortality rates especially among infants and children below the age of 5 years. (Academy of Science 2011).

Nigeria falls short of the first millennium development goals of food security aspirations in seeking to reduce by half the proportion of people experiencing hunger. Due to the population of Nigeria, the upward trend in hunger is close to 30%, whereas the millennium development goal targets only 10%. Over 900 million people experience global food hardship and hunger. (FAO 2010) . Within the context of food security is economic instability, climate change, national and global insecurity. In Nigeria, the incidence of 'Boko Haram' and other terrorist activities continue to threaten the stability of the nation and invariably tamper with family security. If there is instability in any country and constant threat to life and property, then, the worry is not only on food production and consumption but on the access to food during periods of unrest.

Food prices are determined by oil prices. Even though Nigeria is a major exporter of crude oil, its citizens are often under the burden of fuel scarcity. Recently, the Nigerian government announced the removal of oil subsidy, from a pump price of ₦65.00 to ₦141.00 per litre. This change led to uprising from the populace and it is not surprising because it will translate into an increase in almost all the essential commodities of daily living such as food prices, transportation, health, shelter and other basic needs. The uprising brought the country to a stand still and the pump price was reduced to ₦97.00 per litre. People are very unhappy about this because the government was not transparent in this matter. Furthermore, food prices are affected by the seasons of the year. Foods are cheaper during the post-harvest period than the pre-planting season. During periods of festivity such as Christmas and Sallah holidays, the 'festive rush' for food stuff influences food prices. Consumption patterns also change during such periods because of the preparation for delicacies, variety and indigenous types of food. Indeed, it is a period when families try to exhibit their culinary expertise in the cooking and presentation of food. Traders capitalize on these factors and mark up food prices.

Street Food and Food Vendors

Food shops and food vendors are not left out in the bid to make more money during festive periods. Some families depend on food vendors for the provision of their meals especially breakfast and or lunch. Food and Agricultural Organization (FAO, 1990), has defined street foods as ready-to- eat foods and beverages prepared and sold by vendors especially in streets and other similar public places. In many growing urban cities, street food provides a significant percentage of the total intake of many working class people. Yet street foods are largely unregulated and create health risks to people.

Fast food joints, street vendors and mobile food services are now available all over the country. Depending on the locality, multiple street vendors may specialize in specific types of food characteristics of a given cultural or ethnic tradition. In some cultures, it is typical for street vendors to shout the prices and chant the names of food products in a theatrical fashion ('oyi', 'akpukpa', 'okpa' 'doya' 'oyoyo rice' 'suya' 'moimoi' etc) in order to engage the prospective customers. Some of these food vendors have makeshift stalls that they occupy, while others carry their foods on their heads or tricycle trucks or wheel barrows, moving from one part of the town to the other and hawking their foods. In many parts of the country, the majority of persons involved as street vendors are women and children who assist in the carrying of utensils or pushing the trucks. So, in a way the sector contributes to the financial empowerment of women and youths, but keeps the children out of school. Home economists can impact the community through training and advocacy for this vulnerable group.

Increase of Street Food Vendors in Nigeria

Individuals and families recognize the need for eating out of the home due to work and other social factors like the availability of food supplies. That is why it is important that the chain of production provides reliable, safe and nutritious food for the public. There are various reasons why people patronize street food vendors, this patronage gave rise to the increase of street food vendors who see it as a quick way of making a living. Some of the reasons include:

Work style and mobility

Parents now work far from their homes leaving the preparation and selection of family meals in the hands of untrained house helps. Type of job and place of work influences the preparation and choice of food eaten. The traditional method of food selection, preparation and service was such that the mother/women were responsible for the provision of the type of meals that are eaten by family members. With the education of women and subsequent employment into the labour force, most of the household chores including selection and preparation of meals has been commercialized either through the employment of house helps or patronising fast food joints and street vendors. In some large urban centres, it is common place for bank workers and other civil servants to patronise street food vendors for meals due to lack of time for food preparation. Meals require planning in terms of time and other resources. Today many women are engaged in income generating activities and this hardly allows them time to effectively cook their family meals. Such women engage assistance of house helps or live on street food to the detriment of family well-being. (Salami & Uko-Aviomoh, 2005). Highly mobile workers like drivers and salesmen patronise street food vendors because meals served in hotels and restaurants are too expensive.

Economic Factors

Street food vending is significantly related to poverty. Most of the street food vendors are from the low income group who are striving to meet personal or family needs. FAO (2009) observed that the preparation and sale of street food provides a regular source of income to millions of men and women in developing countries. In fact, there is a popular saying that it is only in the business of food that a business man never loses. It requires very little capital to start, and it can be conducted as a family business with other members of the family rendering various form of assistance such as washing of plates after service, clearing and cleaning. It is easy to start especially bearing the fact that Nigeria is endowed with food crops at all seasons such as yams, cassava, rice, beans, cereal crops (maize, millet, and guinea corn), soy bean, different types of fruit crops and vegetables. These food crops are cheap especially when they are in season. So there is a guarantee of the supply of raw materials.

Employment (Youth Empowerment)

The rate of unemployment and youth restiveness has encouraged government agencies to train people in skills for food preparation. They make meat kebabs ('suya' 'kilishi'), pastries, cakes, drinks and beverages and other finger foods. Some of these trainees are given take-off capital and equipment to start their business. This way the government is sure to have taken some youths off the streets. What is missing here is a regulatory policy on sanitation and safety of the food offered to the public.

Rural-urban migration

The lure of the city life and all the good things in the city such as communication, electricity, better housing and menial jobs that are instantly paid for have attracted youths from village farm settlements to the urban cities. During the time for farming one can hardly find the labor and manpower to help even when payment for such labor is available. These youths in urban areas provide commercial motorcycle transport popularly known as 'okada'. Some become political thugs, house helps, bus conductors, street hawkers and shopkeepers. This has implication for food security and family security, it also affects youths who at this age are suppose to be in schools and trained to contribute usefully to the society. This group depends mainly on street food and some of them become street food vendors.

General Complaints about Street Food and Food Vendors

Street food accounts for a significant proportion of the daily food consumption of millions of low and middle income families in Nigeria. In as much as there is the need for street food vendors as a necessity that has come to stay in most urban areas, there are general complaints concerning the safe handling of street foods.

Public Health

Most of the time, fast foods are prepared and served in unhygienic environment. Due to lack of water, serving utensils (which are usually sub-standard) are not properly washed. Food is handled with dirty hands and could be left uncovered. Anyone who appreciates good food and a clean environment and realises that germs cause diseases will know that when foods are prepared with dirty hands and utensils, then left uncovered, infested by flies and dust, it is unsafe for consumption. Foods may be contaminated by disease-causing organism such as viruses, bacteria and parasites which cause common diseases such as typhoid, cholera, dysentery and diarrhoea. These pathogenic organisms results from unhygienic practices in the preparation, cooking, serving and storage of foods. In the preparation of food and through all the process of food from the kitchen to the table, water is a significant factor for proper hygiene and care. If the source of water is not clean and available water is not adequate, then the health of the consumers is compromised. Olufemi (2012) reported that water is a problem confronting street food vendors in most developing countries, Nigeria is not an exception. Potable water for drinking, water for washing plates and utensils and water for food preparation is scarce. Most times the water is not in sufficient quantity, so, it has to be used sparingly. It is not uncommon to see food vendors use the same bucket of water over and over to wash plates and utensils and there is no hot water, which is the ideal for the washing of plates and utensils properly.

Ignorance

Food vendors have little knowledge or appreciation of good cooking practices, food hygiene and sanitation. There is no formal or informal training for this business, they just learn from one another. This activity is related to poverty and a form of employment in the informal sector. There are no regulations or licensing of this aspect of the private sector. Apart from the food vendors, the consumers themselves are sometimes ignorant and show little concern on the type of water used and the environment. The critical factors in the choice of food by consumers are the cost of the food, the taste and variety of food. Consumers assume that these foods are well prepared especially if it is a local delicacy, thus, may not insist on proper heating of the food. These street food vendors do not move about with any source of heat, so it is impossible to heat the food when necessary. Some use food warmers, but food gets cold as hours go by and the food remains at an inappropriate temperature for too long. The food is usually prepared in the morning for the whole day. On a good business day it may be sold out completely, but on other days, this may not be possible. The leftover food is then reheated for the next day.

Environment, Water and Sanitation

FAO identified the following as key factors in street food contamination:
- Insufficient cleaning of raw materials, ingredients and utensils before cooking and of table ware used by customers;
- In appropriate handling of ingredients and raw materials during food preparation and of finished products;
- Poor conditions of storage of raw materials and finished products (exposure to dust, insects and pests) and
- The prolonged holding of prepared food at inappropriate temperature.

From field trip observation, the challenges of food vendors are the absence of basic facilities such as water and toilets, training on hygiene and sanitation and provision of basic infrastructure for the street food industry. These are major deficiencies in food vending. If they are not addressed and regulated, consumers and the general public will continue to be at risk.

Waste generation and disposal scenario is a national problem in Nigeria. Most of these wastes that are generated on the streets are from commercial activities including activities of street food vendors. The quantity and rate of solid wastes generation depends on the population, level of industrialization, socio-economic predominant activities and the kinds of commercial activities, (Babayemi & Dauda,2009). Waste management is not successful because of the unwholesome waste disposal habits of the people, especially as it concerns sanitation. The use of polythene packages and the use of non-degradable solid waste often block the drainage systems thereby causing flooding in some major urban cities. Indeed, environmental sustainability is influenced by individual life styles and ethical consumerism. In order to avoid environmental degradation, there must be management of consumption patterns of individuals and households. That is where Home Economics is relevant in achieving the Millennium Development Goal (MDG) on environmental sustainability. Home Economics is geared towards influencing consumer patterns and external forces impacting on consumer choices. Food handling and attitude change toward healthy eating form an integral part of any Home Economics program. Given the economic trend in Nigeria, individuals and families would need a guided framework on better ways of achieving food security with minimal cost on resources. This is a challenge for home economists.

Some human behavior contributes to health hazards on the streets. Some of these include the dumping of human and house hold wastes on barren land or uncompleted buildings, improper disposal of refuse, littering public places and flipping rubbish carelessly from car windows. Some of these 'refuse sites' are sometimes illegal sites for the occupation of street food vendors. Despite the filth, consumers eat from street vendors in an unhealthy environment. Waste generated by street food vendors end up in gutters blocking the drainage. Sometimes, the used water not finding a passage may accumulate and form an eyesore that encourage the growth of bacteria and breeding of flies, mosquitoes and cockroaches at the sale points. This violates the Millennium Development Goals on environmental sustainability. The proportion of the population with sustainable access to improved water source in both the urban and rural areas is below the MDGs stipulation.

One of the major problems in Nigeria is the inadequate supply of clean water in both rural and urban areas for human consumption and general household use. UNICEF (2009) reported that about 100 million Nigerians out of the 160 million have no access to potable water. Though it seems there is water everywhere, potable water is accessed by only a few. Water is a significant part of the street food vending activities. Drinking water is often sold in polythene sachets (either factory made or home made) and in bottles. Ice cold water as is sold on the streets are often contaminated with pathogens causing cholera, typhoid, dysentery and other water borne diseases. According to the Standard Organization of Nigeria (2007), many street food operators have to use water from wells or rivers or rain water. In many cases, the food vendors contaminate water by inappropriate handling. The major source of contamination of street food in Nigeria is water. Either the water is of poor quality or it had become contaminated during the process of handling.

Home Economics is skill-oriented, therefore it is able to promote the acquisition of skills, knowledge, attitude and practice that can lead to productive ventures without jeopardising the health and well being of families and individuals. If professionals in the field are proactive, then it must be seen to exert certain parameters and work in conjunction with relevant government bodies and through effective advocacy, lobby for the formulation of policies and laws that will control street food vendors.

Repositioning Home Economics in the 21st Century

The ability to develop a framework for the future depends on the capacity of the institutions and professionals to understand the complex nature and requirements of Home Economics. Four dimensions have been identified by IFHE (2008) position statement namely:

- As an academic discipline engaged in research, education and creating new knowledge;
- As arena for everyday living in households, families and communities, identifying potentials for meeting human needs;
- As a curriculum area that facilitate students to discover and develop their professional decisions and actions and

- Finally, as a societal arena to influence and develop policy and advocate for individuals, families and communities to achieve empowerment and wellbeing, to use transformative practices and facilitate sustainable futures.

As much as the above statements can be applied universally, there are regional variations in its application and relevance. In Nigeria, the major concern of home economists is on values of professionalism and recognition by government of contributions of home economists in policy, advocacy and implementation of government laws and policy at all levels of the society. Unless, Home Economics is seen as a profession with laws, ethics and regulations guiding its professionals at whatever level, it will be difficult for practitioners to exert any meaningful influence in ensuring that best practices are adopted in its different careers. Home economists must key into the values of professionalism and ensure that the government recognizes Home Economics contributions to everyday living — a factor that cannot be brushed aside. The role of home economists have been explained variously to include the improvement of quality of life by influencing the social, health, economic and environmental conditions which affect human and social development. This therefore means that home economists can work with street food vendors to develop programs that will help them make positive changes in their environment, sanitation, food preparation and service.

Future-Proofing Home Economics

To future-proof Home Economics is a duty we owe ourselves, the nation and the world of home economists. Our practices must therefore be guided by ethical and professional principles. Home Economics is concerned with the ways in which the quality and content of individual and family life can be enhanced through the optimal utilization of its human and material resources. It is a profession that deals with family values, ideals and goals. A well balanced curriculum prepares students to become responsible citizens in their society. One of the key points for future proofing Home Economics in Nigeria is that training must be relevant, unique and different from the practices received from road side quacks. UNESCO (2009) explained that the three pillars of sustainable development focus on environment, society and economy with the major objective being to "help people to develop the attitudes, skills and knowledge to make informed decisions for the benefit of themselves and others, now and in the future, and to act upon these decisions". The Home Economics curriculum needs to be reviewed to key into the major issues of sustainability.

Effort must be made to encourage young people (both male and female) into the profession for the future is for the youths of today. Young professionals must be engaged in Home Economics and groomed to be good ambassadors of the profession. To achieve this, we need to rebrand Home Economics to give it a new identity, different from cooking and sewing, and make it more visible. Home economists must be concerned about what content is being taught at the secondary schools across the nation and who is teaching what. Are the graduates leaving with employable life skills? Will they choose Home Economics for further studies? We need the expertise of members to work on critical issues. Molokwu (2010) stressed that Home

Economics professionals must mindfully assess the philosophical foundation, objectives, trends, achievements, issues, problems and concerns of Home Economics. Pre-professionals need to know about the status of the profession, career opportunities and the competencies required for entering the job market in Home Economics. We need a new breed of professionals who is confident, assertive, willing to argue and take on major responsibilities for the interest of Home Economics.

Most small-scale businesses are centered round the life skills in Home Economics such as dressing making, cake making, interior decoration, day care/pre-school services, outdoor catering services, bead making etc. Some of these business people are not trained home economists and the best hands are not necessarily Home Economics graduates. There must be some significant difference in curriculum content and approach in what we offer. In order for the profession to continue to be relevant, it must use technology and develop technology that will compete with global standards and ways of promoting products in the global market. The internet and computer aided designs have simplified this task and it is an opportunity that must be adaptable in Nigeria. Entrepreneurship and investments lead to economic growth and well being of individuals and families. Entrepreneurial education introduced in Home Economics must be a practical demonstration of commercial skills, social skills and competences needed in the world of commerce.

Home Economics plays a crucial role in the environment, water and sanitation. Since its major concern is with the wellbeing of families, issues arising from the environment which negatively impact families will therefore become a major concern. Due to inadequate supply of potable water in Nigeria, households depend on unwholesome source of water supply such as ponds, wells and streams. Not many families can afford the borehole that is now common in urban elitist communities. Families spend money to treat avoidable water borne diseases. As home economists, there are a lot of actions that can be taken to proactively address issues that arise from street food vendors and environmental hazards associated with indiscriminate street behaviour. Advocacy, awareness education programmes through seminars, workshops and symposia will be of immense benefit. Home Economics associations like the International Federation of Home Economics (IFHE), Home Economics Research Association of Nigeria (HERAN) and Home Economics Council of Nigeria (HECON) etc need to form regulatory bodies and vanguards for the promotion of good health and family wellbeing. McGregor (2009) explained that togetherness and cooperation is power and power is energy — the capacity generated through relationships.

Summary

This chapter recognises that the issues generated from food security and street food vending directly affect individuals and families and the very centre of family security. The discourse is organized around the highlights with reference to the risks posed by street food vendors to the public. The potential for financial empowerment, wealth creation and employment was highlighted as well as issues in future-proofing Home Economics. There is need for Home Economics to be re-appraised and the functions translated into more proactive activities. Home economists must begin to exert themselves and ensure that the training given to the graduates will be relevant in meeting the requirement of the industry as well as meet individual, family and community needs. Prompts for discussion are included.

- Home economists should be proactive in meeting the needs of families;
- Develop programmes that will be relevant in arresting the inadequacies of street food vending;
- Develop new technologies and use existing approaches that will facilitate the dissemination of Home Economics research findings;
- Review curriculum content that is obsolete and out of context with existing trends in the society;
- Provide a professional body that will regulate Home Economics-related trades and businesses in order to inculcate desirable standards;
- Education is recognised as the most important condition for families to improve their lives and for societies to reach the Millennium Development Goals. Home economists can serve as an advocacy group to promote government policies regarding food security and environmental sustainability and
- Develop field based training programs for some food vendors who would be trained to teach other food vendors best practices in the food business.

Discussion Prompts

- What strategies can home economists adopt to curb the unhealthy practices by street food vendors?
- Identify the benefits of street food as it relates to your own locality?
- How does food security relate to family security?
- What is the total family income spent on street food as compared to homemade meals?
- How can home economists key into the government policy on 'clean hands' and develop a framework that could be used by street vendors in personal hygiene and the environment sustainability?

References

Academy of Science (2011) Agriculture for Improved Nutrition of Women and Children in Nigeria. Advocacy Brief Number 1. Nutritional Status of Women and Children in Nigeria.

Babayemi J. O. and Dauda K. T. (2009) Evaluation of Solid Waste Generation, Categories and Disposal Options in Developing Countries. Journal of Applied Science and Environmental Management, Vol. 13. 3. 83–88

FAO (2010) 825 Million People in Chronic Hunger Worldwide. Though improved, Global Hunger Level 'unacceptable'.

FAO Practical Guide: Basic Concepts of food Security (PDF). http://www.fao.org/docrep/013/al936e/al936e00.pdf. Retrieved nov.13,2011

International Federation of Home Economics (IFHE) (2008). IFHE Position statement Home Economics in the 21st Century. Bonn.

McGregor S. L. T. (2009) Integral Leadership's Potential to Position Poverty within Transdisciplinarity. Integral Leadership Review. Vol. 9. No.2.

Molokwu N. (2010) Home Economics Professionals: The Need for Professionalism and Ethical Values. Nig. Jour. of Home Economics. Vol. 2. No. 1.

Olufemi O. (2012) Will There be Potable water for Nigerians? PM News 4th Jan. 2012

Salamin L. I. and Uko-Aviomoh, E.E.(2005) Home Economics and Family Crisis Management. Journal of Home Economics Research. vol. 6. No.1. pp. 79-83.

Standard Organization of Nigeria (2007) Nigerian Standard for Drinking Water Quality. Abuja Retrieved 13th December, 2011. http://en.wikipedia.org/wiki/World Health Organization.

UNESCO (2009) Education for Sustainable Development. Review of Context and Structure

UNICEF (2009) Joint WHO/UNICEF Meeting on infant and young child feeding. Geneva. WHO.

World Bank (2012) Nigerian Population. World Development Indicators. Updated Jan. 24th 2012

CHAPTER
19

What did we Learn from the 3–11 Disaster and How do we Need to Reconsider a Sustainable Life?

Midori Otake, MichioMiyano, Kei Sasai, Kuniko Sugiyama, Yoko Ito and Noriko Arai

The catastrophic earthquake that struck Japan in March 2011 has forced us to reconsider our affluent and convenient life styles. In the period following the disaster, we had no choice but to return to basic living, relying on as few things and items as possible, which have made us realize what makes a truly worthwhile community. In such a community, people help each other and guarantee each other's safety and security. Simply put, it is community in which its members pursue "a sustainable life." It is time for scholars of Japanese Home Economics to share the insights that we have gained from this rare, painful experience. In this chapter, we consider the importance of a sustainable life and the processes by which Japanese citizens are now trying to restore their lives. Firstly, we identify the basic requirements for survival in the stricken area immediately after the calamity. Secondly, we discuss several issues relevant to each area of Home Economics, including housing, families, children, food, clothes and education.

Insights into sustainable lifestyle gained from the Great East Japan Earthquake

The main priorities of the Johannesburg Plan of Implementation adopted at the World Summit on Sustainable Development (WSSD) held in 2002 included, among others, (1) eradication of poverty, (2) water sanitation, (3) sustainable consumption and production, and (4) energy. In the midst of the confusion faced by Japanese citizens in their daily lives as a result of the 2012 Great East Japan earthquake, the importance of the items listed in the Plan for securing a sustainable lifestyle was reconfirmed.

The two greatest problems facing the country are the issues of energy and radiation pollution, which have resulted from the nuclear accident. Not only did the city functions come to a standstill as a result of the power outage immediately following the earthquake, but the frequent partial outages in the many months that followed have led to delays in production and distribution of goods needed for daily life, and the contamination of fields and ocean by radiation threatens the safety of the food and water supply. In order to be able to guarantee safe and secure living conditions, it is of highest priority that we rethink our system of production and consumption, including the issue of energy supply.

The earthquake also taught us what constitutes the most basic, minimal needs in our lives. It reaffirmed that the minimal requirements for carrying on a human-like lifestyle include warm food to provide us with a balanced nutrition, clothes to protect us from the heat or cold, shelter to guarantee privacy and a quiet place to sleep and water — not only for food, but also to maintain sanitary conditions through bathing and washing of clothes.

The keyword of the recovery is "linkages." It is the strength of these linkages between family and community members that led the rescue of people from the tsunami and that have enabled people to survive the difficult conditions of life in evacuation shelters. In communities with strong ties between members, elderly citizens who would have been overtaken by the tsunami on their own were aided by younger community members. In evacuation shelters, such mutual assistance relationships sustain the lives the elderly, who are prone to becoming isolated, through the delivery of meals and groceries. The experience has also led to a reaffirmation of the importance of family, in as much as it is cooperation among family members that guarantees a stable life.

At present, along with growing concerns related to guaranteeing the livelihood of those who have lost their jobs, poverty has once again become an important issue. The impact has been particularly prevalent on women. The employment structure and systems to guarantee a minimum income are important components of a sustainable lifestyle.

Osaka City University's Interdisciplinary Earthquake Preparedness Study Following the Great East Japan Earthquake Disaster

The Great East Japan Earthquake (M9.0) occurred off the coast of Japan's Tohoku (northeast) region at 2:46 p.m. of March 11, 2011. The earthquake and ensuing tsunami caused extensive damage over a wide area including Iwate, Miyagi and Fukushima. The faculty of Osaka City University has, historically, conducted research on urban areas. It is against this historical backdrop that the university as a whole initiated a project to study urban disaster prevention immediately following the Great East Japan Earthquake. The project involves 22 researchers from various fields organized into three research groups, each with their own theme. The first group, whose theme is "behavior and support mechanisms for survival," is studying the evacuation and human casualties from the tsunami as well as the life-support system for evacuees and refugees. The second group, whose theme is "the creation of disaster-resistant

Figure 19.1

Osaka City University (OCU) interdisciplinary earthquake preparedness study framework.

cities and community reconstruction," are examining the relationship between change in livelihood basis and lifestyle. The third group, whose theme is "monitoring geographically extensive multiple-earthquake disasters and earthquake preparation and disaster mitigation," approaches these issues from physical and engineering standpoints. Studies under the rubric of this project focus not only on emergencies but also daily life. That is, the various themes are examined from the time point prior to, during, and immediately following a disaster (Figure 19.1).

In the present study, we conducted verbal and written surveys in Miyako and Kamaishi Cities in Iwate Prefecture, which both suffered severe damage from the tsunami caused by the earthquake. Our objective was to understand the Great East Japan Earthquake in terms of human casualties and to examine the behavior of those who survived the earthquake and ensuing tsunami. In Miyako City, 10 meter-high seawalls with evacuation passages leading to a perch above the city had been built in the Taro district to protect the town from tsunamis. In the recent disaster, however, one of the seawalls was breached and nearly all of the houses in the town were washed away. Although over 100 people lost their lives in Miyako City, many were able to escape through the evacuation passages. The mortality rate in the main residential area was relatively low because the seawall hindered the progress of the tsunami. It appears the elderly were the main victims of the tsunami, similar to previous tsunami disasters such as those caused by the 1946 Nankai and 1993 Hokkaido Nansei Oki earthquakes. In contrast, the mortality rate of children was not so high. Generational disparity in mortality may be considered one characteristic of this tsunami disaster.

The victims who lost their houses in Great East Japan Earthquake disaster have had to move successively from emergency shelters (school gymnasiums and other public facilities) to temporary housing to their own homes. During their time as evacuees, they required a variety of assistance and support. It is important to recognize that the needs of disaster survivors' changes with time, and that the systems supporting survivors must, accordingly, change with time as well.

Because each local jurisdiction is responsible for providing emergency shelter, housing conditions vary considerably across communities as well as across prefectures. Another concern is that, due to the extensive devastation in some areas, shelter residents have little access to shopping and other activities. Shelters were not selected with consideration of optimizing such access but, rather, were simply structures of convenience that survived the tsunami. Transportation is difficult for shelter residents, particularly if they have disabilities or mobility limitations. Transportation continues to be a challenge for those who moved into temporary housing and especially the elderly, who are targeted in many temporary housing programs. Temporary housing also presents a major challenge. Public space on which such housing can be established is in short supply. Many of the most devastated areas are located on coastal plains, bounded by steep slopes that are unsuitable for building. The clear preference is to locate temporary housing in areas with ready access to utilities, but finding such space is problematic. Even if suitable locations are identified, they may lack amenities such as shopping, banks and transportation. Housing may be located adjacent to areas severely impacted by the tsunami. In short, the ability to provide suitable, convenient temporary housing is severely constrained (ISSS, 2010).

Sustainable Living: Clothing

The Great East Japan Earthquake and Clothing

Great East Earthquake of March 11, 2011 has forced us to reconsider the function of clothing and what we expect from clothing. Much of the disaster area was not only inundated by the tsunami but subsequently experienced cold and snow. Under these circumstances, the most immediate need for saving lives was clothing. The disaster reminded us of the importance of clothing for survival, an aspect that is not a major concern in times of peace in which clothing is the object of design and fashion. Meanwhile, growing concerns over environmental issues requires us to consider how to practice sustainable living. At this juncture, after experiencing this unprecedented disaster, it is important for us to reconsider the nature and function of clothing in addition to pursuing the development of new, eco-friendly materials.

The '5Rs' in Making and Buying Clothing

To clarify the challenges of sustainable living in the field of clothing, it is helpful to refer back to the oft-cited "3Rs" of environmentalism: reduce, reuse and recycle. These 3Rs form the basis of policy adopted by the Japanese government to create a sustainable society. The first R, reduce, refers to the reduction of waste. Manufacturers are required to reduce waste in the course of production. The second R, reuse, refers to the re-use of previously-used items. In terms of clothing, items that we no longer need can be passed on to others who do. Such recycling can be undertaken by both individuals and manufacturers. In Japan, a large volume of used clothing is sent to developing countries. The third R, recycle, involves the use of recyclable resources as raw materials for the manufacture of new products. Recycling can be divided into two categories: material recycling and chemical recycling. There are numerous examples of material recycling: discarded cotton products can be recycled and reused as scrubbing cloths for industrial machinery; discarded wool products can be restored to wool yarn and used in the manufacture of other products; other fibers are made into felt to be used in the interior of automobiles. Chemical recycling is applicable to synthetic fibers, which can be transformed into new synthetic fibers.

In terms of clothing, there are two more important Rs, namely "repair" and "remake." The fourth R, repair, refers to the long-term use of clothing through repair; and the last R, remake, refers to the transformation of used clothing into new clothing by combining it with other used or new materials. The 5Rs listed above, then, constitute the basic principles for achieving sustainable living with regard to clothing.

Clothing and Sustainable Living — Challenges

In the aftermath of the Great East Japan Earthquake, volunteer groups and manufacturers provided many items of clothing to disaster victims. Individuals also donated clothing through official and unofficial channels. However, much of this donated clothing still sits in warehouses because it is either the wrong size or fails to meet the needs of the disaster survivors. This circumstance provides us an opportunity to rethink our attitudes toward clothing.

The problem of size can be solved by disaster victims and volunteers remaking the donated clothing. To support such efforts, the Japan Society of Home Economics donated sewing sets to disaster victims. Students from universities around Japan assembled and distributed sewing sets containing needles, thread, and scissors to disaster victims along with letters of encouragement. As mentioned above, the principle of "remaking" is important not only in the disaster area but also in our everyday efforts to achieve sustainable living. The problem of size also highlights the need for universal clothing. Today, unisex fashion has gained popularity worldwide, bringing down manufacturing cost and increasing the availability of homogeneous and inexpensive clothing. This situation is welcome in the sense that a given article of clothing can be worn by both men and women, young and old — a point worth considering given the fact that a great deal of the donated clothing has not been used because of its lack of universality.

The issues of clothing size and style aside, the fact that much of the donated clothing has not been used because it does not meet people's needs indicates that people require certain types of clothing for certain occasions and that the availability of universal clothing in and of itself is insufficient. We need a variety of clothing in order to live our everyday lives comfortably. We must consider the 5Rs when buying clothing with the goal of achieving sustainable living.

As in other aspects of our lives, in order to achieve sustainable living, it is necessary to choose activities related to the manufacture, selection and wearing of clothing that are eco-friendly and that can be easily put into practice. Taking the lessons from the Great East Japan Earthquake to heart, we must rethink our clothing habits in Japan.

The ability to critically analyze information regarding food and make good dietary choices

In the areas affected by the Great East Japan Earthquake, basic lifelines such as power, gas, water, and food, among others, were shut off for several weeks following the disaster. There was, in addition, the accident at Tokyo Electric Power Company (TEPCO)'s Fukushima Dai-ichi Nuclear Power Station. Japan depends greatly on nuclear power for electricity, which accounts for approximately 30% of the total electric power supply. In the Kanto area, where electricity is supplied by TEPCO, regular planned blackouts continued into the summer due to shortage of electricity supply. Japan's staple food is rice, typically cooked using an electric rice-cooker. Due to the shortage of electricity, the practice of boiling rice using gas heat has gained the attention of the public. We have all become conscious of the need to save electricity and energy. In Japan, when children reach the upper grades of elementary school, they learn how to cook rice and to practice eco-cooking.

In the Fukushima accident, explosions at the Dai-ichi nuclear power plant resulted in leakage of radioactive materials. On March 17, 2011, the Ministry of Health, Labor and Welfare established provisional regulation values for radioactive materials in food based on the Food Sanitation Act. Food is tested for radiation in all Japanese prefectures and the data is published on each prefecture's official website. When food is found to have radiation levels exceeding the provisional regulation values, shipments from that source are restricted. However, people remain concerned about the risk of internal exposure by air, water or food as well as external exposure. To better ensure the safety and security of food on the market, new standard values, which are approximately 1/5 of the current provisional regulation values, are scheduled to be adopted in April, 2012. Japan has 54 nuclear power generation facilities, placing it third in the world in terms of number of nuclear power plants. Most Japanese have a poor knowledge of the potential risks of radioactive materials to begin with, with little chance of learning more. We must take greater interest in this new technology that has supported our daily life.

Recent years have witnessed a dramatic change in the dietary habits of the Japanese people. To address issues emerging from this change, the Basic Act on Shokuiku (food and nutrition education) was enacted in June 2005. The term shokuiku is defined in the law as "food and nutrition education" over people's entire life spans. According to the Basic Act on Shokuiku, shokuiku is a fundamental aspect of our lives and is considered to be the foundation for the three pillars of education, these being: intellectual, moral and physical education. The goal of shokuiku is to enable people, through a variety of experiences, to select proper food and to nurture people's awareness of healthy food habits. What are really needed in this multimedia society are individuals who are able to critically analyze the flood of information regarding food and make good dietary choices on their own.

Sustainable Society and Communities for Child Well-being

Impacts on children of the Great East Japan Earthquake

The Great East Japan — Earthquake followed by the massive tsunami caused terrible damage, and its victims included many children and their families in the stricken area. Most of the children who survived the tsunami have been forcibly displaced from their hometown because their homes and schools were swept away. There was, of course, another disaster. Three reactors at the Fukushima Dai-ichi nuclear plant were severely damaged. Although the total amount of radiation released from the plant is still unknown, some residents, including children, living in the communities near the nuclear plant were evacuated for fear of the impacts of chronic radiation exposure.

The pain of the children who lost their family members and close friends is unfathomable. The affected children have suffered, and continue to suffer, severe stress, especially due to protracted anxiety over the radiation disaster, the endpoint of which remains uncertain. High incidences among infants and toddlers of episodic crying at night, bedwetting and regressive thumb sucking have been reported. Those in middle childhood have tended to act out their stress, exhibiting symptoms such as aggressive behavior, avoidance and inattentiveness. Efforts were made to deal immediately with their symptoms of Post-Traumatic Stress Disorder (PTSD) with the goal of recovering mental health. It should be recognized that the national government, municipalities, NPOs and volunteer groups swiftly dispatched mental health care specialists including psychiatrists, clinical psychologists and school counselors to carry out these efforts.

Protecting and promoting children's mental and physical well-being

We have learned the importance of establishing a society and communities that guarantee the safety and security of children through the bitterest of experiences. The unprecedented disaster makes us realize that the younger members of our society are unable to deal with such situations by themselves. In addition, it forces us to recognize that infants and toddlers are vulnerable to radiation exposure. It is the responsibility of the present generation, which includes not only parents, families and caregivers but also all citizens, to once again create a safe and secure environment in which children can play outside freely.

We must start supporting efforts to ensure a safe and secure environment in which to raise our children. This will require comprehensive support including hard to soft measures and continuing efforts in the short, medium and long term. To realize reconstruction, we need to promote cooperation between the national government, municipalities and various domestic and overseas organizations. The manner in which adults reconstruct and recuperate our country and communities will serve as a model of sustainable society for our children who represent the future generation.

We Japanese have maintained a lifestyle and a traditional wisdom that allows us to live in commune with nature. We have endeavored to cultivate a foundation for balanced development of mind and body by encouraging our children's interest and curiosity in nature and the world around them. In addition, we have emphasized the bonds between children and others to cultivate an attitude of independence and cooperation. We should reaffirm and impart these values (regarding childrearing). It is the realization of a society based on such values that a sustainable society true to Japan's nature will be created.

The 2011 East Japan Earthquake and Home Economics Education: Lessons from the Disaster on Competencies to Be Developed

The 2011 East Japan Earthquake left an indelible mark on Japan's educational system. Approximately 600 children died in the tsunami, and approximately 6000 school buildings were destroyed. Many children who lost their family members are currently living in temporary housing. Many other children are unable to play outside in schoolyards or parks due to potential risks to their health posed by radioactive contamination resulting from the explosions at the Fukushima nuclear power plant.

The highest priorities of school education, for the time being at least, are undoubtedly to support children who have suffered emotional damage and to extract practical lessons from the recent experience to protect against possible future disasters. However, in this paper, I will discuss how the discipline of Home Economics specifically relates to the educational imperatives brought to the fore by the recent earthquake disaster and examine the ways in which our profession can potentially help student develop competencies to manage their lives positively.

Independent living

Water, electricity and gas supplies were cut and food supplies halted because of the earthquake. Under such circumstances, many schools in the communities became shelters for evacuees, and Home Economics rooms were used to prepare and serve simple hot meals like rice balls and miso soup. It is reported that many students helped to cook and serve dishes and assisted the elderly by bringing water, gathering wood for fuel. These skills all required effective utilization of Home Economics knowledge. The disaster brings into clear focus the fact that Home Economics competencies, including coping with supply shortages and maintaining health and preparing well-balanced meals under challenging conditions, are indispensable for independent living.

Care, communication, and living together

In the shelters, many instances of people helping and caring for each other were observed. It is reported that older students played with younger children and helped them with their studies. Such experiences have had a positive impact on students' self-respect and increased their willingness to both rely on and help others. Teachers have reported that instances of bullying in classes have decreased or completely disappeared since the earthquake. Nurturing fluency in caring, helping, and communication is a fundamental objective of Home Economics education. Many youths have become fluent in these areas after living through such extraordinary experiences.

Critical thinking and consumer citizenship for sustainable development

The sheer magnitude of the two simultaneous disasters, the giant tsunami and the explosion of the nuclear power plant, which far exceeded any forecasts, is such that it is difficult for people to obtain accurate information about the situation. Lacking sufficient knowledge of how to deal with possible radioactive contamination and without thinking critically, some consumers simply stopped buying rice and vegetables produced in Fukushima while others in Tokyo began to stockpile food and water based on unfounded rumors. Meanwhile, the various energy conservation measures enacted in the summer have led ordinary citizens to discuss the concept of sustainable living. Critical thinking, as well as the concepts of consumer citizenship and sustainable development is intrinsic to the discipline of Home Economics (Arai 2005). It is hoped that by studying Home Economics, students will develop the ability to analyze information carefully, discern what is accurate and choose an appropriate course of action based on this information.

Practical reasoning and problem solving
Since the earthquake, the future of Japanese energy policy, and especially Japan's reliance on nuclear energy, has become a topic of heated debate. Previously, the nuclear power issue was discussed from political and economic perspectives. However, it was human lives and everyday needs such as food, water and health that were most severely affected by the radioactive contamination resulting from the accident. It is now apparent that the accident will continue to impact people's lives for many years to come. The accident clearly reveals the crucial lack of consideration of the lives of individuals and families in the nuclear policy decision-making process. In so far as it is imperative that young people to consider the advantages and disadvantages of nuclear energy from the viewpoint of their own and others' lives, the issue of nuclear power may be one for developing practical reasoning and problem-solving skills in Home Economics curricula.

In summary, the Great East Japan Earthquake has highlighted the essential need for students to develop competencies in independent living, caring, critical thinking and practical reasoning and the fact that the perspectives and discipline of Home Economics have great potential to nurture these competencies. In fact, since the earthquake, many home economists have developed and executed various lessons plans built around the four competencies listed above. We should take greater initiative and be more proactive in developing such lessons, sharing these widely among home economists and demonstrating to others outside the discipline the potential sizable contribution of our profession.

Summary

Japan, which was severely impacted by the earthquake, is presently beginning to return to normal life while jury-rigging the minimal goods and services necessary for daily life. In this process, we are beginning to get a sense of the elements that constitute a sustainable lifestyle. The basis of a sustainable lifestyle is community that includes not only the strongest members of society but also the weakest and is based on a sharing of resources and mutual assistance. Such a lifestyle can be said to be a natural extension of the Japanese style that, despite the state of confusion following

the earthquake disaster, resulted in no rioting and citizens acting calmly to help each other. In summary, the key elements of a sustainable society are as follows.
- Establishment of conditions where the most vulnerable members of society, the children and the elderly, are able to live safely and without fear;
- Safe and nutritionally balanced food, clothing and shelter to protect us from heat and cold and to provide us with a safe place to sleep and privacy, and a guarantee of income to enable access to these and
- Linkages between family and communities members that enable mitigation of risk and stabilization of life.

The following is a list of challenges facing the regions affected by the disaster in achieving the guarantee of a stable life.
- In order to guarantee incomes and to maintain the minimal requirements for life, there is an urgent need to recuperate the productive function of the affected region and to link this to employment;
- In order to establish safe and secure living conditions, it is necessary to first repair the damaged nuclear reactor and remove the resulting radiation contamination, to reevaluate our energy supply, and to develop a new lifestyle that will lead to a new energy future;
- In order to develop healthy and stable living conditions, it is necessary to guarantee access to minimally safe clothing, food, and for all citizens and
- In order to create a system of mutual assistance among family and community members capable of supporting the children and the elderly, it is important to promote the formation of relationships between people that are consistent with the idea of "linkages".

References

Arai, N. (2005). The new paradigm of Home Economics curriculum creation and implementation: Nurturing independence, cooperation and citizenship in everyday life. In N. Arai & K. Aoki (Eds), A new paradigm for the curriculum and educational strategy for Home Economics education in the changing world (pp. 75-91).Tokyo: Japan Association of Home Economics Education.
ISSS. (2010). Report of Closing Workshop for the Great Eastern Earthquake Study Trip.

CHAPTER
20

Capacity-Building in the Home Economics Profession: The Maltese Experience

Suzanne M. Piscopo and Karen S. Mugliett

Throughout its history as a discipline, Home Economics has constantly striven to help develop societies comprised of healthy, productive and responsible citizens. This goal has been achieved through providing knowledge and skills to individuals of different ages, through conducting research related to different specializations within Home Economics, as well as through working with different stakeholders, including industry, media, members of civil society and policymakers.

Home economists have been successful in their work because they identify and respond to individual, family and community needs, offer targeted and practical education, counseling and guidance, and advocate for appropriate infrastructure, products and services. This strategy needs to continue in order to future-proof the Home Economics profession, keeping in mind the 10 emerging megatrends as outlined by Pendergast, McGregor and Turkki as a stimulus for this book. Simultaneously, there needs to be continuous marketing of the Home Economics profession so that the perception and status of Home Economics is enhanced and legitimized.

Home economists can build on their successes by strengthening and developing competences to work with each other and to work with others. This process requires capacity-building on different levels, the focus of this chapter. The outcomes of building capacity can be short, medium and long-term serving, not only the intended, ultimate beneficiaries, individuals, families and communities, but the profession itself. The resultant increased respect for the knowledge and skills of professional home economists in the public, academic, industrial, civil society and political arenas will open further avenues for home economists to get involved in research, development and implementation initiatives. Home economists could play a particularly stronger role in advocacy and in educating policymakers in viewing issues from a more integrative, holistic perspective, ensuring individual, family and community wellbeing.

What are home economists good at?

Over the years, home economists have moved beyond their original confined focus on the home and household and acknowledged that individual and family choices and actions impact at all levels — from the family home, to the local neighborhood and to the global community. Thus, home economists are concerned with the empowerment of individuals, families and communities to become responsible, healthy and productive citizens. They facilitate the development of attributes for lifelong learning for paid, unpaid and voluntary work and for the development of the necessary environments to promote optimal and sustainable living.

Of interest to home economists is UNESCO's (2010) document entitled *Teaching and Learning for a Sustainable Future,* wherein four sets of principles are identified, which need to be ensured as often as possible through education initiatives. People must:

- care for each other and value social justice and peace;
- protect natural systems and use resources wisely;
- value appropriate development and satisfying livelihoods for all and
- make their decisions through fair and democratic means.

The document further underlines that, "developing the capacity and commitment to apply these principles at the level of personal and family actions, and in decisions for local, national and global communities, is the task of educating for a sustainable future" (UNESCO, 2010, online).

Undeniably, the goals of Home Economics and the content of Home Economics' courses are very much akin to these principles. It is therefore clear that home economists' have a crucial role in 'teaching' for sustainable futures, whether in the classroom or around the boardroom table. Home economists vision can follow that of UNESCO (2010): building capacity to think in terms of 'forever.' Although home economists can be seen as catalysts for societal transformation focused on 'forever', they must learn to view themselves as 'expert novices', recognizing that society is constantly changing and that they themselves need to be 'good at learning' about and for the new issues and challenges continually emerging (Pendergast, 2006). To quote the IFHE (2008) Position Statement "...the profession is constantly evolving, and there will always be new ways of performing in the profession" (p. 1). This statement means home economists must work on building their own capacity as practitioners who promote wellbeing and quality of life. This process is the focus of the rest of this chapter.

What is capacity-building?

If optimal and sustainable living is the goal of Home Economics practice, capacity-building is a means to achieving it. The United Nations Development Programme (UNDP, 1997, online) has defined "capacity development" as "the process by which individuals, groups, organizations, institutions and countries develop their abilities, individually and collectively, to perform functions, solve problems and achieve objectives in a sustainable manner". The UNDP goes on to say that "capacity-building then builds on the pre-existing capacity base" (UNDP, 1997, online). The United Nations Environmental Programme (UNEP) expands on this definition, stating that capacity-building is:

> "a holistic enterprise, encompassing a multitude of activities. It means building abilities, relationships and values that will enable organizations, groups and individuals to improve their performance and achieve their development objectives. It includes strengthening the processes, systems and rules that influence collective and individual behavior and performance in all development endeavors. And it means enhancing people's technical ability and willingness to play new developmental roles and adapt to new demands and situations." (UNDP, 2002, p. 11).

This comprehensive definition reflects the different levels and contexts in which capacity-building takes place and hints at key elements of the process. Indeed, capacity-building involves further training and retraining of individuals who are members of a profession and who will be conducting research, creating policy, developing interventions and/or delivering services. This training may be required, for example, to extend knowledge and skills related to the discipline, to use new technology in the field, or to apply new research that has emerged in the discipline. All this capacity-building will not only improve the delivery of professional practice, but also enhance the credibility of the profession in the academic, political, industrial and public spheres.

Capacity-building also involves nurturing and extending networks of individuals within the profession and those outside the profession who have similar goals or who can contribute their expertise and services in achieving Home Economics goals and mission. Similarly, capacity-building also involves establishing partnerships with non-governmental organizations (NGOs) or civil society organizations (CSOs), with local and national governments, within industry and the mass media. The goal is to collaborate in different ways for creating new policy, offering new services and developing new products. Through such alliances and partnerships, with multiple groups working together, capacity shortcomings can be overcome more effectively, and with more assurance of efficacy. Moreover, such teamwork gives legitimacy to the establishment of research and policymaking bodies and centers.

One outcome of networking and strategic partnering is an improvement in the understanding of the profession. This outcome is particularly crucial as capacity-building often has a slow, but positive, ripple effect. Taking Home Economics as an example, once governments appreciate the valid role of Home Economics professionals within various tasks, what follows is greater public visibility for the profession. This visibility, in turn, will generate interest among personnel in the mass media industry that then creates opportunities for home economists to appear, present or write using various vehicles. This exposure further creates interest and understanding among the general public, who gradually become sensitized to the scope of the Home Economics discipline, acknowledging its value and seeking the services of home economists, individually or via places of work or other agencies.

The above introduction to capacity-building comes with a note of caution, however. One cannot truly build capacity — the knowledge, skills and resources needed to perform a function — unless one is clear about one's function, goals and existing capacity, both individually or collectively. Here is where the crux of the matter lies. Home economists are, in reality, a means to an end — to build capacity for individuals and families to realize their potential for better lives. Two factors make this goal most challenging. Firstly, what constitutes 'better lives' is very subjective. Secondly, whilst home economists work with individuals to meet their current needs and enhance wellbeing, often, especially in the education and political arenas, home economists have to anticipate future needs and make their recommendations or develop their own training in light of this uncertainty.

Home economists need to be able to educate, deliver services, conduct research, develop products and services, create policy and promote wellbeing in the context of a changing future which is shaped by megatrends. Such capacity-building will help to future-proof the profession, as described by McGregor (2011, p. 561):

> "A future-proofed profession can handle the future because members of the profession take steps now in order to avoid having to make radical changes to practice in order to remain viable in the future. A profession that is future-proofed will not stop being effective because something newer or more effective comes in to replace it. A future-proofed profession is strategically planned so it can remain effective even, especially, when things change."

Capacity-building in the Home Economics profession

Borrowing from Pendergast (2010), home economists must continually ask if they can improve on what has been done so far and at times repeat what has worked well for them, or change to respond to newer trends in society. In the light of this statement, and the earlier discussion on capacity-building, one can say that the Home Economics profession must grow fourfold by: (a) ensuring that curricula, programmes and services are in line with current and future societal needs (meeting societal needs); (b) providing more Home Economics instruction and courses at different levels and beyond formal education (expanding education and training); (c) providing professional training for participation of home economists in different career settings and sectors (diversifying the profession); and (d) embracing collegiality, collaboration, continuing professional development (CPD) and networking (strengthening the profession). All of these elements of capacity-building can develop simultaneously and alongside continuous and aggressive marketing of the profession. The following text is organized using these four elements of capacity-building (see Figure 20.1).

Meeting societal needs

The future is difficult to predict, but change is inevitable. It is essential to educate and prepare individuals, families and communities for the assimilation of inevitable changes which are taking place globally, regionally and nationally. Home economists are no strangers to this need. They have always been at the forefront of change management, either by suggesting change in behaviour to make better use of current individual or family resources, or anticipating future needs and educating to help individuals and families cope with, adapt to and effect social change for the betterment of all (McGregor, 2009). In this regard, a sensitivity towards the interdependence of human activity and the different factors in the different levels of the environment, as motivated by key human eco-systems theoretical perspectives (Bronfenbrenner, 1989; McGregor, 2009), has emerged strongly in Home Economics syllabuses and programmes around the world. This approach has lead to a refocusing from the transmission of knowledge and skills to the positive and transformative

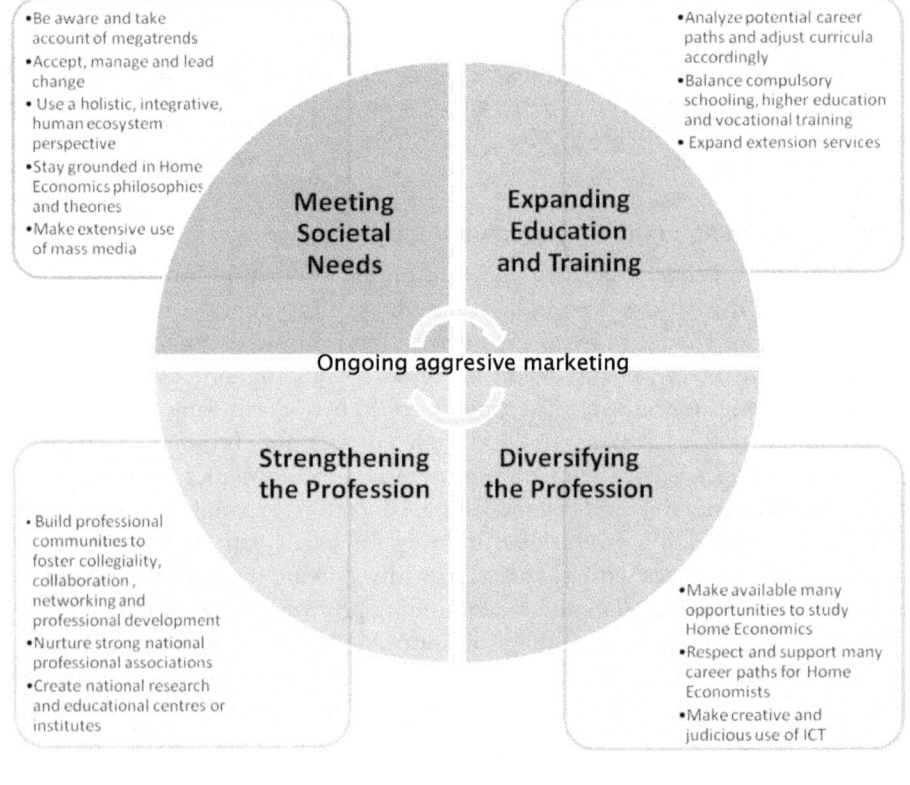

Figure 20.1

Features of capacity-building in the Home Economics profession.

actions of humans towards preserving and making the best use of resources in the broadest sense.

From the perspective of capacity-building, it is essential that Home Economics programmes are grounded in societal needs. For example, the United States National Standards for Family and Consumer Sciences address the need for education to develop learners' capacities to analyse and use information, collaborate with others and make reasoned ethical decisions, skills that are necessary in today's affluent societies (National Association of State Administrators of Family and Consumer Sciences, 2008). It is equally important that home economists increase their own knowledge and skills to be able to respond to the trends emerging in society and live as informed, reflective and responsible individuals. Home economists must also remain faithful to the theories and paradigms that frame and form the philosophy(ies) of the profession.

To see how this capacity-building works in reality we chose a few examples from Maltese society, reflecting several megatrends namely: prosperity, acceleration, health and environment, globalization and technological development. A recent Eurobarometer (European Commission, 2007) placed Maltese adults as among the happiest people in Europe, with 90% of respondents saying they were happy and 94% saying they enjoyed a good quality of life. Additionally, all respondents said that family came above everything else in their lives, giving it 100% importance. Health, leisure time and friends followed closely at 99%, 90% and 88% respectively. Maltese home economists need to take advantage of these values and attitudes, firstly to market the potential role of Home Economics education in nurturing happy, satisfied families and secondly to deliver education and training to fulfill this goal — which is the backbone of our profession.

Malta has also been described as a country quickly-changing towards a more regional and modern Euro-Mediterranean 'island-city' (Abela, 2006), which has emerged from its previous, strict non-permissive moral society (Abela, 2001). There is a growing trend in Malta for more women to remain in employment, even during the child-rearing years, despite the employment rate for working women in the 25–54 age group in Malta being the lowest in Europe at 33.4% (Hantrais, Philipov & Billari, 2006). This working mother trend in Malta has brought with it big challenges for young families, working mothers and older grandparents — the latter often acting as the child carers.

A major societal concern in many countries, which could be addressed by home economists, is how to manage family life and employment challenges in order to enable families to achieve a workable balance. Increasingly, families are finding it difficult to reconcile a traditional belief system based on traditional gender roles with the emotional wellbeing of the family (Abela, 1998; Borg Xuereb, 2008). Whilst there is a clear move towards gender equality in parenting, there is still a measure of asymmetry between the expected roles of women and men in the family and Maltese society. Home economists can be of particular support to young families through educational interventions on time and organizational skills, healthy and economical meal planning and the practical use of technology.

Indeed, technology hit Malta most forcefully in the late 1990s, followed by the formulation of policies in 2004 that were meant to "transform Malta into a regional technology centre of excellence for systems development, training specialisations and service provision in the Euro-Mediterranean region" (Inzelt, n.d., p. 2). Technological development is visible in different ways in Malta. For example, most children are avid computer users and technological game experts. Schools have introduced a number of educational technologies to facilitate the teaching and learning experience, such as recently-introduced interactive whiteboards in every class, as well as a national eLearning platform.

Due to the fact that Maltese consumers are asked to utilise eGovernment facilities when they are required, technological literacy has become a crucial skill in the country. Home economists need to help children, parents, industry figureheads and policymakers to become aware of the implications of all of this technology on family life. Home economists can make consumers aware of certain e-services, offer consumers comparative information on new products and services, and demonstrate and encourage use of new beneficial technology. They can also recommend more user-friendly technological developments to policymakers and to industry. Meanwhile, home economists working in education within Malta need to hone their own skills in using the new technology to enhance teaching and learning for their students.

Based on these few examples of dominant megatrends, the Home Economics profession clearly has sufficient cause to lobby more strongly for making Home Economics education available nationally within Malta, for both sexes, and at different periods of their schooling. The goal is to help students understand and manage their specific needs, make appropriate decisions and actions and use available resources as efficiently as possible while retaining their efficacy and empowerment. The new National Curriculum Framework in Malta proposes that Home Economics studies will be included in primary and secondary curricula as a core component under the Health Education learning area and still be offered as a specialisation subject in the third year of secondary schooling (Ministry of Education, Employment and the Familiy, 2011). This recognition of Home Economics as an entitlement for all students is extremely positive, and has come about after many years of direct and indirect lobbying in different forums.

Of course, one could also advocate for increasing the presence of Home Economics education in adult, lifelong learning initiatives. Home economists must lobby policy makers (education, health, agriculture, consumer affairs, tourism and industry), entrepreneurs and other industry professionals to convince them to favor the role of the discipline in empowering individuals and families to optimize their lifestyles and life skills for the short, medium and long-term amelioration of society. This empowerment can happen through improved health, more financially secure households and a better consumer-retailer relationship.

The potential impact of the mass media cannot be ignored in this capacity-building exercise. In Malta, extensive marketing in the media by leading local home economists has been of great benefit to the profession overall. Anecdotal evidence suggests that heavy media participation has improved the perception of Home Economics in Malta. The knowledge and skills gained from Home Economics studies seems to now be perceived as an entitlement for individuals and families. After a concerted effort in recent years by local home economists to gain regular media presence via radio and TV participation and the contribution of articles to national newspapers and popular magazines, the media is now seeking Home Economics professionals for one-off and more regular commitments. Should home economists develop a more strategic awareness-raising plan, such as using social marketing principles, this impact may be even more effective and long-term.

Expanding education and training

Internationally, Home Economics permeates different sectors of society, with trained home economists being employed in education, government departments, NGOs, industry and the media (Shields & Williams, 2000). These diverse career paths have come about through the provision of curricula during compulsory schooling, which caters to basic knowledge related to different vocations and further specialisation at post-secondary (high school) and university degree level.

Pendergast (2010) recently suggested that Home Economics should refocus curricula towards vocational outcomes. In the United States, analysing career paths is considered integral to Family and Consumer Sciences (FCS) education (National Association of State Administrators of Family and Consumer Sciences, 2008). In Malta, the present Home Economics syllabi (SEC and Advanced level) also address vocational areas, such as hospitality, care of the elderly, childcare and food technology, but coverage is limited (University of Malta, n.d., online). However, whilst Home Economics qualifications are accepted, or even prefered, as entry requirements to a variety of post-secondary and tertiary level courses, there are no Bachelor of Arts or Bachelor of Science degrees in Home Economics in Malta. The only directly related degree available at the tertiary level is a teaching degree in Nutrition, Family and Consumer Studies (University of Malta). This fact alone can lessen the appeal of the subject for a broad range of students and for their parents, who often look at employability when guiding their children on school subject choice. Developing new curricula and courses at secondary, post-secondary and teriary levels can lead to a variety of employment options, facilitating the future-proofing of the Home Economics discipline.

In countries such as Malta where Home Economics has been taught primarily within the formal education setting and has mainly provided lifeskills or led to careers in education, further work is required so that home economists are in touch with individuals beyond students in compulsory education. In Malta, such extension education happens formally only via the Home Economics Seminar Centre — a state-funded initiative that provides seminars and day courses in nutrition, finance and sustainability education for primary school children, parents, the elderly and NGOs (Directorate for Quality and Standards in Education, 2010). More informally, as mentioned earlier, a number of home economists regularly educate through different mass media vehicles, including TV, radio, print, blogs and websites. Home Economists in Action (HEiA, n.d. online), a Maltese professional organization, has also recently started playing a role in extension work, collaborating with NGOs on community events, courses and web-based education.

Diversifying the profession

There are various strategies that could be adopted by the Home Economics professional community to become stronger and to develop professionally. First of all, the profession must grow in size, quality and diversity. Individuals must be able to qualify in Home Economics at different levels — certificate, diploma, bachelor, masters, doctoral — to be able to address the needs of various sectors of society, especially megatrends. By developing different qualifications, multiple career paths can be created within the Home Economics discipline. For example, Home Economics professionals can run and teach community courses or certificate courses in childcare, elderly care, parenting, healthy eating, food technology, furnishings or crafts producton, family budgeting and finance and consumer studies. Home economists with more advanced and specialist training can get involved in the training-of-trainers, or in management roles, for example in childcare and elderly care centres.

Home economists could work with government, NGOs, industry or as freelancers as authors of brochures, magazine articles, textbooks, cookbooks or 'educational' storybooks as well as teaching and learning material and websites. They could become speakers, seminar organizers or TV and radio producers and presenters, translating scientific knowledge into understandable and practical knowledge for school-aged students and for the general public.

One recent European project, involving a number of Home economists, is the European-wide consumer education website called *Dolceta* (see www.dolceta.eu), originally focused on adult learners, but since expanded to all educational levels. Home economists were engaged to develop informational sections and the *Teachers' Corner*, writing hundreds of webpages and a series of downloadable teaching and learning resources to be used cross-curriculary in schools, or as part of community adult education programmes (Piscopo, 2010). Other home economists could expand upon these various activities, and even use modern techonological facilities, such as blogs and phone apps, to continue giving essential data and practical guidance to consumers on nutrition, food, textiles, fashion, family, finance and consumer issues. This educational role would take a different slant if home economists were to become advisors and consultants to policymakers.

Strengthening the profession

The final element of capacity-building to be discussed is strengthening the profession. Capacity-building involves working as a professional community to enhance practices through collegiality. Thus, home economists must be able to work together within and across levels. For those who have access to it, Infomation Communication Technology (ICT) is an important tool to encourage the formation of a stronger professional community. Online communities and blogs can be used to build a community of Home Economics practice that can provide the medium for collegial co-operation, collaboration and the sharing of knowledge and perspectives amongst home economists (Mugliett, 2009). All of these initiatives will help build capacity among participants, also contributing to pride in their discipline and profession, prompting them to self-identify with and support the profession (a major aspect of future-proofing).

Any professional community aiming to act collegially and to foster professional development and growth must have a professional body. In Malta, *HEiA* is an active, national association aimed primarily at Home Economics and textiles studies educators. It organizes information-giving, skill-building and networking activities and issues a newsletter several times throughout the year. Where this is not already the case, professional associations such as HEiA could develop in parallel to regional or national developments of new Home Economics qualifications, areas of specialization and job opportunities, thus undertaking a more important role in building an integrated professional community. These associations could seek official national education authority recognition for CPD provision and accreditation (like the American Association of Family and Consumer Sciences), and initiate best practice awards among home economists in different sectors.

On a small island such as Malta, one of the ways of strengthening the profession and widening its scope would be through the creation of a national centre or insitute that could offer a national focal point for the discipline. This centre could offer various courses, for different audiences at different levels, as well as CPD for home economists. This centre or institute could also partner with government entities, industry, NGOs, CSOs and research and development bodies to initiate and implement local, national and international projects in areas related to Home Economics. The centre or insitute could be housed within the main national university, adding to its status, and offer the multitude of services listed in Figure 20.2. Some of the courses identified in Figure 20.2 could also be delivered online, thus even reaching international home economists, particularly, but not limited to, populations with similar Mediterranean contexts.

Summary

This chapter has suggested that a more diverse but integrated Home Economics professional community, with an awareness of global megatrends and a holistic sensitive and practical approach to societal needs, can more successfully fulfil Home Economics goals in the coming years and help future-proof the profession. The different branches of the Home Economics professional community must continuously build their own capacity — knowledge, skills and networking and partnerships — to promote and support wellbeing among individuals, families and communities. They must get involved at the policy level as much as at the grassroot level, to address all areas of everyday living. The future of the Home Economics profession lies in reaching individuals of different ages, different life stages and in different settings to help build stronger families, more responsible consumers and more sustainable nations.

This chapter has focused on the different features of capacity-building, discussing them in light of emerging megatrends and future-proofing of the Home Economics profession. We suggested that home economists can only continue to be successful in

- Bachelor degrees in Home Economics or Nutrition, Family and Consumer Studies with sub-specialisations;
- Bachelor of Education in Home Economics or Textile Studies;
- Master degree in Home Economics-related areas;
- Diploma and Certificate courses in areas such as consumer studies, parenting skills, childcare, elderly care, healthy aging, healthy food preparation, culinary skills, and food technology;
- Short courses for individuals involved in family counseling or hospitality such as courses on family budgeting for low income earners, or healthy meal planning for chefs;
- Short continuing professional development (CPD) courses for home economists, to respond to trends and megatrends in society and to acquire skills in new teaching and learning technology;
- Workplace seminars on topics such as health, food and nutrition, home design, fashion, finance, sustainable lifestyles, and preparation for retirement;
- Participation in or initiation of local and international Home Economics-related projects and
- Consultancy services to government departments, national institutes, industry, NGOs, CSOs and the mass media.

FIGURE 20.2

The potential offerings of a national Home Economics centre or institute.

their primary goal of facilitating individual, family and community wellbeing if they ground their practice in societal needs, give school curricula a vocational orientation, get more involved in lifelong learning provision, diversify with regards to their own training, continue to develop professionally throughout their career, strengthen collegiality within the profession, partner with other professions and entities on research and projects and market the profession through different vehicles.

- As educators, counselors, product developers, service providers, researchers, policymakers, and members of NGOs, home economists are effective as they address current and future needs of individuals, families and communities;
- Capacity-building, which revolves around (a) strengthening and acquiring knowledge, skills and perspectives, (b) enhancing networking and (c) establishing partnerships will help to future-proof the Home Economics profession and ensure effective practice;
- Home economists need to (a) ground their practice in the needs of different population groups within society, (b) diversify and enhance Home Economics education and training, (c) expand courses and career paths for home Economists, and (d) build professional collegiality and collaborate with other professionals and

entities to achieve Home Economics' goal of nurturing stronger families, more responsible consumers and more sustainable nations;s and
- Increasing the positive presence of home economists in different public (civil), commercial, academic and political forums can help to improve understanding, recognition and the status of the discipline.

Discussion Prompts

- What do you feel are the strengths of home economists in building capacity among their 'clients' or, from a family strengths perspective, their 'partners' in problem posing and solving?
- To what extent, and in what format, does formal capacity-building in the Home Economics profession exist in your country or region? How could it be initiated and/or improved to future-proof the profession?
- What do you consider important to add to current Home Economics professional training and socialization processes in your country or region in order for home economists to be able to respond to different megatrends?
- How can you contribute to developing networking within your Home Economics professional community and to building partnerships with other professions, entities and the mass media for facilitating individual, family and community well-being and future-proofing the profession?

References

Abela, A. (1998). *Marital conflict in Malta.* (Unpublished doctoral dissertation). University of Malta, Msida.

Abela, A. (2001). *Youth participation in voluntary organisations in Malta: A comparative anaylsis of European values studies.* Paola, Malta: Printwell.

Abela, A. (2006). Shaping a national identity: Malta and the European Union. *The International Journal of Sociology, 35*(4), 10–27.

Brofenbrenner, U. (1989). Ecological systems theory. *Annals of Child Development,* 6, 187–249.

Borg Xuereb, R. (2008). *The needs of Maltese first-time parents during their transition to parenthood: Initial stage for the development of an educational programme.* (Unpublished doctoral dissertation). University of Malta, Msida.

European Commission. (2007). *Special EUROBAROMETER 273 — European social reality.* Brussels: Author. Retrieved from http://ec.europa.eu/public_opinion/archives/ebs/ebs_273_en.pdf

Hantrais, L., Philipov, D., & Billari, F. (2006). *Policy implications of changing family formation [Population Studies #49].* Belgium: Council of Europe Publishing. Retrieved from http://www.coe.int/t/e/social_cohesion/population/N%B049_Family_Formation.pdf

Home Economists in Action. (n.d.). *News and events.* Malta: Author. Retrieved from http://www.wix.com/heiamalta/home#!

Inzelt, A. (n.d.). *Private sector interaction in decision making processes of public research policies: Country profile, Malta.* Brussels: European Commission. Retrieved from: http://ec.europa .eu/invest-in-research/pdf/download_en/psi_countryprofile_malta.pdf

IFHE. (2008). *IFHE position statement 2008: Home Economics in the 21st century.* Bonn, Germany: Author. Retrieved from http://www.ifhe.org/175.html

Mugliett, K. (2009). ICT integration in Home Economics classrooms: A study using an online community of practice. (Unpublished doctoral dissertation). University of Sheffield, Sheffield.

McGregor, S. L. T. (2009). Home Economics as an integrated, holistic system: Revisiting Bubolz and Sontag's 1988 human ecology approach. *International Journal of Consumer Studies, 35*(1), 26–34. doi: 10.1111/j.1470-6431.2010.00920.x

McGregor, S. L. T. (2011). Home Economics in higher education: Pre professional socialization. *International Journal of Consumer Studies, 35*(5), 560–568.

Ministry of Education, Employment and the Family (Malta). (2011). *Towards a quality education for all: The National Curriculum Framework 2011*. Valletta, Malta: Author. Retrieved from https://www.meef.gov.mt/Page.aspx?pid=543&depid=2&pageid=9

National Association of State Administrators of Family and Consumer Sciences. (2008). *National Standards for Family and Consumer Studies (2nd ed.)*. Retrieved from http://www.doe.in.gov/sites/NASAFACS/ProcessFramework.html

National Statistics Office. (2003). *Lifestyle survey 2003*. Valletta, Malta: Author. Retrieved from http://www.nso.gov.mt/statdoc/document_file.aspx?id=1600

Pendergast, D. (2006). Sustaining the home economics profession in new times — A convergent moment. In A-L. Rauma, S. Pöllänen and P. Seitamaa-Hakkarainen (Eds.), *Human perspectives on sustainable future No 99* (pp. 3–20). Savonlina, Finland: University of Joensuu, Faculty of Education.

Pendergast, D. (2010). Home economics: The next 100 years. *Victorian Journal of Home Economics, 49*(2), 26–33. Retrieved from http://www98.griffith.edu.au/xmlui/bitstream/handle/10072/39203/65725_1.pdf?sequence=1

Piscopo. S. (2010). DOLCETA: An online treasure trove for teachers. *The Teacher, 99*, 9–10.

Shields, R. & Williams, A. (2000). *Opportunities in home economics careers*. Chicago, IL: NTC/Contemporary Publishing Group

UNDP. (1997). *Governance for sustainable human development. A UNDP policy document –Glossary of key terms*. New York: Author. Retrieved from http://mirror.undp.org/magnet/ policy/glossary.htm

UNEP. (2002). *Capacity-building for sustainable development*. Nairobi, Kenya: Author. Retrieved from http://www.unep.org/Pdf/Capacity_building.pdf

UNESCO. (2010). *Principles for a sustainable future*. Paris, France: Author. Retrieved from http://www.unesco.org/education/tlsf/mods/theme_gs/popups/mod_c_s01.html

University of Malta, MATSEC Examinations Board. (n.d.). *Choose a syllabus*. Msida, Malta: Author. Retrieved from http://www.um.edu.mt/matsec/

Capacity-Building in the Home Economics Profession: The Maltese Experience

www.ingramcontent.com/pod-product-compliance
Lightning Source LLC
Chambersburg PA
CBHW070029010526
44117CB00011B/1763